SRA Reading Mastery Plus

Textbook B

Level 3

Siegfried Engelmann
Susan Hanner

SRA
A Division of The McGraw·Hill Companies
Columbus, Ohio

Illustration Credits

Dave Blanchette, Mark Corcoran, Susan DeMarco, John Edwards and Associates, Kersti Frigell, Simon Galkin, Meryl Henderson, Susan Jerde, Loretta Lustig, Steve McComber, Pat Schories, Lauren Simeone, James Shough, Rachel Taylor, and Gary Undercuffler.

www.sra4kids.com

SRA/McGraw-Hill

A Division of The **McGraw-Hill** *Companies*

Send all inquiries to:
SRA/McGraw-Hill
8787 Orion Place
Columbus, OH 43240-4027

Printed in the United States of America.

ISBN 0-07-569121-3

7 8 9 RRW 06 05 04

Table of Contents

A

1	2	3
1. finally	1. cheered	1. brighter
2. fuel	2. peeked	2. wearing
3. weigh	3. shaped	3. lower
4. early	4. traveled	4. feeling
5. November	5. waved	5. colder
6. thirstier	6. checked	6. bothered

4	5
1. fairly	1. million
2. Italy	2. Earth
3. Jerry	3. China
4. Turkey	4. aisle
	5. sparkling
	6. grew

B The Air Around the Earth

There is air all the way around the earth. Here's a rule about the temperature of that air: When you go higher, the temperature gets lower.

Let's say that the temperature on the ground is 70 degrees. You go up 1 mile. The temperature is now less than 70 degrees. It may be only 55 degrees.

You go up another mile. The temperature is less than 55 degrees. It's 30 degrees.

Use the rule about temperature to answer the questions below:

- Tom is 1 mile high.
- Jerry is 3 miles high.

  Who is colder?

  Why?

C Herman Flies to Italy

Herman was on a seat back of a jumbo jet. The inside of the plane had become very cold.

Herman watched a big dark move toward him. Herman tried to get out of the way, but his legs would hardly move. Very slowly, he crawled into a crack on the seat back. The big dark moved past him. Then another big dark moved past. The big darks were really crew members getting ready for the next flight. They were walking down an aisle of the plane.

Herman was on a seat right next to the aisle. The crew members walked right past Herman. One crew member was wearing a coat that brushed against the spot where

Herman had been. But Herman was in the crack of the seat, feeling very slow, very slow.

Then Herman began to feel faster. Herman could move his front feet faster. He peeked out of the crack and noticed that the plane was brighter now. He thought about flying, but it was too cold for that. So he crawled out on the seat and waited and waited for his body to get warmer.

By the time the passengers got on the plane, Herman was able to fly fairly fast. The plane was now 65 degrees. Some of the passengers said, "Oh, my, it's cold in this plane." When the plane moved down the runway, ★ the inside of the plane was 70 degrees, and Herman was flying very fast. He was feeling quite good now and was looking for good things to smell and eat.

The plane took off and went up 6 miles. The inside of the plane was still 70 degrees. But the outside air was now 80 degrees below zero. The captain talked over the loudspeaker and told the passengers about the temperature outside the plane. "Wow," some of the passengers said. Herman said, “Bzz,” as he headed toward the galley.

The captain told the passengers, “Look at your map and you can follow our flight today. We left Japan and we’re flying straight to Italy. We will fly over China and Turkey on our way to Italy. The flight to Italy is 6 thousand miles and should take 13 hours.”

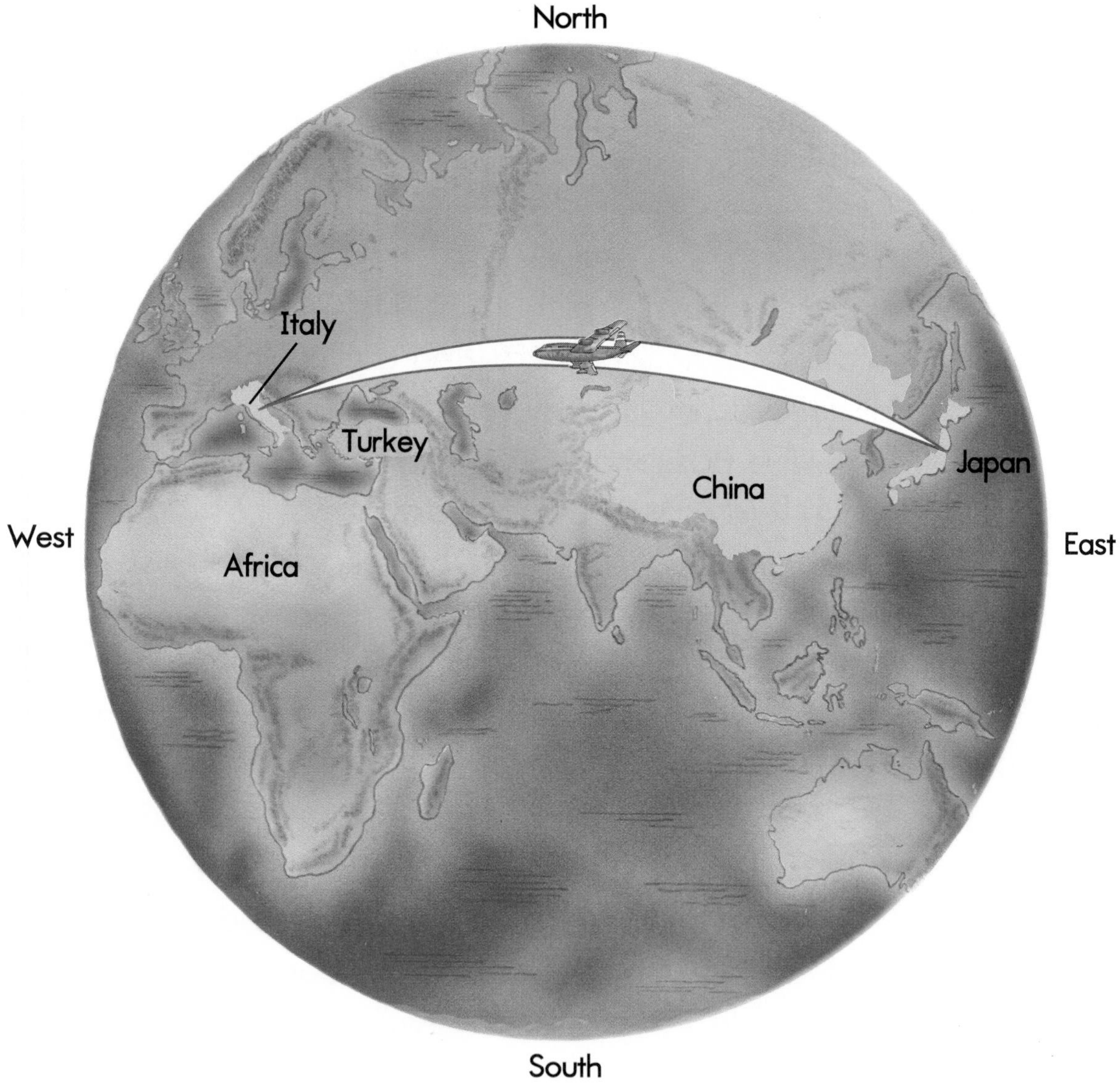

The country of Italy is very small compared to the United States. Italy is about the same size as Japan. So Italy is smaller than the state of Alaska. Italy is small, but 60 million people live there.

Italy is shaped something like a boot.

The jumbo jet circled several times and then landed. The passengers cheered and waved as they got off the plane. Nobody cheered for Herman. But Herman had just traveled farther than any other insect that ever lived.

MORE NEXT TIME

D **Number your paper from 1 through 26.**

1. Write the letter of the plane that is in the coldest air.
2. Write the letter of the plane that is in the warmest air.

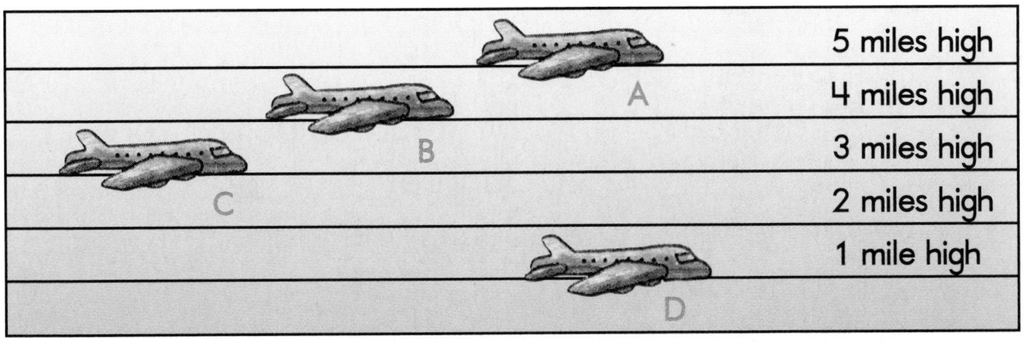

Story Items

3. Why was Herman moving so slowly at the beginning of the story? Write the letter that answers the question.
   a. He was tired. b. He was cold.
   c. He was hot.
4. What made Herman start moving faster? Write the letter that answers the question.
   a. The plane got warmer.
   b. The plane got colder. c. Herman woke up.

5. After the plane took off, how high did it go?
6. Write the letter of the temperature inside the plane.
   a. 70 degrees b. 80 degrees below zero
   c. 90 degrees
7. Write the letter of the temperature outside a plane that is 6 miles high.
   a. 70 degrees b. 80 degrees below zero
   c. 90 degrees
8. Write the letter of the country the plane left.
   a. United States b. Japan c. Italy
9. Write the letter of the country where the plane was going.
   a. United States b. Japan c. Italy

10. Write the letters of the 9 places that are in the United States.

a. Lake Michigan
b. Alaska
c. Japan
d. Chicago
e. California
f. San Francisco
g. Texas
h. Ohio
i. Italy
j. China
k. Denver
l. New York City
m. Turkey

Skill Items

The lifeboat disappeared in the whirlpool.

11. What word names an emergency boat that's on a large ship?
12. What word tells what happened to the lifeboat when you couldn't see it any more?
13. What word refers to water that goes around and around as it goes down?

Review Items

14. The United States is a ___.
   - country
   - city
   - state
15. Japan is a ___.
16. How many states are in the United States?

17. The biggest state in the United States is .
- Texas
- Alaska
- Ohio
- California

18. The second biggest state in the United States is .

19. Write the name of the state in the United States that is bigger than Japan.
- New York
- Alaska
- Ohio

20. Let's say you are outside when the temperature is 35 degrees. What is the temperature inside your body?

21. Let's say you are outside when the temperature is 70 degrees. What is the temperature inside your body?

22. Let's say a fly is outside when the temperature is 70 degrees. What is the temperature inside the fly's body?

Write **warm-blooded** or **cold-blooded** for each animal.

23. beetle
24. cow
25. cat
26. spider

A

1

1. giant
2. special
3. enormous
4. announcement
5. disappeared

2

1. frisky
2. blocks
3. bothered
4. freezing
5. checked
6. sparkling

3

1. grandchildren
2. sidewalks
3. bulkhead
4. whirlpool

4

1. swirled
2. tanks
3. smelly
4. weighs
5. billows

5

1. bow
2. stern
3. frost
4. grew
5. November

6

1. early
2. fuel
3. thirsty
4. thirstier

B

Herman's Last Trip

Herman ate and slept and felt warm and napped and smelled good things. For Herman, there was light and there was dark. There were things that smelled good and things that smelled bad. There were warm things and cold things. He didn't know that he had traveled farther than any other insect. And he didn't know that the plane was on its way back to New York City.

The plane had landed in Italy. Passengers got off and passengers got on. The crew got off and a new crew got on. People serviced the plane. They checked the tires and filled the plane with jet fuel.

Do you know where the fuel tanks are on a big jet? They are in the wings. All the parts of the plane were checked. Then the plane took off. It was on its way back to an airport that Herman had seen before.

Look at the map. It shows the last part of the jet's trip.

Herman had gone west from New York City and west from San Francisco and west from Japan. Now Herman went west from Italy. And Herman was on his way back to New York City. By going west, Herman had gone all the way around the world.

When the plane landed in New York City, Herman caught a good smell and followed it. He left the plane. For the next couple of hours he buzzed around inside the airport. Then he went outside. It was hot and the air was filled with good smells. He landed on top of an airport bus. And that bus stopped a few blocks from the place where Herman was born. Herman didn't know that he had come back to his home. He just knew that the sun felt very good and that it was time to eat. So he ate.

For the rest of the summer, he buzzed around with other flies, doing the things that flies do. He bothered

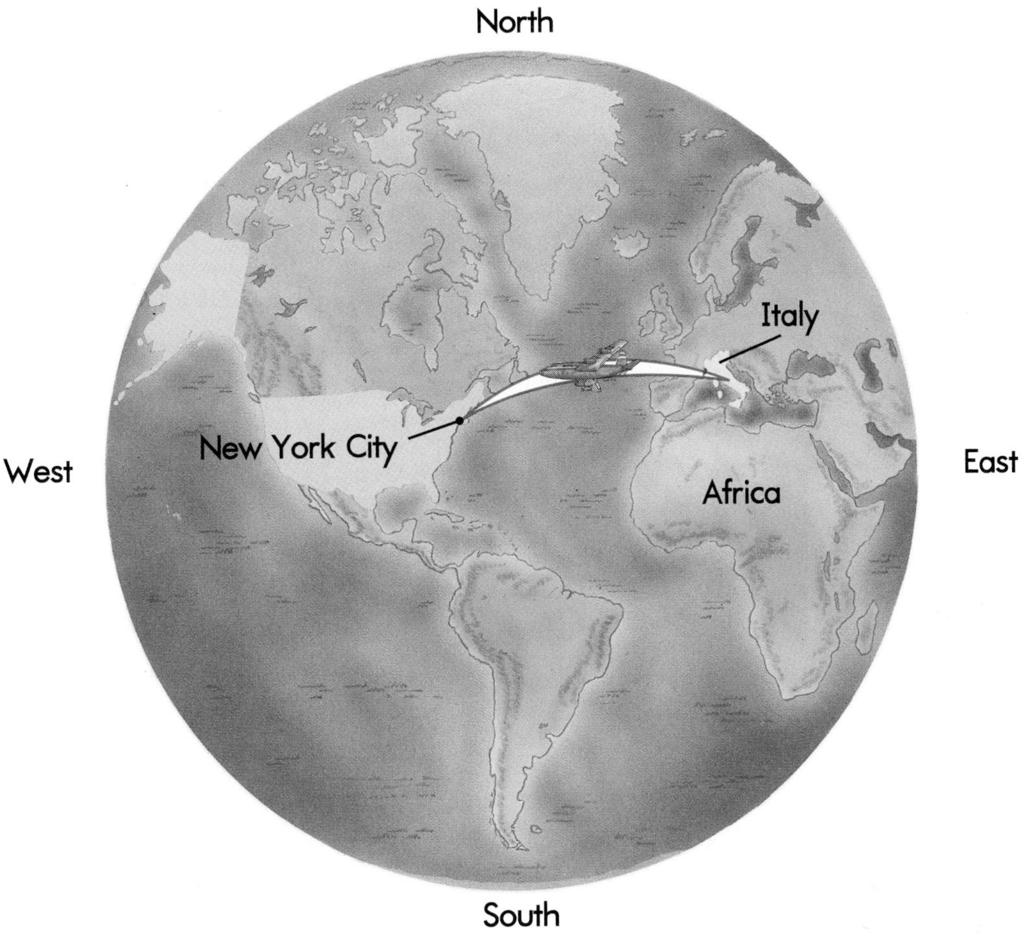

people, and he joined crowds of flies in garbage cans and other smelly places. He had a good time.

Then the days became colder and colder, and it was harder for Herman to move around. Summer was over. It was fall now. Every now and then, a warm day would make Herman feel frisky again, but most of the time, he moved very slowly.

One night early in November, the temperature dropped below freezing. The low temperature killed Herman and millions of other flies. The next morning people woke up and looked outside. They saw frost sparkling on the sidewalks and on the cars. "Look at the frost," they said. "It's beautiful." But for Herman there would be no more beautiful things—no smells and bright lights. There would be no fear of spiders. The insect that had traveled farther than any other insect was dead.

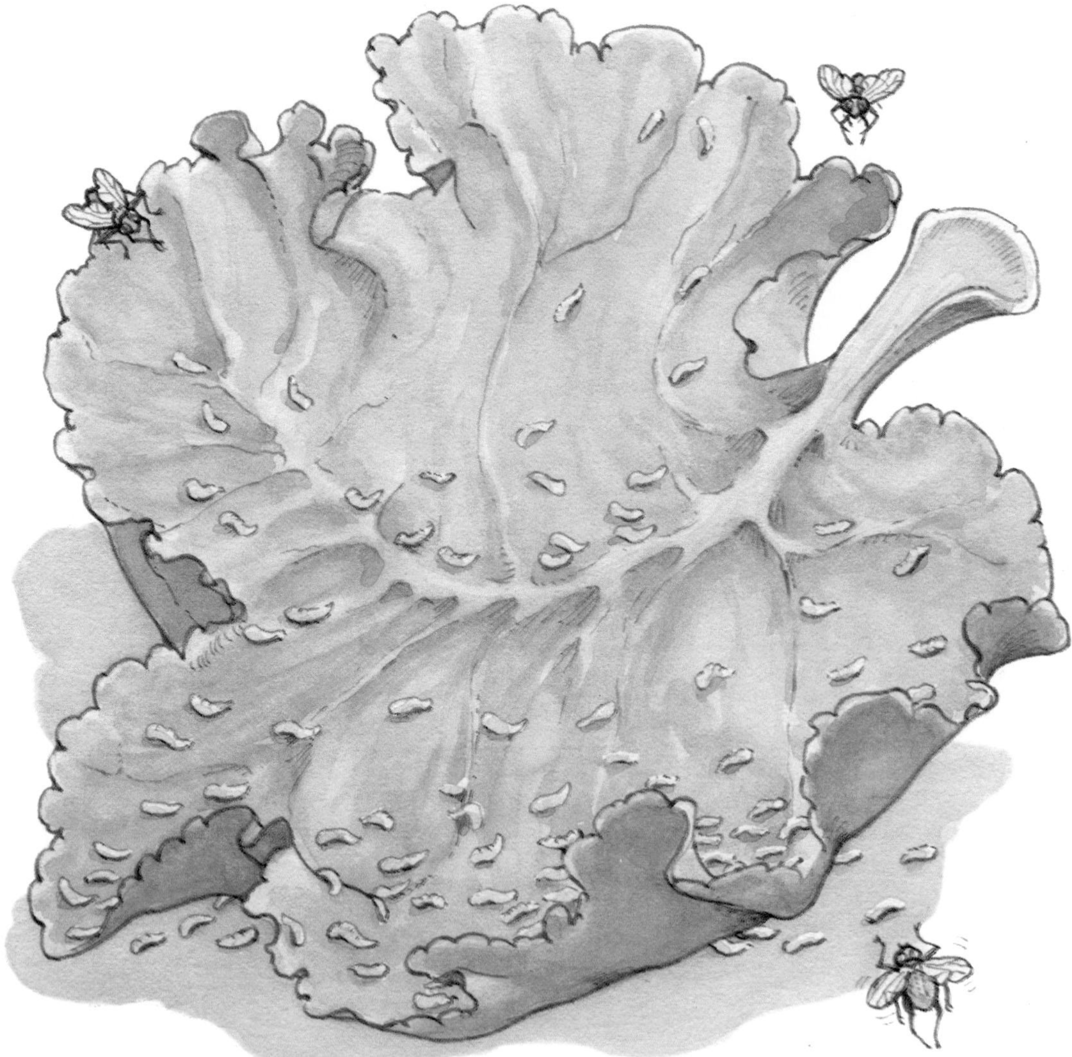

But Herman had a lot of children and grandchildren. In fact, the next spring, when the days got warm, Herman's 8 thousand children and grandchildren were born. They were maggots, and they looked just like Herman had looked when he was a maggot. And many of these maggots grew up to be flies, just like Herman.

The next time you look at a fly, take a good look. Maybe that fly is one of Herman's children or grandchildren.

THE END

C Number your paper from 1 through 26.

Skill Items

Write the word from the box that means the same thing as the underlined part of each sentence.

froze	figured out	weren't	boiled
continued	distance	thawed	moments

1. The snow <u>melted</u> when the sun came out.
2. The girls <u>were not</u> at home.
3. He <u>kept on</u> reading as he ate.

4. Look at object A and object B. Write one way that both objects are the same.
5. Write **2** ways that tell how object A is **different** from object B.

Object A

Object B

Use the words in the box to write complete sentences.

finally	whirlpool	eager	colder	lifeboat
announcement	traveled	disappeared	early	

6. They were ______ to hear the ______.
7. The lifeboat ______ in the ______.

Review Items

8. When we talk about miles per hour, we tell how ______ something is moving.

9. Which arrow shows the way the air will leave the jet engines?
10. Which arrow shows the way the jet will move?

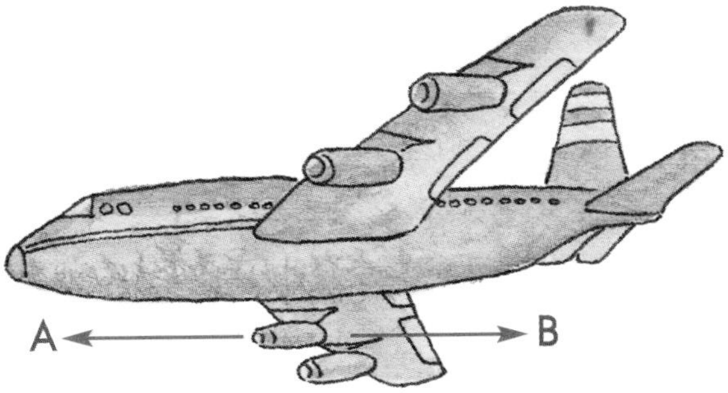

Write **warm-blooded** or **cold-blooded** for each animal.

11. flea 12. dog 13. horse 14. spider

15. Write the letter of the plane that is in the **warmest** air.
16. Write the letter of the plane that is in the **coldest** air.

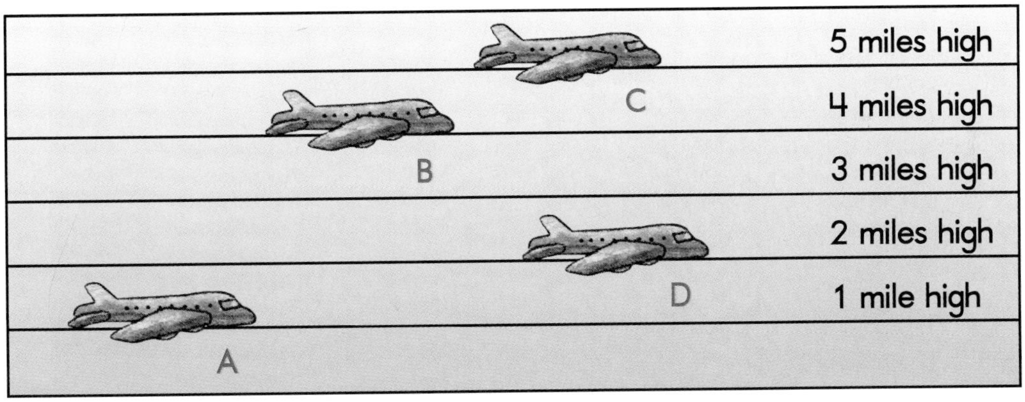

17. Name a state in the United States that is bigger than Italy.
18. Italy is shaped something like a ____.

19. Let's say a fly is outside when the temperature is 85 degrees. What is the temperature inside the fly's body?
20. Let's say you are outside when the temperature is 85 degrees. What is the temperature inside your body?
21. Let's say you are outside when the temperature is 50 degrees. What is the temperature inside your body?

22. What part of the world is shown on the map?
23. How far is it from **A** to **B?**
24. How far is it from **C** to **D?**

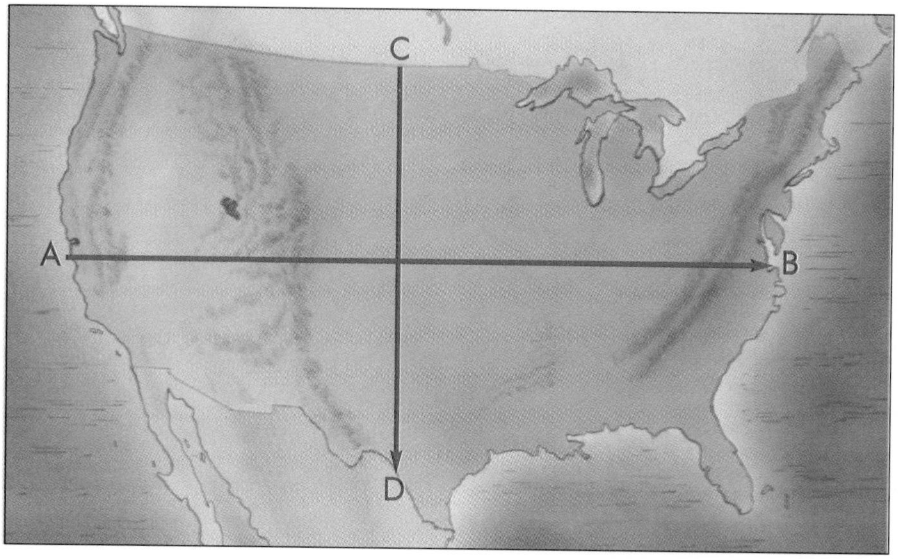

25. Would it be easier to catch a fly on a **hot day** or a **cold day?**
26. Would a fly move faster on a **hot day** or a **cold day?**

END OF LESSON 52 INDEPENDENT WORK

SPECIAL PROJECT

Use a large beach ball to make a globe of the earth. Cut out countries and paste them on your globe. Make labels for the following places:

- the United States
- Japan
- Italy
- New York City
- San Francisco
- Turkey
- China

◆ Show where Herman was born.

◆ Make an arrow to show where he went next.

◆ Make an arrow to show where he went after he left San Francisco.

◆ Make an arrow to show where he went after he left Japan.

◆ Make an arrow to show where he went after he left Italy.

53

A

1

1. objects
2. spins
3. tastes
4. weighs
5. bulkheads

2

1. closest
2. finally
3. easier
4. farthest
5. disappeared
6. announcement

3

1. carries
2. decks
3. drains
4. liners
5. whirlpools
6. currents

4

1. stern
2. bow
3. announce
4. giant
5. enormous
6. special

B Facts About Whirlpools

In the next lesson, you will start a story that tells about ocean liners, ocean water, and a giant whirlpool.

You have seen whirlpools in sinks. As the sink drains, the water near the drain moves around in circles. Anything caught in the whirlpool goes around and around faster and

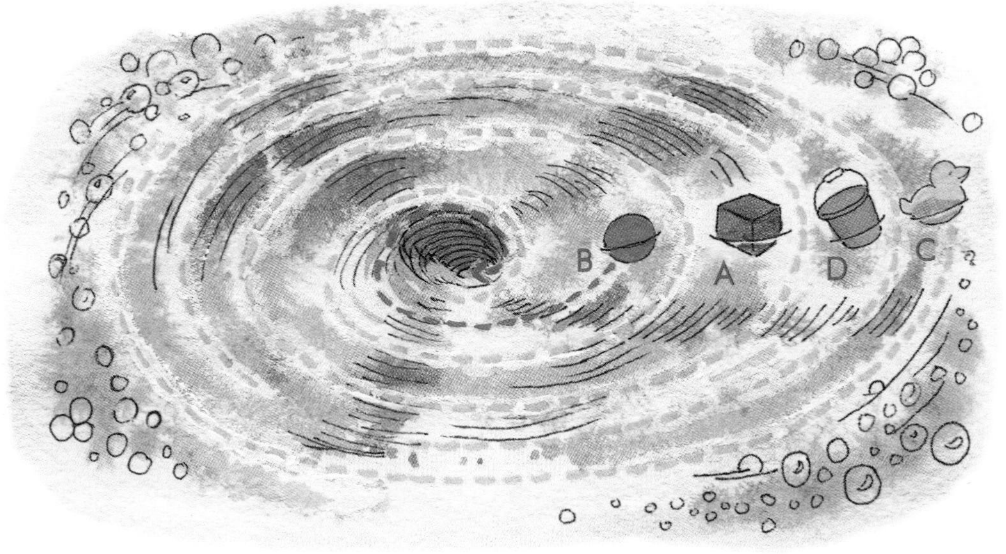

faster as it gets closer to the drain. Finally, it goes down the drain.

The water in a whirlpool spins around and around. It also goes down.

Look at the objects caught in a whirlpool. The object farthest from the drain moves the slowest. Which object is that?

The object closest to the drain moves the fastest. Which object is that?

The object closest to the drain goes down the drain first. The object farthest from the drain goes down the drain last. In the picture, which object will go down the drain first?

Which object will go down the drain last?

Sometimes, large whirlpools form in the ocean. They are like giant drains that pull things around and down.

C Facts About an Ocean Liner

Here are facts about an ocean liner:

- An ocean liner is a very large ship.
- An ocean liner carries passengers. Not all ships carry passengers. Most of them carry things like food, cars, stoves, or logs. But ocean liners carry passengers.
- Special names are used to talk about parts of a ship.
- The front of the ship is called the **bow.** The bow in the picture is marked with a **B.**

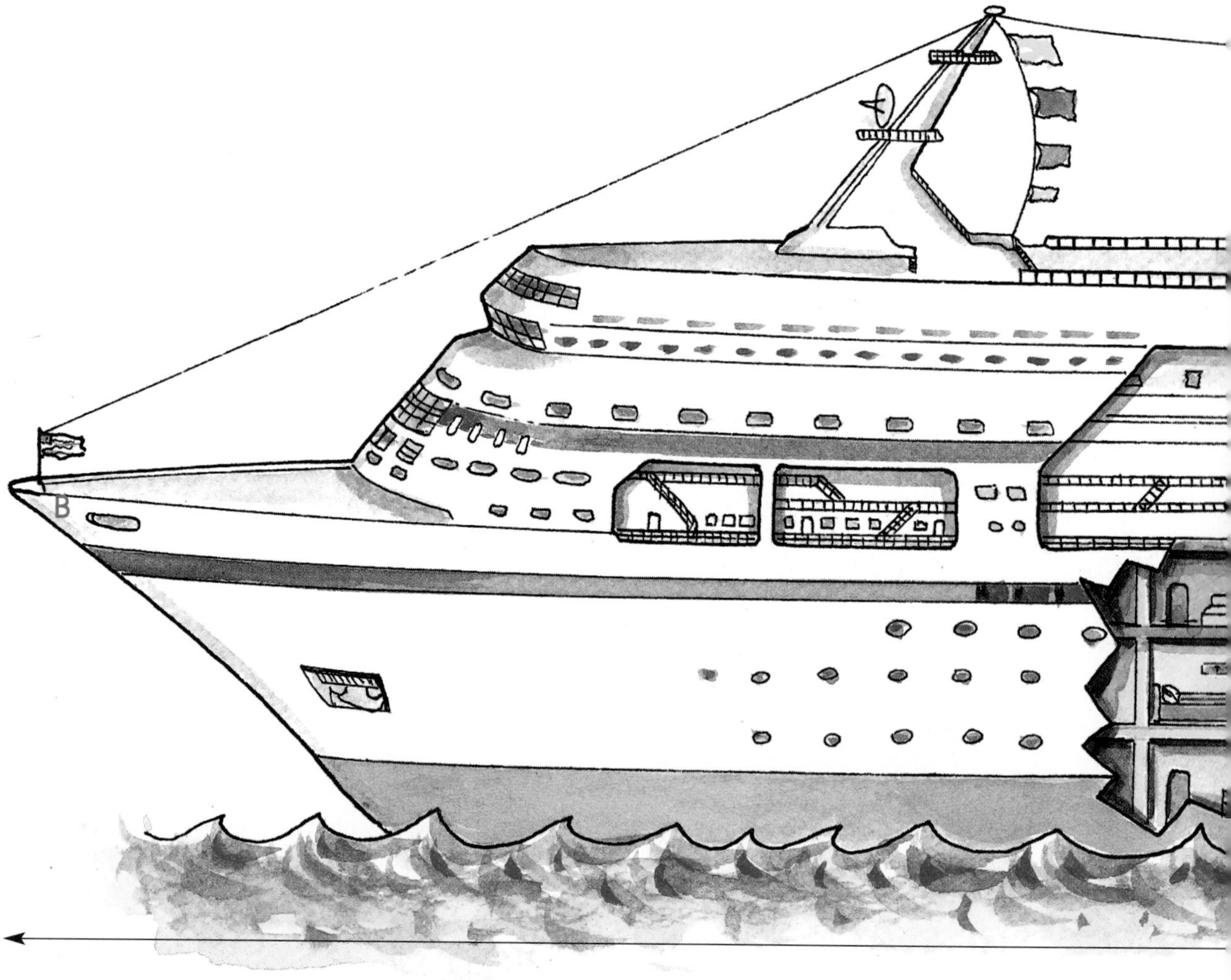

- The back of the ship is called the **stern.** The stern is marked with an **S.**
- The floors of a ship are called **decks.** One deck is marked with a **D.**
- The walls are called **bulkheads.** One wall is marked **BH.**
- Notice that the ocean liner in the picture is 200 meters long.

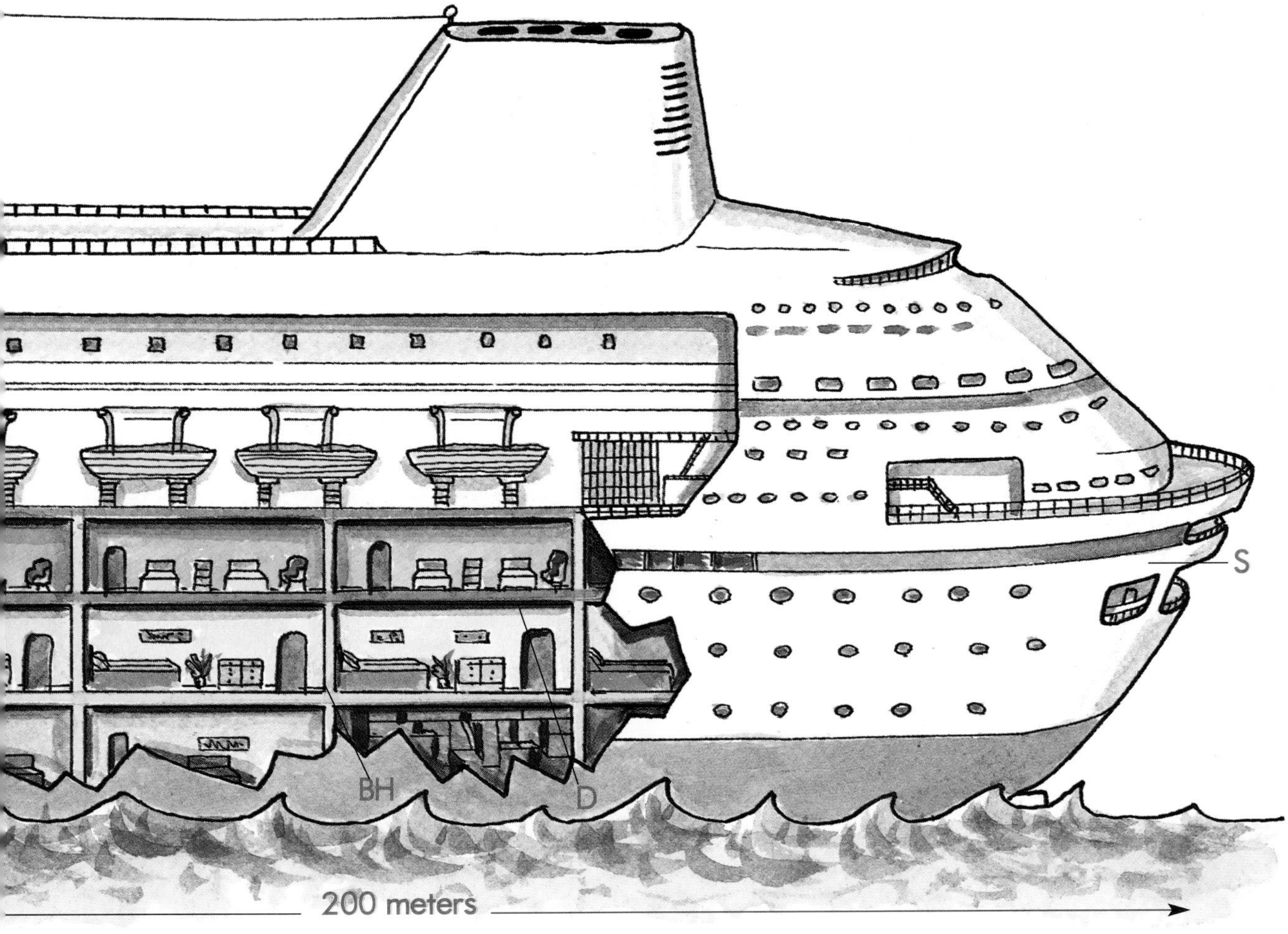

D Facts About Ocean Water

Here are some facts about ocean water:

- Ocean water tastes salty because it has salt in it.
- If you drink a lot of ocean water, you'll get thirstier.
- A bottle of ocean water weighs more than a bottle of fresh water because the ocean water has salt in it.
- It's easier to float in ocean water than in fresh water.
- Ocean water must get colder than fresh water before it will freeze.

Look at the jars in the picture below. Figure out which jars are filled with ocean water.

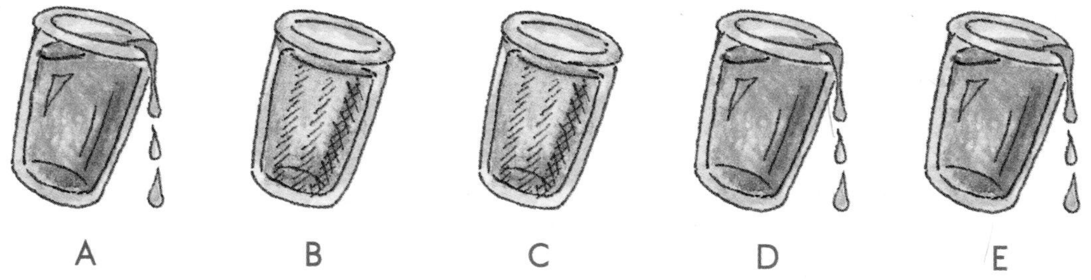

E Comparing Things

When you compare two things, you tell how the things are the same. Then you tell how they are different. When you tell how they are different, you use the word **but.**

Look at object A and object B.

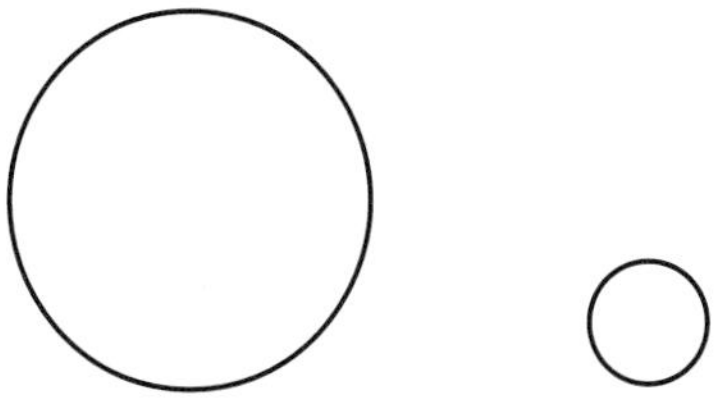

Object A Object B

When you compare object A and object B, first you tell a way they are the same: **They're both circles.** Then you tell a way they are different: **Object A is big, but object B is not big.**

Compare object C and object D. First tell a way they are the same. Then tell a way they are different.

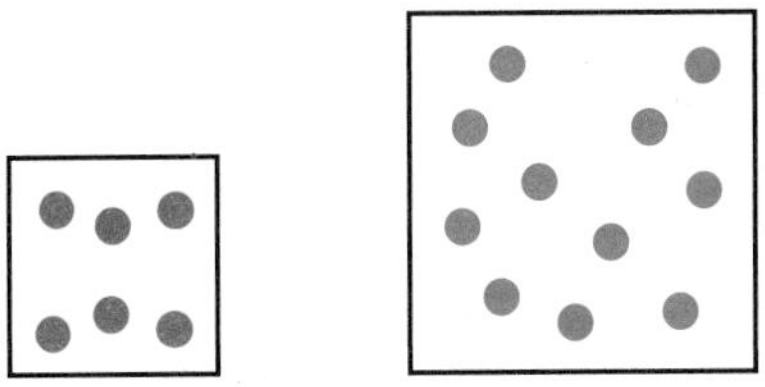

Object C Object D

Compare object E and object F. First tell a way they are the same. Then tell a way they are different.

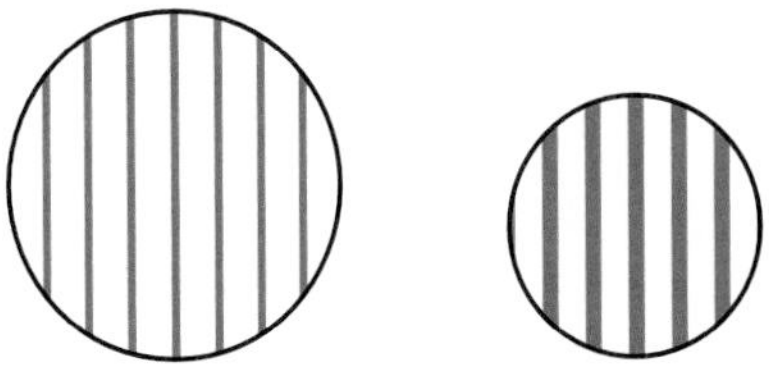

Object E Object F

F Number your paper from 1 through 28.

1. Look at the picture. Jar A is filled with ocean water. Jar B is filled with fresh water. Which jar is heavier?
2. Which jar will freeze at 32 degrees?
3. Will the other jar freeze when it is **more than 32 degrees** or **less than 32 degrees?**

ocean water fresh water

Skill Items

Look at object A and object B. Compare the objects.

4. Tell a way the objects are the same.
5. Tell a way the objects are different.

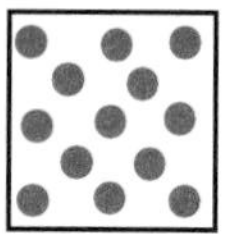

Object A

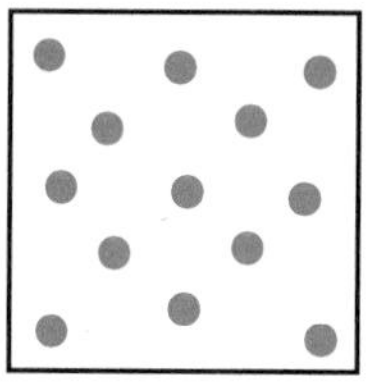

Object B

Here's a rule: **Dogs have hair.**

6. Sam is not a dog. So what does the rule tell you about Sam?
7. Rex is a dog. So what does the rule tell you about Rex?
8. A jay is not a dog. So what does the rule tell you about a jay?
9. A poodle is a dog. So what does the rule tell you about a poodle?

Review Items

10. How far is it from New York City to San Francisco?
11. What ocean do you cross to get from San Francisco to Japan?
12. How far is it from San Francisco to Japan?
    - 15 hundred miles
    - 5 thousand miles
    - 3 thousand miles

13. How many legs does an insect have?
14. How many legs does a fly have?
15. How many legs does a bee have?
16. How many legs does a spider have?
17. How many parts does a spider's body have?
18. How many parts does a fly's body have?

19. Which letter shows where Italy is?
20. Which letter shows where China is?
21. Which letter shows where Turkey is?
22. Which letter shows where Japan is?
23. Is the United States shown on this map?

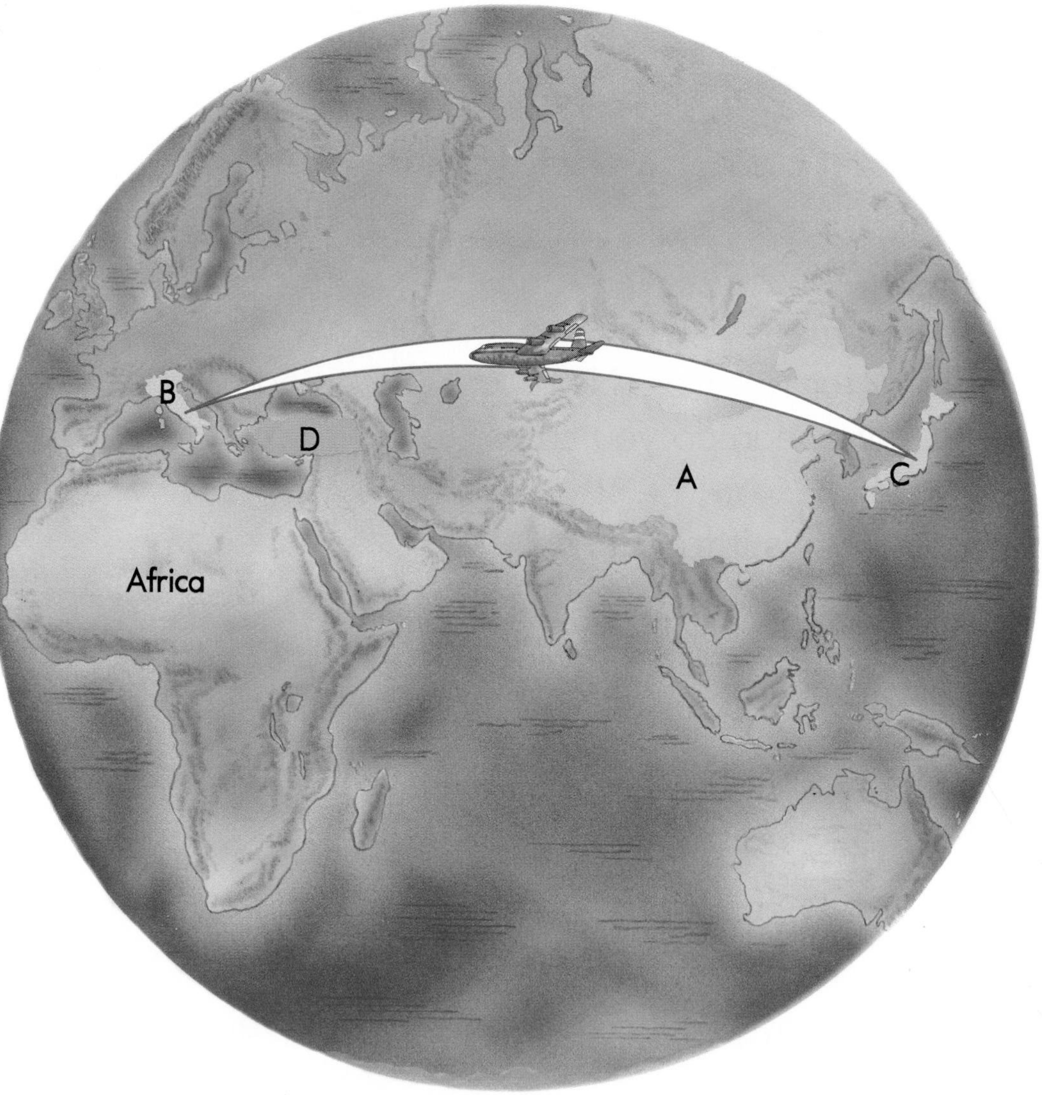

24. A plane that flies from Italy to New York City goes in which direction?
25. Where are the fuel tanks on a big jet?
26. It was hard for Herman to move around in the fall because ______.
27. What killed Herman?
28. Write the letters of the 5 places that are in the United States.

a. Denver
b. California
c. Japan
d. New York City
e. Alaska
f. Lake Michigan
g. Italy
h. China

54

A

1	2	3
1. except	1. announcement	1. crate
2. island	2. announced	2. crowd
3. heard	3. rushing	3. Kathy
4. sign	4. currents	4. enormous
5. occasional	5. disappeared	5. Linda

4	5	6
1. lifeboats	1. younger	1. normal
2. somewhere	2. tumble	2. myna
3. outline	3. thirteen	3. palm
4. footprint	4. pushed	4. swept
	5. patch	

B

Linda and Kathy Escape from a Sinking Ship

"Fire! Fire!" a voice announced over the loudspeaker. "The forward deck is on fire," the announcement continued. "Everybody, leave the ship. Get into the lifeboats!"

Linda and her sister were on their way from the United States to Japan. Linda was thirteen years old, three years older than Kathy. Their father was in Japan, and they were on their way to visit him. Three days before, they had left California on a great ship called an ocean liner. They were now somewhere in the middle of the Pacific Ocean.

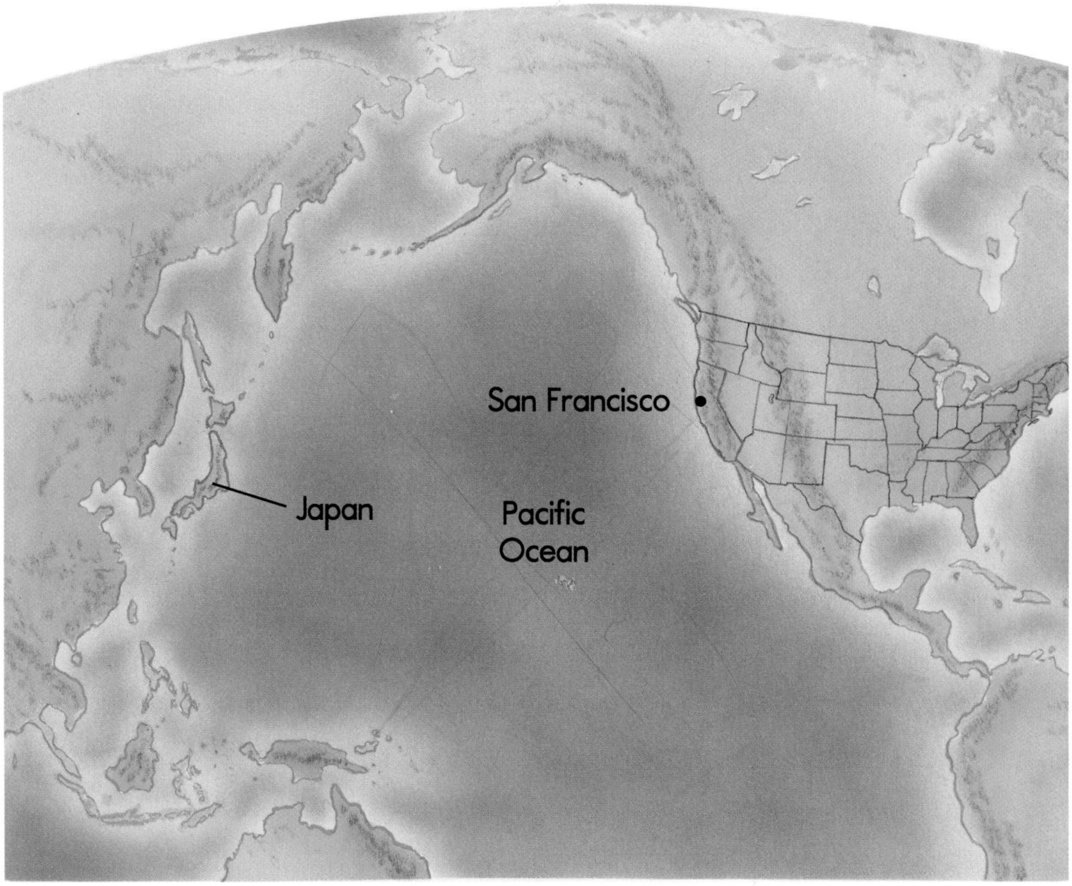

"Fire! Fire!" the voice shouted. "Everybody get into the lifeboats!"

People were running this way and that way on the deck of the ship. They were yelling and crying.

"Hold on to my hand," Linda said. The girls went to the lifeboats. People were all around them, pushing and yelling. Linda could not see much. She was afraid. Suddenly she was no longer holding Kathy's hand.

Just then a strong pair of arms grabbed Linda. "In you go," a voice said. A big man picked Linda up and put her in the lifeboat.

"Where's my sister?" Linda asked. Linda looked but she couldn't see her younger sister.

"Kathy!" Linda called. Linda jumped from the lifeboat to the deck and started to look for her sister.

"Kathy! Kathy!" she called. There was so much noise on the deck that Linda could hardly hear her own voice.

Then she saw Kathy, who was standing behind a crowd of people. Kathy was crying. Linda ran over to her. "Hold my hand and don't let go," Linda said.

Linda noticed that the deck of the ship was leaning more and more. The ship was sinking.

She grabbed Kathy's hand and ran to the rail. "We've got to get into a lifeboat," Linda said out loud. She rubbed

her eyes and tried to look for a lifeboat, but the front of the ship was hidden in smoke—enormous clouds of black, rolling smoke.

"Hello," Linda shouted, "here we are." But the smoke and the roar of the fire made her voice sound very thin.

Linda and Kathy walked along the rail at the stern of the ship. They looked into the water and called. But they couldn't see much. Once in a while, the smoke would clear and they would see the water below.

Suddenly, the girls almost tripped over a large wooden crate that was on the deck. "We'll use this for our lifeboat," Linda said. She and Kathy pushed the crate over the side. The boat was leaning so much now that it was easy to push the crate over the side. The crate disappeared in the water.

"We need life jackets," Kathy shouted.

Linda replied, "I don't know where they are." Then she said, "Hold your nose and jump." Together, the girls jumped into the water. The water was very warm and it tasted salty. Linda was a good swimmer, but Kathy wasn't.

Behind them were great rushing sounds of water as the huge ocean liner continued to sink. As the ship went down, water rushed toward the ship, pulling everything in its path down with the ship. It was a giant whirlpool. The currents of water were pulling Linda and Kathy. Where was that crate?

MORE NEXT TIME

C Number your paper from 1 through 24.

Skill Items

1. Compare object A and object B. Remember, first tell how they're the same. Then tell how they're different.

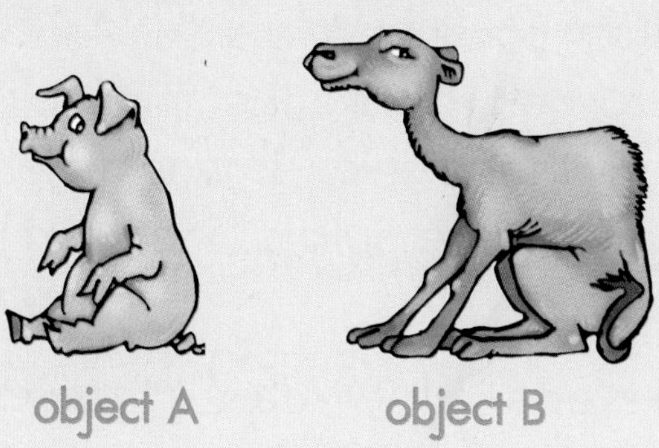

The smoke swirled in enormous billows.

2. What word means that the smoke spun around and around?
3. What word means **very, very large?**
4. What word means that the clouds were swelling up?

Review Items

The picture shows objects caught in a whirlpool.

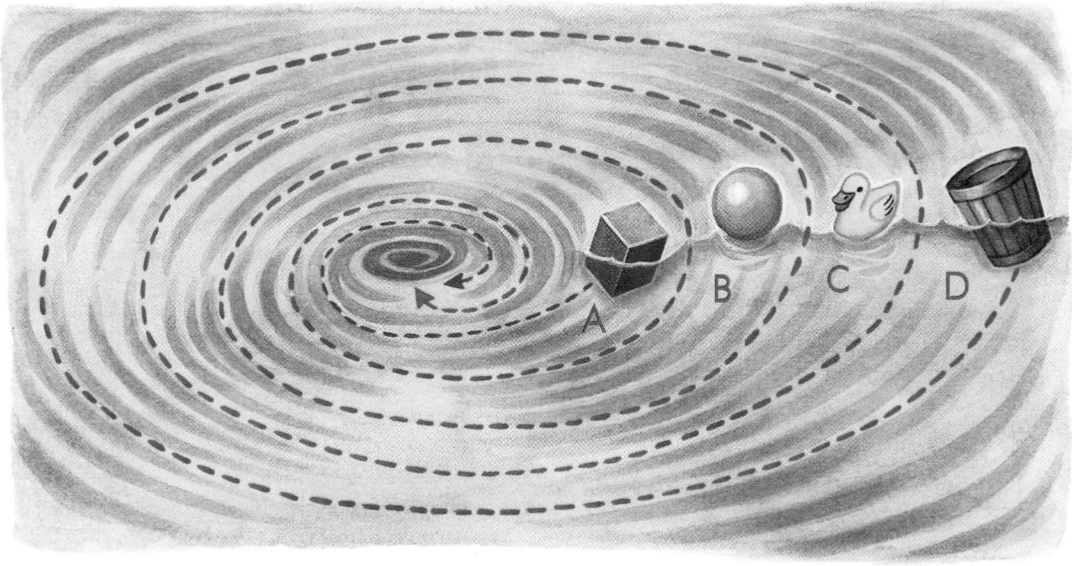

5. Write the letter of the object that will go down the whirlpool first.
6. Write the letter of the object that will go down the whirlpool next.
7. Write the letter of the object that will go down the whirlpool last.

8. Write the letter of the plane that is in the warmest air.
9. Write the letter of the plane that is in the coldest air.

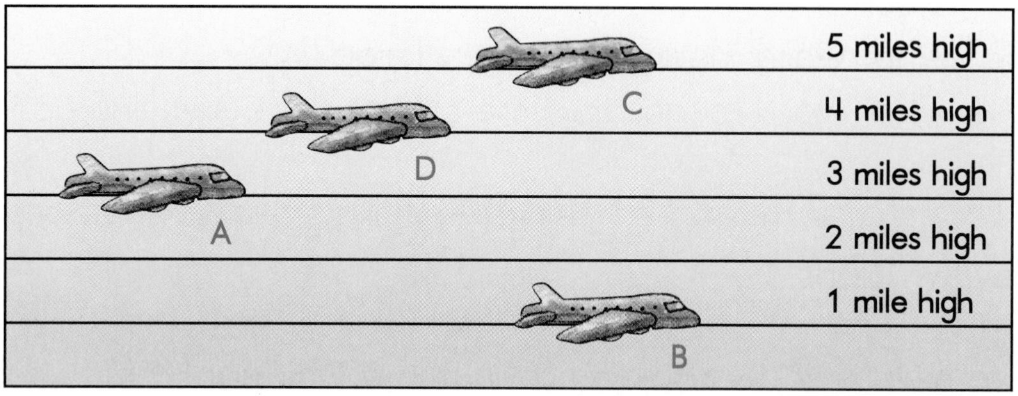

10. Name a state in the United States that is bigger than Italy.
11. Italy is shaped something like a ____.
12. The biggest state in the United States is ____.
13. The second biggest state in the United States is ____.
14. Write the name of the state in the United States that is bigger than Japan.
    - Ohio
    - Alaska
    - New York

15. Which eye works like one drop, a human's eye or a fly's eye?
16. Which eye works like many drops, a human's eye or a fly's eye?
17. Which eye can see more things at the same time, a human's eye or a fly's eye?

18. Write 2 letters that show bulkheads.
19. Write 2 letters that show decks.
20. Which letter shows where the bow is?
21. Which letter shows where the stern is?

22. What is the temperature of the water in each jar?

23. Write the letter of each jar that is filled with ocean water.

24. Jar B is filled with ocean water. How do you know?

32 degrees 32 degrees 32 degrees 32 degrees 32 degrees 32 degrees

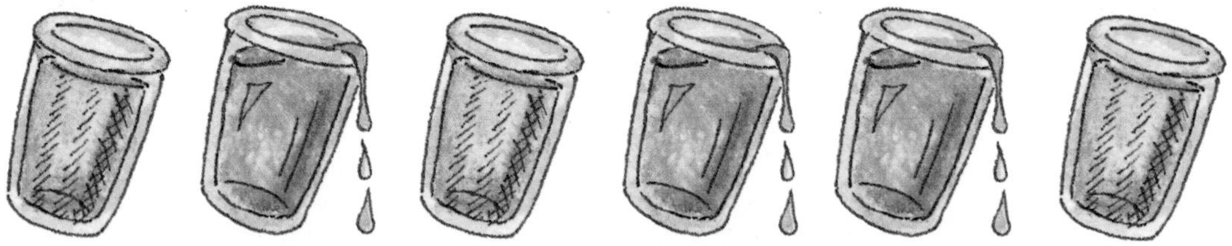

A B C D E F

A

1	2	3
1. palm	1. swam	1. bubbles
2. coconut	2. swirled	2. billows
3. myna	3. swept	3. bellies
4. thirsty	4. swimmer	4. paddles

4	5	6
1. faded	1. island	1. occasional
2. tumbled	2. except	2. stretch
3. drifted	3. outline	3. foul
4. beginning	4. heard	4. normal
	5. patch	5. frond
	6. sign	

B Facts About Islands

You're going to read a story about an island. Here are facts about islands:

- Islands are small.
- There is water on all sides of an island.

There are three islands on the map below. Find them.

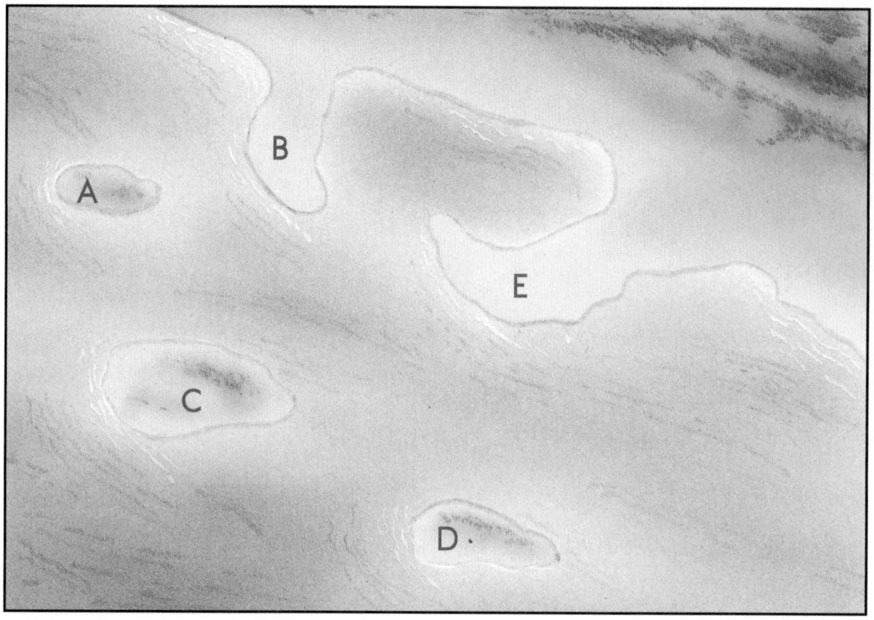

C Linda and Kathy Find Land

The sinking ship was making a whirlpool. Great currents of water were pulling Linda and Kathy toward the ship. Only the bow of the ship was now above water. The bow was pointing into the air, and it was beginning to slip down into the water. The huge billows of smoke were beginning to clear. The currents were pulling things closer and closer to the sinking ship.

Linda and Kathy were swimming in the water. "There," Linda said, pointing to the crate. It was only a few meters from them. Linda swam as fast as she could. She swam and swam, but she couldn't seem to move in the current.

At last Linda reached out and grabbed a corner of the crate. She climbed on. The crate was floating high in the water. Linda pulled Kathy onto the crate. "Let's paddle out of here before the current sucks us down with the ship," Linda said.

So she and her sister got on their bellies and used their hands for paddles. They paddled as hard as they could. Behind them were loud rushing sounds of the sinking ship. Linda turned around and saw just the tip of the bow sticking above the water. The rushing sounds suddenly faded, and the ocean became quiet.

A huge trail of smoke still hung over the ocean, but there was no sign of the ship, except for a patch of water where bubbles were still coming up. Linda and Kathy looked and looked, but they could not see any of the lifeboats.

The girls sat on the crate with their feet in the salt water. Linda tried to sleep, but the sun was too hot. The salt water was starting to burn Linda's feet.

"I'm thirsty," Kathy said.

Linda said, "You can't drink the ocean water. It is full of salt. And salt water will just make you thirstier. You'll have to be brave. Someone will find us soon."

The girls waited for somebody to find them. But nobody did. They drifted farther and farther away from the place where the ocean liner had sunk. Slowly the sun went down. The air became cooler. Linda put her arm around

Kathy and tried to sleep. She tried and tried, but she was too thirsty and her feet hurt too much.

Then she heard something in the dark: "Wish-coooooo, wish-coooooo, wish-coooooo."

"Those are waves," Linda said. "Those are waves on a beach. We must be near land. Kathy, we're near land." The girls looked in the direction of the sound. Linda could see the outline of trees. Yes, they were near a shore.

A wave crashed over their crate. The wave swept the crate faster and faster toward the shore. Linda had a nose full of water. She grabbed her sister and held on as hard as she could. The girls tumbled from the crate. They were in the water, but the water was not deep. In fact, they were sitting in water that was only a few inches deep.

They waded from the water and walked along the beach. It was so dark that they could hardly see where they were going.

"I'm thirsty," Kathy said. She sounded as if she was ready to cry.

"So am I," Linda said. "But it won't do us any good to cry."

MORE NEXT TIME

D **Number your paper from 1 through 23.**

1. There are 3 islands on the map. Write the letter of each island.
2. **A** is not an island. Tell why.

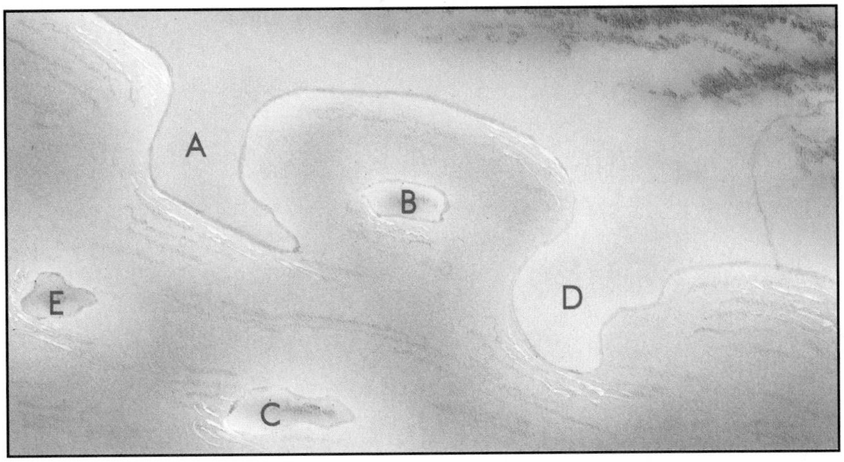

Skill Items

Use the words in the box to write complete sentences.

swirled	announced	enormous	smelly
lifeboat	billows	crowd	whirlpool

3. The ___ disappeared in the ___.
4. The smoke ___ in ___ ___.

5. Compare object A and object B. Remember, first tell how they're the same. Then tell how they're different.

Object A

Object B

Review Items

The closer an object is to the center of a whirlpool, the faster it moves.

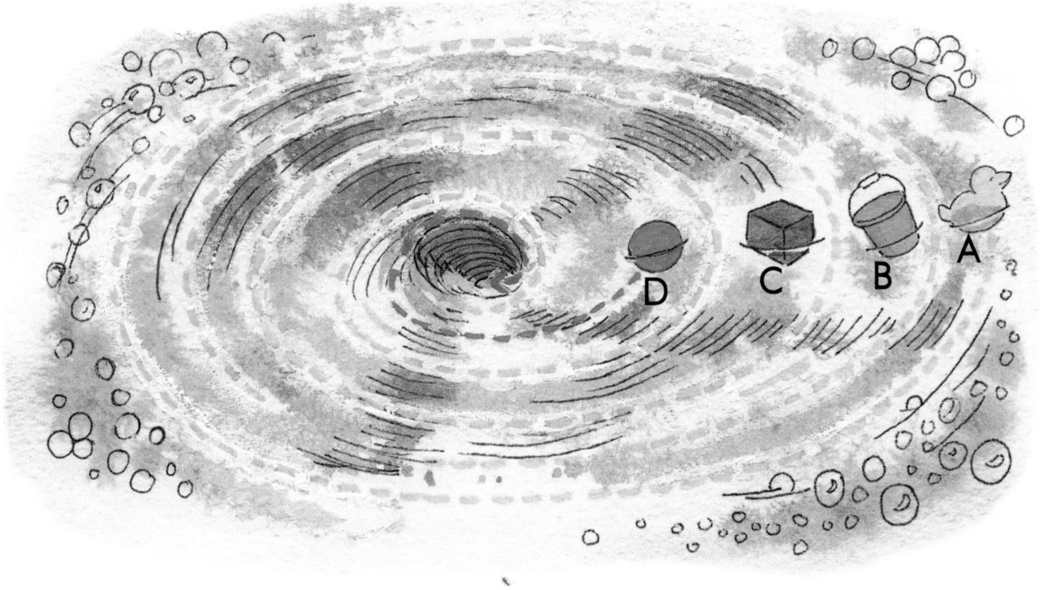

6. Write the letter of the object that is going the fastest.
7. Write the letter of the object that is going the slowest.
8. The path is shown for objects A and D. Which object will go around more times, A or D?
9. Which path will go around the most times, the path for B, C, or D?

10. When we talk about how hot or cold something is, we tell about the ▭ of the thing.
- weight
- length
- temperature

11. When the temperature goes up, the number of ▭ gets bigger.
- miles
- degrees
- hours
- miles per hour

12. Write the name of the city that's on the east coast.
13. Write the name of the city that's on the west coast.
14. Which letter shows where Denver is?
15. Which letter shows where Chicago is?

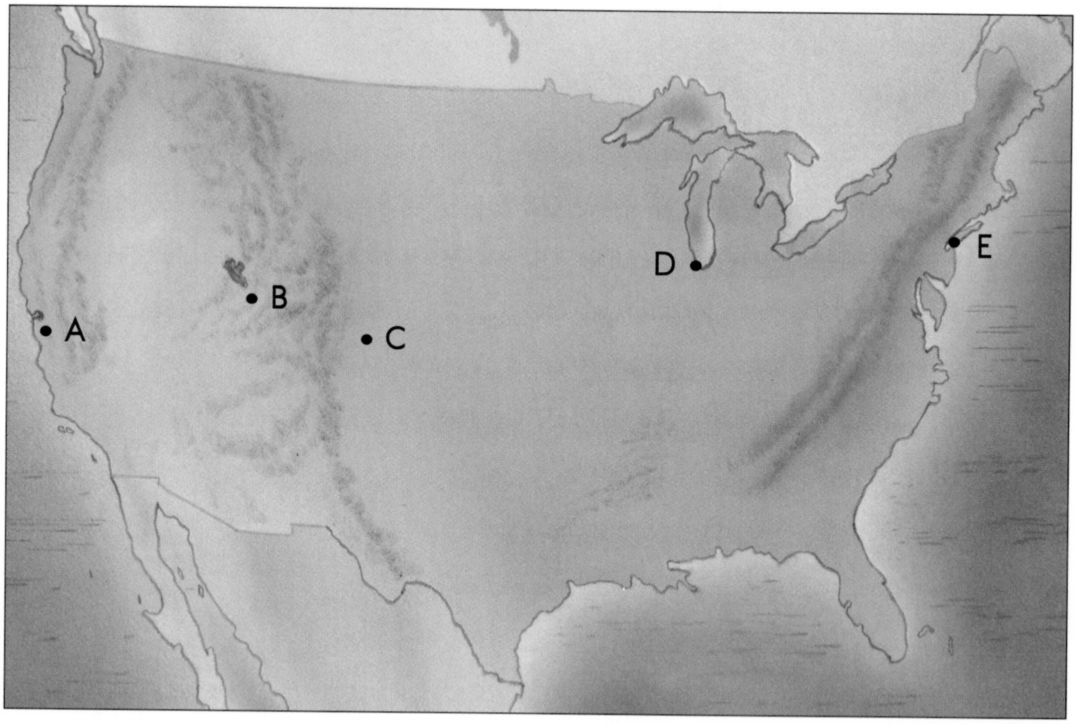

16. Which letter shows where Italy is?
17. Which letter shows where New York City is?
18. Which letter shows where Turkey is?

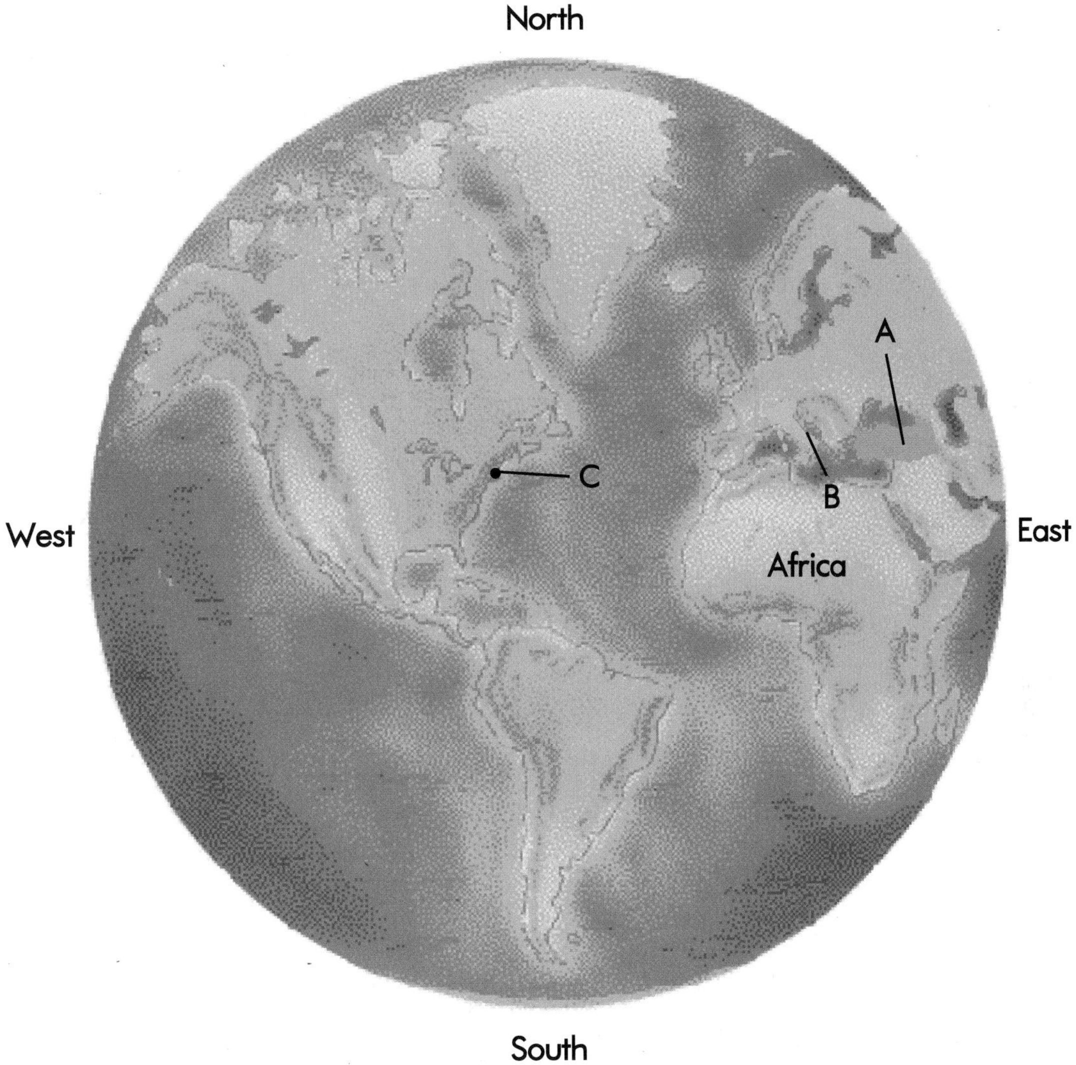

19. A plane that flies from Italy to New York City goes in which direction?

Jar X is filled with fresh water. Jar Y is filled with ocean water.

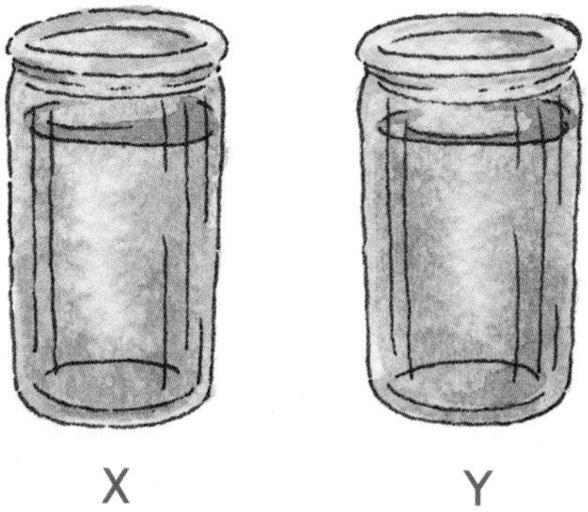

20. Which jar is heavier?
21. Which jar will freeze at 32 degrees?
22. Will the other jar freeze when it is **less than 32 degrees** or **more than 32 degrees?**

23. Linda and Kathy were on a ship that was going from the United States to ___.

A

1
1. fronds
2. break
3. echoed
4. enough
5. bananas

2
1. coconuts
2. ankles
3. dates
4. bunches
5. trunks

3
1. footprints
2. outcome
3. raindrops
4. football

4
1. beyond
2. stretching
3. edge
4. fluffy
5. ladder

5
1. raise
2. juice
3. shelves
4. means

B Facts About Palm Trees

Today's story tells about palm trees. Here are facts about palm trees:

- Palm trees grow in places that are very warm.
- Palm trees cannot live in places that get cold.
- Palm trees have very small roots.

- The branches of palm trees are called fronds.
- Some palm trees grow dates. Some palm trees grow coconuts.

Bananas grow on plants that look something like palm trees. But banana plants are not trees.

C Alone on an Island

Linda and Kathy walked along the beach. It was very dark, so they walked close to the waves. The waves washed up and swirled water around the girls' ankles. Then the waves fell back, pulling sand from under the girls' feet. Suddenly, Linda stepped into some very cold water, much colder than the water in the ocean. That cold water was running into the ocean. The girls were standing in a stream. Linda bent down and tasted the water. It was fresh water. "Kathy! Water!" she announced.

Kathy and Linda drank water until they couldn't drink any more.

Then they found a place near the palm trees where they could sleep. Linda didn't know how long she slept.

But when she woke up it was morning. A strange sound woke her: "Caw chee, caw chee."

There were many large birds around the girls and many trees. Some trees were palm trees, with trunks that have shelves like a ladder. The birds were different colors. A few were white, many were red and yellow. Small black birds with yellow beaks made most of the noise. "I think those are myna birds," Linda said. "They're very smart."

"I'm hungry," Kathy said.

Linda stood up and looked around. She could see a beach of bright sand. She could see a blue sky and fluffy white clouds. She could see the ocean, stretching out until it met the sky. And she could see the crate, about twenty yards from the water. But she could not see a house, a boat, or any person other than her sister.

Linda and Kathy looked around for something to eat. The girls found a plant that had large bunches of bananas.

After the girls ate all the bananas they could eat, Linda said, "Let's walk down the beach and see if we can find out where we are."

"My feet hurt," Kathy said.

"We'll walk slowly," Linda said. So the girls started walking along the beach. They didn't go into the trees beyond the beach, because they were afraid that they would get lost. They walked and walked. They walked until the sun was high in the sky. Linda said, "It must be around noon time." But they did not see a house or a boat or any people.

They walked and walked until they came to a large rock. Linda climbed up on the rock and looked around. She saw footprints on the beach in front of her. The girls ran over to the footprints. Kathy said, "Other people are here. I see lots of footprints."

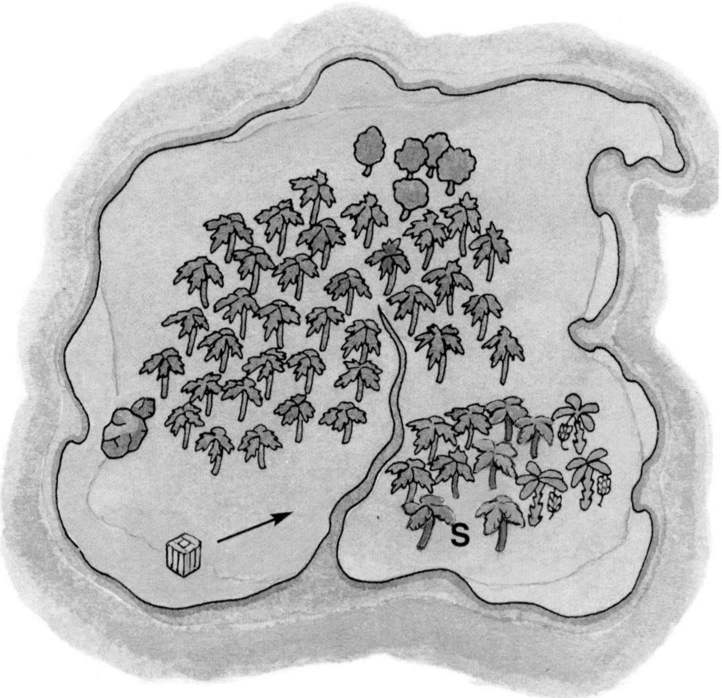

Linda looked at the footprints. She noticed a crate near the edge of the water. Linda said, "Those are our footprints. We have been walking in a circle. That means we're on an island. We walked all the way around the island."

Kathy started to cry.

Linda said, "Don't cry. Everything will be all right."

Linda didn't cry, but she felt like crying, too. She and her sister were all alone on an island. There was nothing on that island but trees and sand and a stream. How would they let anybody know where they were? How would they ever get off the island?

MORE NEXT TIME

D Number your paper from 1 through 26.

1. Name 2 things that grow on different palm trees.

2. What part does the A show?
3. What part does the B show?
4. What part does the C show?
5. What part does the D show?

Skill Items

Here's a rule: **Birds have feathers.**

6. A crow is a bird. So what does the rule tell you about a crow?
7. A bass is not a bird. So what does the rule tell you about a bass?
8. A jay is a bird. So what does the rule tell you about a jay?

Review Items

9. What does ocean water taste like?
10. If you drank lots of ocean water, you would get ▇▇▇.

Jar M is filled with fresh water. Jar P is filled with ocean water.

11. Which jar is heavier?
12. Which jar will freeze at 32 degrees?
13. Will the other jar freeze when it is **more than 32 degrees** or **less than 32 degrees?**

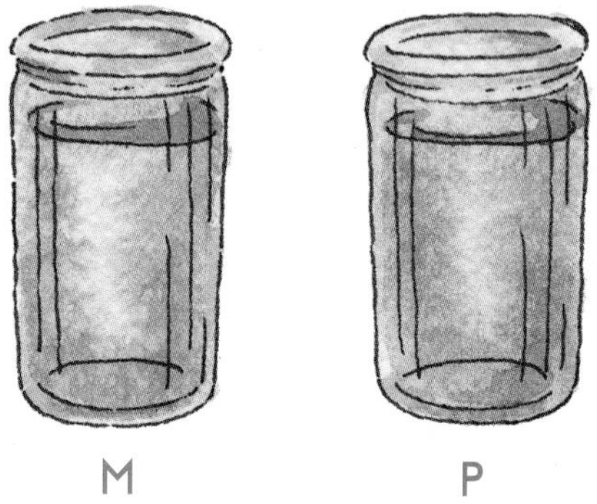

The ship in the picture is sinking. It is making currents as it sinks.

14. Write the letter of the object that will go down the whirlpool first.
15. Write the letter of the object that will go down the whirlpool next.
16. Write the letter of the object that will go down the whirlpool last.

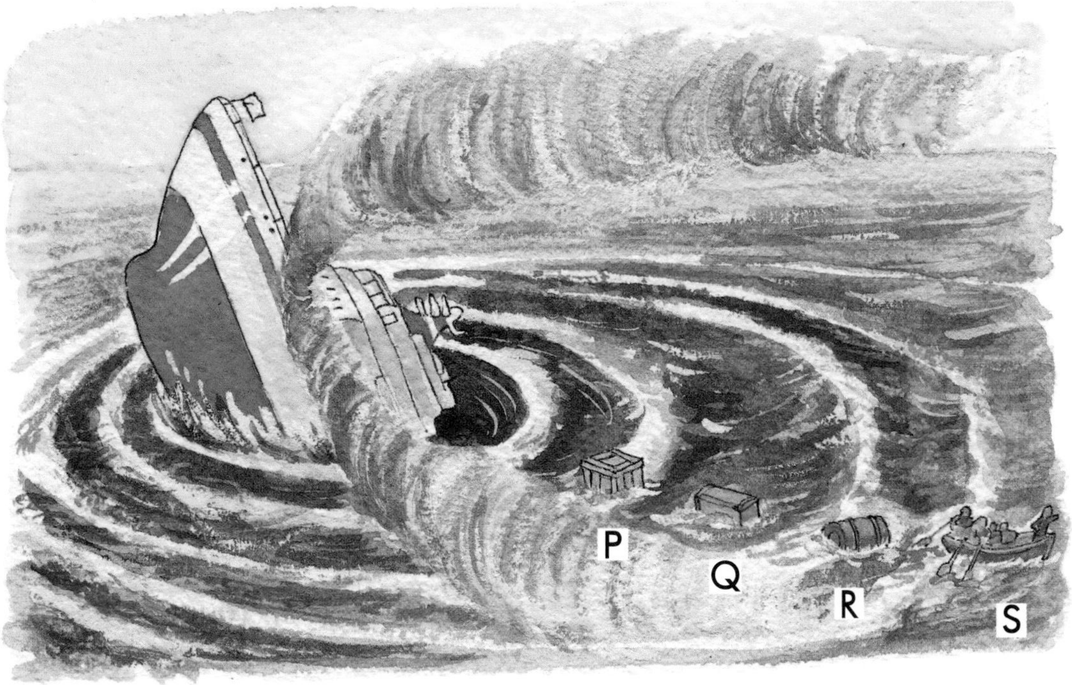

17. When a plane flies from New York City to San Francisco, is it flying in the same direction or the opposite direction as the wind?
18. A mile is a little more than ____ feet.

19. Write the letter of each island on the map.
20. **C** is not an island. Tell why.

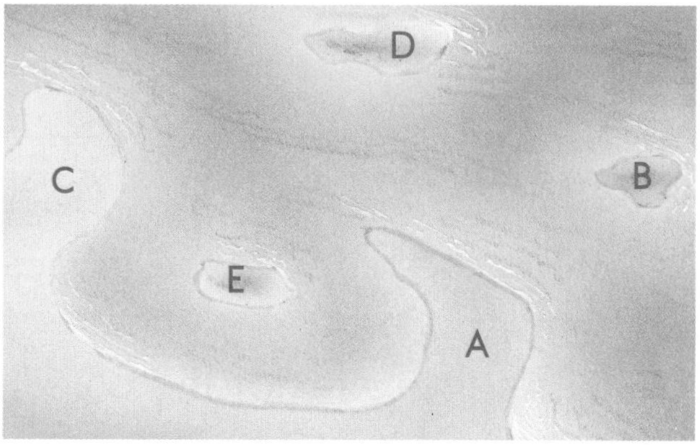

21. Write the letter of the animal that is facing into the wind.
22. Which direction is that animal facing?
23. So what's the name of that wind?

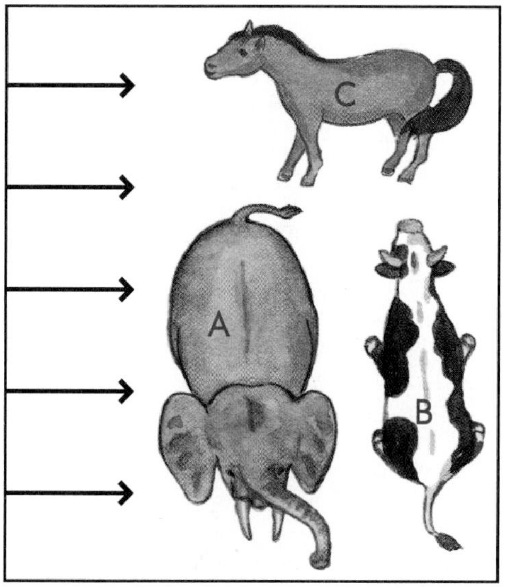

24. Let's say you are outside when the temperature is 40 degrees. What is the temperature inside your body?
25. Let's say a fly is outside when the temperature is 85 degrees. What is the temperature inside the fly's body?
26. Let's say you are outside when the temperature is 85 degrees. What is the temperature inside your body?

A

1
1. contest
2. attach
3. though
4. machine
5. automobile
6. construct

2
1. echoed
2. explained
3. screeched
4. peeled
5. raised

3
1. monkeys
2. babies
3. shells
4. raindrops
5. knives

4
1. threw
2. outcome
3. enough
4. football
5. haul
6. power

5
1. hammer
2. inner
3. juice
4. silver
5. vine

B Facts About Coconuts

Here are facts about coconuts:

- A coconut is about as big as a football.
- Coconuts are not easy to open.
- Coconuts have two shells, one inside the other.
- Each shell is so hard that it wouldn't break if you hit it one time with a hammer.

- Inside the second shell is sweet, white coconut meat.
- Inside the coconut meat is sweet juice, called coconut milk.

The picture shows a coconut that is cut in half. The parts of the coconut are labeled.

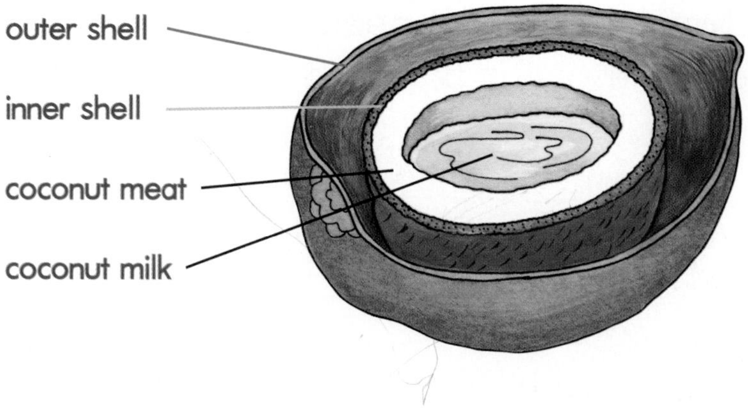

C Linda and Kathy Find More Food

Linda and Kathy were all alone on an island. Linda said, "Stop crying, Kathy. We are both very smart, and if we use our heads, we will get out of here."

Linda looked around and started to think. Then she pointed to the trees near the beach. "Those are coconut palm trees," she said to her sister. "Coconuts are good to eat. You can see them in the middle of the fronds," Linda pointed.

The girls ran to the trees and started looking under them. There were some coconuts on the ground, but they smelled foul and were covered with bugs. These coconuts

were rotten. The girls kept looking. At last they found two good coconuts.

Kathy picked up one of the good coconuts and shook it. It sounded like a bottle that had water in it. Kathy said, "I'll break it open." She threw it down on the sand as hard as she could. The coconut made a dent in the sand, but there was no mark on the coconut.

Kathy picked up the coconut and slammed it down in the sand again. But the outcome was the same.

"I don't know how to do this," Kathy said.

"I've got an idea," Linda said, and she explained her idea to Kathy.

The girls walked along the beach until they came to the large rock. It was almost six feet across. Linda climbed up on the rock and held the coconut in both hands. She raised her hands over her head, and she threw the coconut against the rock as hard as she could. Kwack—the sound of the coconut echoed. But there was no crack in the outer shell. After two more tries, the outer shell cracked open.

After the girls peeled off the outer shell, Kathy said, "Let me do it now." Kathy slammed the coconut against the rock four times before it cracked. Linda grabbed the cracked inner shell and held it so that not much juice leaked out. Then Linda carefully removed part of the shell. The girls ate all the coconut meat and shared the coconut milk.

"I'm still hungry," Linda said, "What about you?"

"Yes, me, too."

So the girls went to the banana plants and filled up on bananas.

Later, Linda said, "I'm tired of bananas. The trees are full of coconuts. We have to think of some way of getting them."

"We can't climb up there," Kathy said. "The trees are too tall and the coconuts are too high."

Linda pointed to monkeys in a tree and said, "I think I know how to get the monkeys to help us."

The girls walked along the beach until they came to a place where there were many monkeys in the trees. The monkeys were making a lot of noise. They were jumping and running through the trees.

"Let's make them mad," Linda said. Linda walked over to the trees. The mother monkeys picked up their babies and screeched at Linda. "Choo, choo, cha, cha, chee, chee, chee," they screeched.

Linda made a face and waved her arms at them. The monkeys got madder and madder. Linda went over to one of the trees and tried to shake it.

One of the monkeys picked a coconut and threw it down at Linda. Linda tried to shake the tree again. Another monkey threw a coconut at her. Other monkeys started to throw coconuts. Coconuts were coming down like raindrops.

Linda ran away from the trees. By now the ground was covered with fresh coconuts.

Kathy laughed. "We will have enough coconuts to last us for days and days," she said.

MORE NEXT TIME

D **Number your paper from 1 through 27.**

1. How many shells does a coconut have?
2. Is it easy to break open a coconut?
3. What is the juice inside a coconut called?

The picture below shows a coconut that is cut in half.

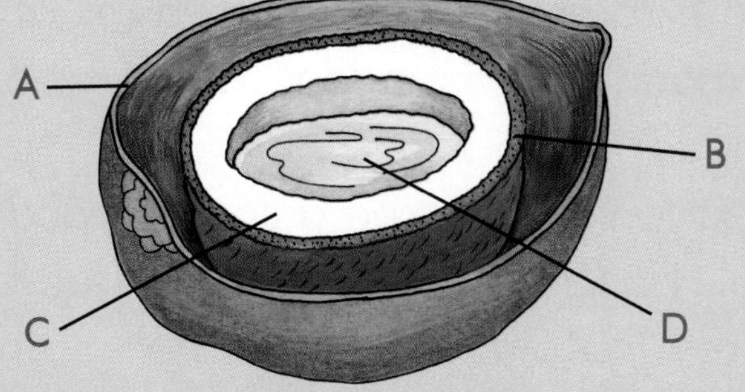

• inner shell	• coconut milk	• outer shell
• fronds	• coconut meat	• dates
• trunk	• coconuts	• roots

4. What part does the **A** show?
5. What part does the **B** show?
6. What part does the **C** show?
7. What part does the **D** show?

Skill Items

8. Compare object A and object B. Remember, first tell how they're the same. Then tell how they're different.

Object A

Object B

The occasional foul smell was normal.

9. What word means **once in a while?**
10. What word means **bad?**
11. What word means **usual?**

Review Items

The picture below shows a coconut tree.

• inner shell	• coconut milk	• outer shell
• fronds	• coconut meat	• dates
• trunk	• coconuts	• roots

12. What part does the **A** show?
13. What part does the **B** show?
14. What part does the **C** show?
15. What part does the **D** show?

16. Write **A, B, C** or **D** to name the arrow that shows the way the cloud will move.
17. That wind is blowing from the ____.
18. So that wind is called a ____ wind.

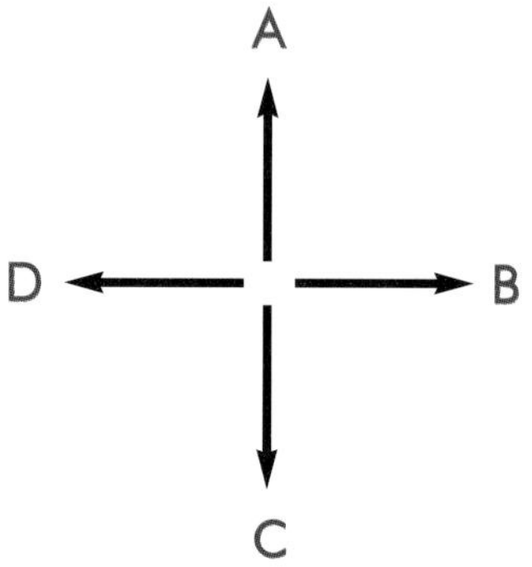

19. Which eye works like one drop, a human's eye or a fly's eye?
20. Which eye works like many drops, a human's eye or a fly's eye?
21. Which eye can see more things at the same time, a human's eye or a fly's eye?

Some of the objects in the picture are insects, and some are spiders.

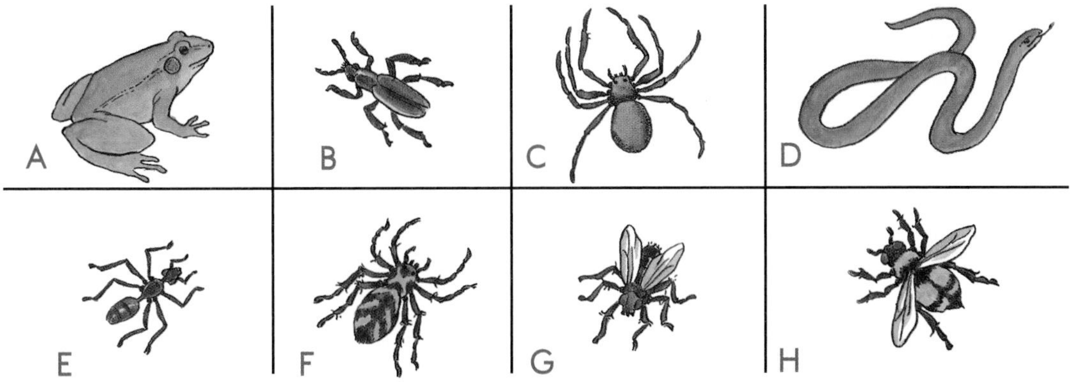

22. Write the letters of the spiders.
23. Write the letters of the insects.

24. Write the letters of the 9 places that are in the United States.

a. Denver
b. Turkey
c. Chicago
d. New York City
e. Texas
f. China
g. Alaska
h. Italy
i. Lake Michigan
j. California
k. San Francisco
l. Japan
m. Ohio

25. When something tries to move in one direction, something else tries to move ___.

26. Which arrow shows the direction the canoe is moving?
27. Which arrow shows the direction the paddle is moving in the water?

A

1

1. support
2. force
3. steady
4. contest

2

1. jungle
2. rocky
3. silver
4. power
5. stronger
6. startle

3

1. ledge
2. attached
3. though
4. haul
5. knives
6. twice

4

1. raw
2. machine
3. vines
4. motor
5. automobile
6. constructed

B Facts About Machines

Some machines have engines or motors. A washing machine has a motor. An automobile is a machine that has an engine. Drills and blenders and lawn mowers are machines.

Some machines are very simple. Here's the rule about all machines: **All machines make it easier for you to do work.**

The machine in these pictures is a long branch. The girl is using the branch to make it easier for her to move the large rock. That rock is far too heavy for her to move without the help of a machine.

Here's another kind of machine.

The two people are having a contest. Each person is pushing and trying to turn the log. The arrows show that person A is trying to move the log in one direction. Person B is trying to move it in the opposite direction. Which person is bigger and stronger?

Even though person B is much smaller than person A, person B will win this contest. Person A is pushing on the log. Person B is pushing on a handle that is attached to the log. That handle is a simple machine. It gives person B a lot more power than person A.

Remember, a long stick or a handle can be used as a simple machine. It gives a person a lot of power.

C Making Tools

The only things Linda and Kathy ate for two days were coconut meat and bananas. On the third day Kathy said, "I want to eat something else."

"Me, too," Linda said. "I think that we should catch some fish."

Kathy said, "I'm not hungry enough to eat raw fish."

"Well," Linda said, "maybe we can figure out some way to cook the fish."

Kathy said, "How can we catch fish without any fishing poles or hooks?"

Linda said, "We can take the wooden crate apart and use the nails for hooks. We can take vines from the jungle and use them for lines."

So the girls took the wooden crate apart. They pulled the nails out and bent them by hitting them with rocks.

Then the girls found thin vines. They tied the vines to the nails. Linda said, "Now we need to put worms or bugs on our hooks."

They caught some big bugs and stuck them on the bent nails.

Linda and her sister walked to a rocky place on the beach. They put their lines in the water and waited. They waited and waited. They could see many fish in the water—big fish, little fish. Some fish were green with red marks around their heads. Some fish were long and silver, like knives cutting through the water. Once in a while, a dark form of a large fish would move through the light green water.

The girls could see the fish, but the fish did not go after the bugs on the hooks. The girls fished for almost two hours. Finally, Kathy caught a fish, but it was only about three inches long.

Kathy said, "We will never catch enough fish to have a fish dinner."

Linda said, "We have to think of another way to catch fish."

The girls sat there on the sunny rocks and thought and thought. Finally Linda said, "I've got an idea. We will use a net. We will put the net in the water. When fish swim into the net, we will pull the net out of the water."

The girls went back into the jungle and got lots of vines. Then they tied the vines together. Soon they had a net. It was very heavy. Kathy and Linda could hardly haul it along the beach.

They finally hauled the net to a ledge of rocks over the water.

The girls dropped the net into the water and waited for fish to swim into it. Soon, there were many fish inside the net. Some of them looked nearly as big as Kathy.

"Let's pull the net up," Linda said. "Pull fast."

The girls tried to pull the net out of the water. But the fish were pulling the net in the opposite direction. The fish pulled the net farther into the water. "We're slipping!" Kathy cried. Splash! Both of the girls fell into the water.

As the girls climbed back onto the rocks, Linda said, "We'll have to think of a better way to pull the net out of the water."

MORE NEXT TIME

D Number your paper from 1 through 27.

Skill Items

Use the words in the box to write complete sentences.

foul	swirled	echoed	normal	enough
billows	juice	enormous	inner	occasional

1. The smoke _____ in _____ _____.
2. The _____ _____ smell was _____.

Write words from the box that mean the same thing as the underlined parts of the sentences.

- the reason
- coconuts
- fronds
- echo
- crate
- finally
- the outcome
- frost

3. She was happy with how things turned out.
4. Many of the palm trees' branches broke off in the storm.
5. He filled the wooden box with dishes.

Review Items

Write **W** for **warm-blooded** animals and **C** for **cold-blooded** animals.

6. dog
7. cow
8. pig
9. spider
10. bee

The picture shows objects caught in a giant whirlpool.

11. Write the letter of the object that will go down the hole in the whirlpool first.
12. Write the letter of the object that will go down the hole in the whirlpool next.
13. Write the letter of the object that will go down the hole in the whirlpool last.

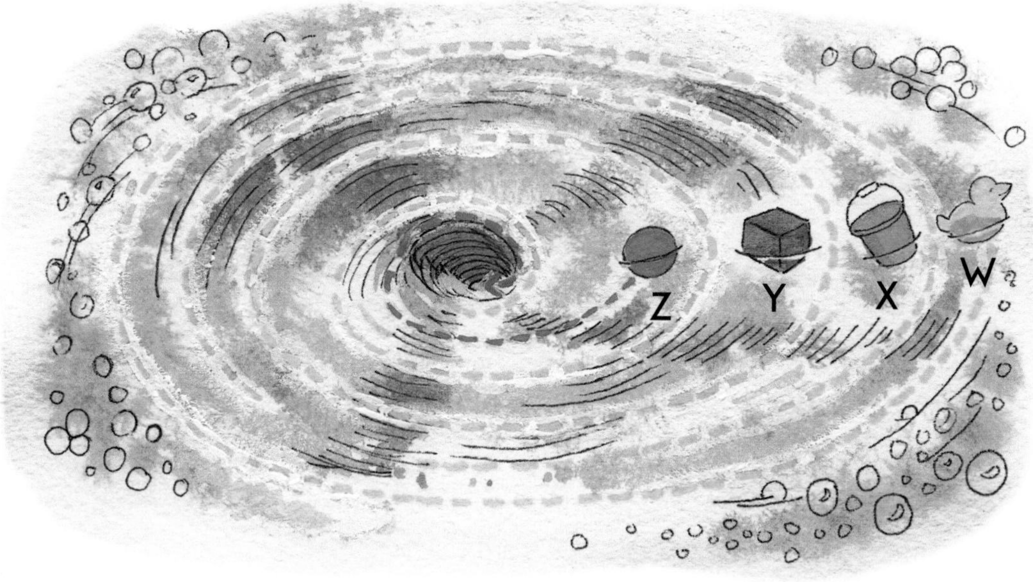

14. Palm trees cannot live in places that get ______.
15. What are the branches of palm trees called?
16. Name 2 things that grow on different palm trees.

17. What part does the **H** show?
18. What part does the **G** show?
19. What part does the **E** show?
20. What part does the **F** show?

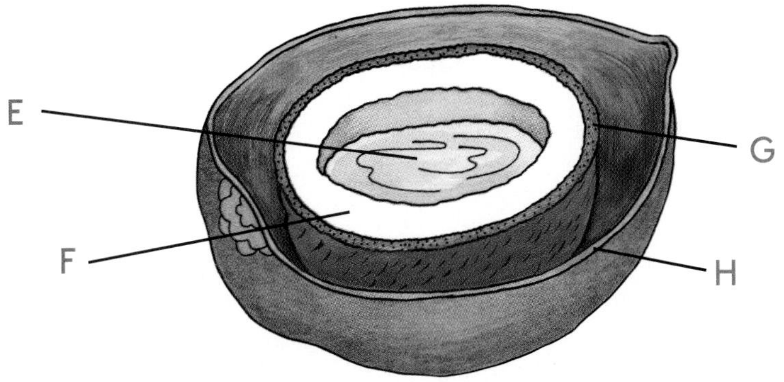

21. Lee is 8 miles high. Sam is 6 miles high. Who is colder?
22. Tell why.

23. The United States is not a state. It is a ___.
24. Japan is a ___.
25. How many states are in the United States?
26. When we weigh very small things, the unit we use is ___.
27. You can see drops of water on grass early in the morning. What are those drops called?

59

A

1	2	3	4
1. imagine	1. support	1. raw	1. splashed
2. neither	2. startled	2. force	2. twigs
3. beauty	3. seconds	3. burst	3. steady
4. unpleasant	4. gather	4. tied	4. overhead
5. occasionally	5. seashell	5. twice	5. straightened
6. shoulders		6. scale	6. scraped

B

Linda and Kathy Construct a Machine

Linda and Kathy were not able to pull the net from the water when it was filled with fish.

Linda began to think of a way to solve this problem. She sat on the rocks near the edge of the ocean and thought. Waves rolled in and splashed against the rocks.

Suddenly, Linda jumped up and said, "I've got it."

Linda continued, "We will make a machine for pulling the net out of the water."

Kathy said, "I don't know what kind of machine that could be."

Linda said, "It's just a log with a long handle. We'll tie vines to the log. We'll turn the handle around and the vines will pull the net out of the water."

The girls found a small straight tree trunk. Then they got boards from the crate and they pulled nails from the crate.

Suddenly Kathy pointed to something floating in the water and said, "Look. There's a white box."

Linda got a stick and pulled the box to shore. It had a big red cross on it. Linda said, "This is a first-aid kit. It must be from our ship."

The girls opened the kit and looked inside. Everything was dry.

"Look," Linda said and held up a small plastic box. Four matches were inside.

"Wow," Kathy said. "If those matches work, we'll be able to start a fire. Should we test one to see if it works?"

"No," Linda said. "There are only four of them. We may need all four to get a fire going."

Linda said, "Let's get back to work. Our next job is to use the boards from the crate to support the tree trunk."

An hour later, the girls had completed these supports.

PICTURE 1

Next, the sisters put the log in place and attached a handle to one end of the log. The handle was a board from the crate. They hammered three nails into it.

Now the machine looked like this:

PICTURE 2

Next, the sisters went into the jungle and found long vines. They tied them together and nailed one end of the vines to the log. They tied the other end to the net. Now their machine looked like this:

PICTURE 3

Linda explained, "We'll put the net out in the water and wait for fish to swim into it. Then we'll just turn the handle on our machine. The vines will wind around the log, and we'll pull the net up onto the beach."

So the girls put their net in the water. They went back up on the rock and waited. But no fish swam into the net. The day was hot and the wind was not blowing. The girls waited for more than an hour. Then a wind started to blow, and in a short time lots of fish started to gather close to the shore—some very large fish.

When there were lots of fish in the net, Linda said, "Okay, let's pull our net out of the water."

The girls ran up the beach to their machine. They grabbed the handle and turned it. It took a lot of force, but each time they turned the handle all the way around, the net got closer and closer to the shore.

PICTURE 4

The girls kept turning the handle. Linda's hands were sore, but she kept turning the handle and slowly, the net came out of the water. When the net was about 10 feet up the beach, the girls stopped turning and ran back to see what was in the net. It had lots of fish in it. Some of them were bigger than Kathy.

"Wow," Linda said.

Kathy said, "Let's put some of them back."

The girls kept four fish and put the rest back. The fish were glad to be back in the water, and they swam quickly from the shore.

Kathy said, "It's time to see if the matches work."

Linda said, "We'll need some dry grass and twigs." The girls found some and made a pile behind the big rock. Most of the time there was no wind here, but once in a while a hard gust of wind swirled through the grass and twigs.

The girls waited until the wind wasn't blowing. Quickly, Linda lit the first match and held it against the grass. Just then a gust of wind blew it out. The same thing happened to the second match. The third match worked. Within a few seconds, the whole pile of grass and twigs burst into flames.

"We did it," Linda said. "We're going to have a fish dinner."

MORE NEXT TIME

C Number your paper from 1 through 27.

Skill Item

1. Compare object A and object B. Remember, first tell how they're the same. Then tell how they're different.

Object A

Object B

Review Items

2. Let's say you are outside when the temperature is 40 degrees. What is the temperature inside your body?
3. Let's say you are outside when the temperature is 85 degrees. What is the temperature inside your body?
4. Let's say a fly is outside when the temperature is 85 degrees. What is the temperature inside the fly's body?
5. The stream water that Linda and Kathy found was different from the ocean water. **Tell 2 ways it was different.**
   The stream water was ____ and ____.
6. How many shells does a coconut have?
7. What is the juice inside a coconut called?
8. All machines make it easier for someone to ____.
9. Name a state in the United States that is bigger than Italy.

10. Italy is shaped something like a ___.

11. Write 2 letters that show bulkheads.
12. Write 2 letters that show decks.
13. Which letter shows where the bow is?
14. Which letter shows where the stern is?

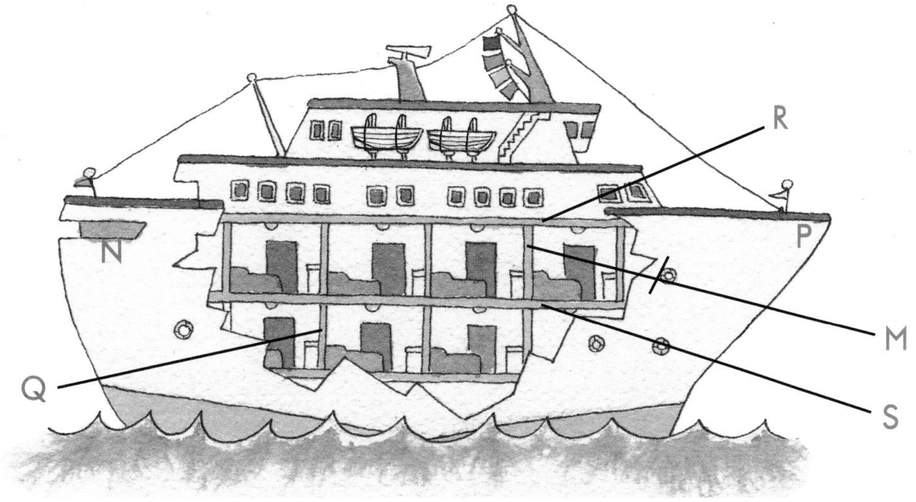

15. Which arrow shows the way Linda's hand will move?
16. Which arrow shows the way the crate will move?

E ←

G →

17. The biggest state in the United States is ____.
18. The second biggest state in the United States is ____.
19. A mile is a little more than ____ feet.
20. Write the name of the state in the United States that is bigger than Japan.
    - Ohio
    - Alaska
    - New York

21. You would have the least power if you pushed against one of the handles. Which handle is that?
22. Which handle would give you the most power?

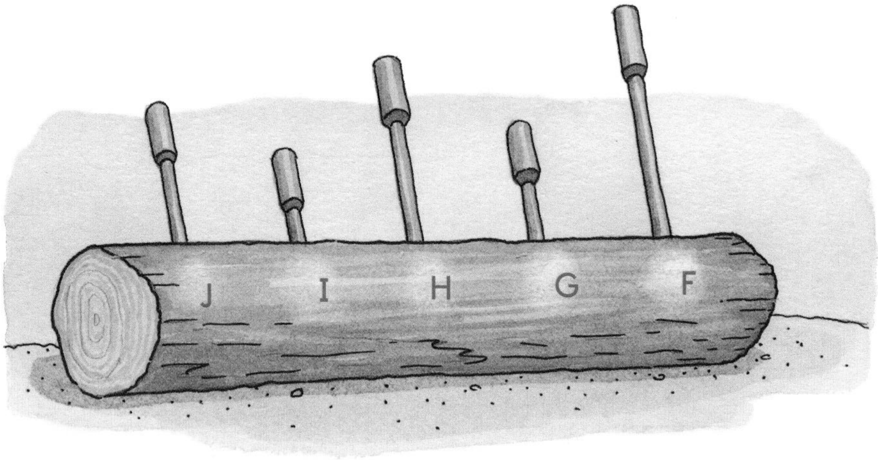

23. Write the letter of the plane that is in the warmest air.
24. Write the letter of the plane that is in the coldest air.

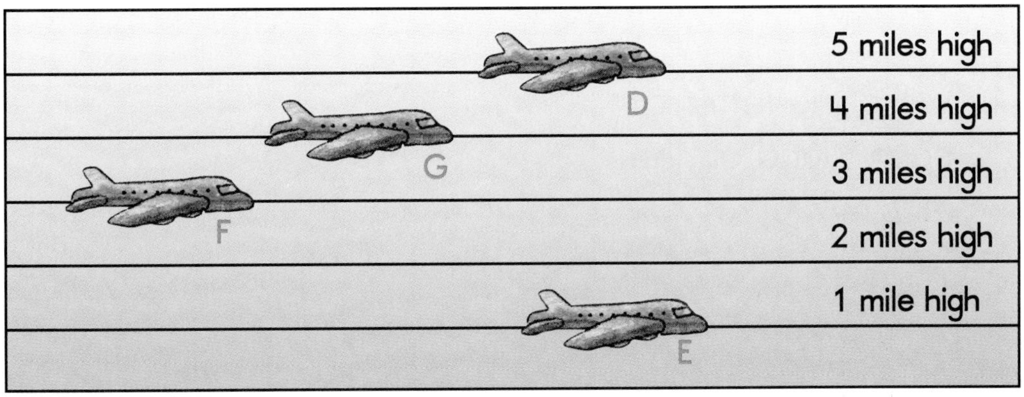

25. Does dew form in the middle of the day?
26. Dew forms when the air gets ___.
    - cooler
    - windy
    - warmer
27. What's the boiling temperature of water?
    - 212 miles
    - 212 degrees
    - 112 degrees

60

TEST 6

Number your paper from 1 through 32.

1. Write the letter of each island on the map.

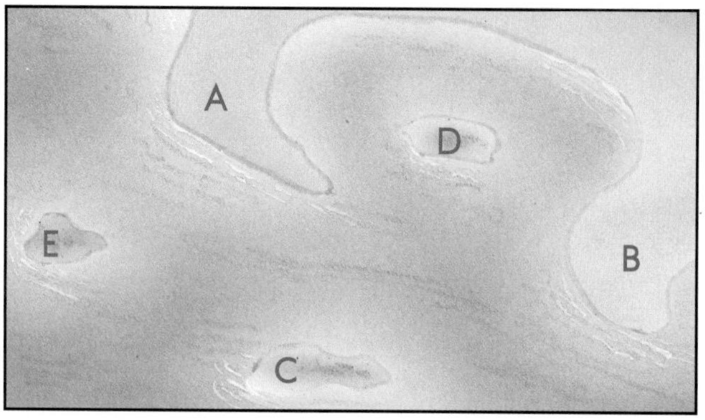

2. Jar A is filled with fresh water. Jar B is filled with ocean water. Which jar is heavier?
3. Which jar will freeze at 32 degrees?
4. Will the other jar freeze when it is **less than** 32 degrees or **more than** 32 degrees?

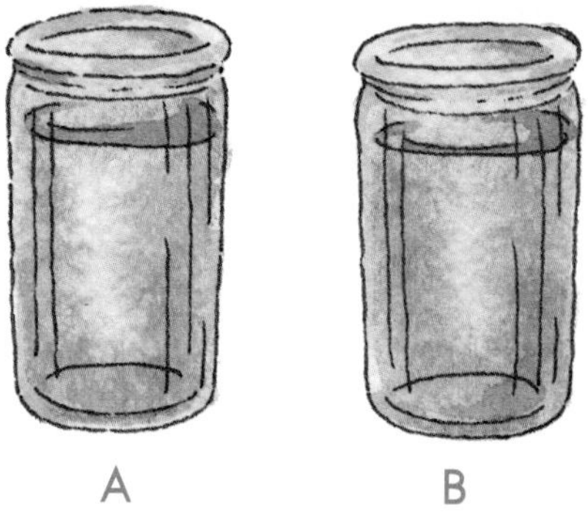

5. Write the letters of the 9 places that are in the United States.

a. Denver
b. Lake Michigan
c. China
d. Alaska
e. New York City
f. Chicago
g. Texas
h. San Francisco
i. Ohio
j. Japan
k. Turkey
l. California
m. Italy

6. The ship in the picture is sinking. It is making currents as it sinks. Write the letter of the object that will go down the whirlpool first.
7. Write the letter of the object that will go down the whirlpool last.

8. A plane that flies from Italy to New York City goes in which direction?

9. Which letter shows where Italy is?
10. Which letter shows where China is?
11. Which letter shows where Turkey is?
12. Is the United States shown on this map?

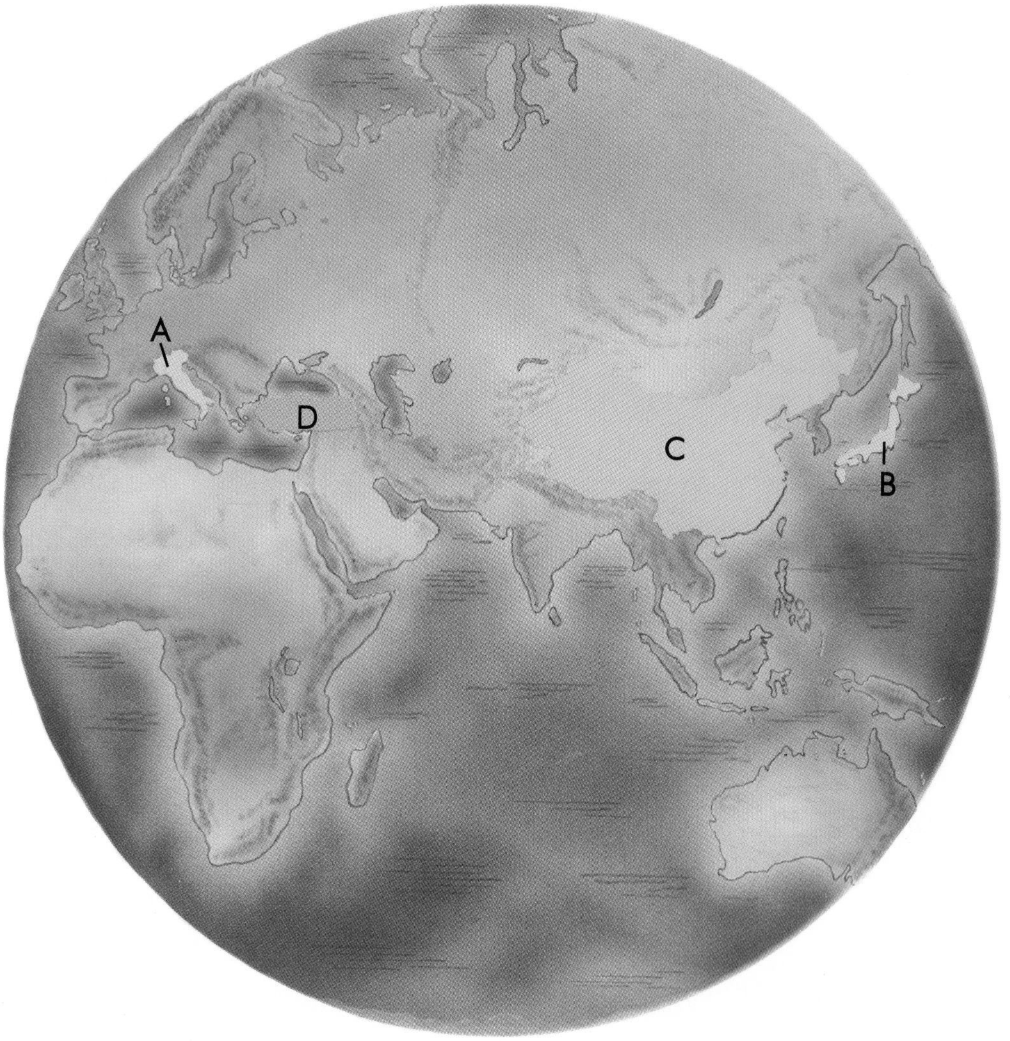

13. Which arrow shows the way Linda's hand will move?
14. Which arrow shows the way the crate will move?

15. Write the letter of the plane that is in the warmest air.

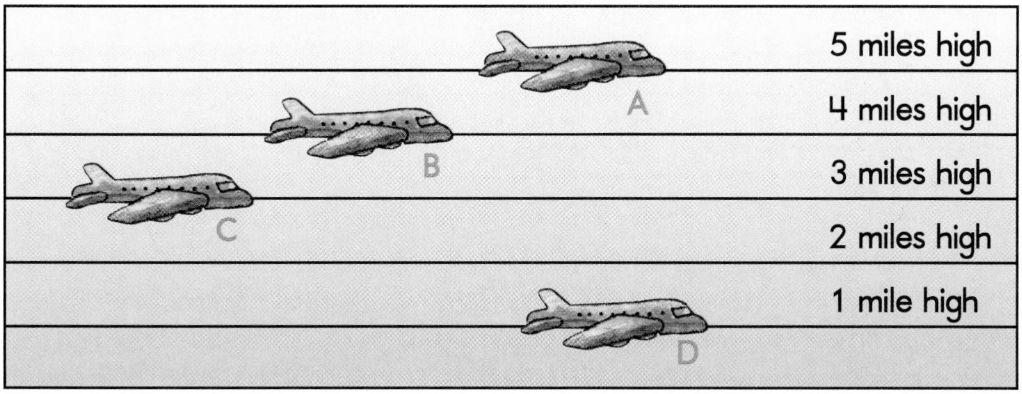

16. Palm trees cannot live in places that get ___.
17. Name 2 things that grow on different palm trees.

18. All machines make it easier for someone to ____.

19. You would have the most power if you pushed against one of the handles. Which handle is that?
20. Which handle would give you the least amount of power?

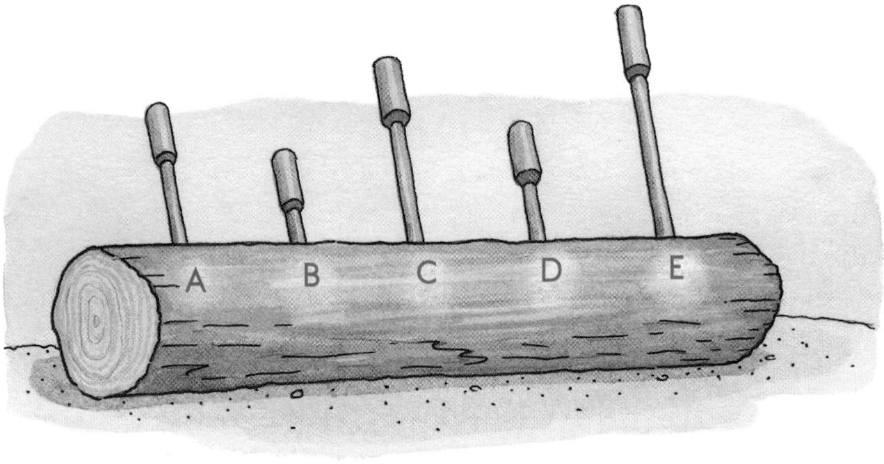

The arrow on the handle shows which way it turns.

21. Which arrow shows the way the log moves?
22. Which arrow shows the way the vine moves?

23. What part does the **G** show?
24. What part does the **H** show?
25. What part does the **K** show?
26. What part does the **J** show?

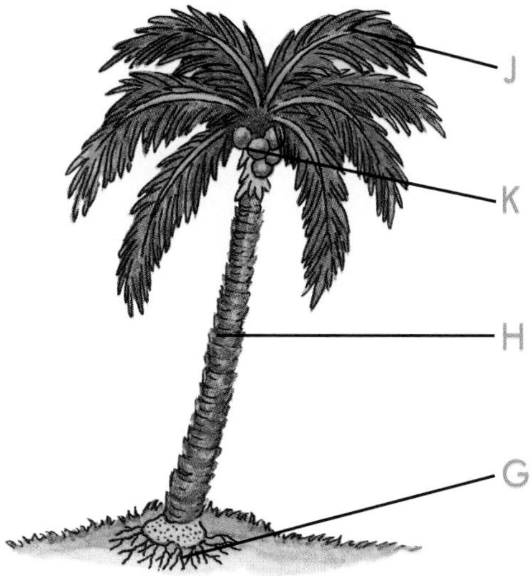

Skill Items

27. Compare object A and object B. Remember, first tell how they're the same. Then tell how they're different.

Object A

Object B

For each item, write the underlined word from the sentences in the box.

The lifeboat disappeared in the whirlpool.
The smoke swirled in enormous billows.
The occasional foul smell was normal.

28. What underlining names an emergency boat that is on a large ship?
29. What underlining means **usual?**
30. What underlining names water that goes around and around as it goes down?
31. What underlining means **very, very large?**
32. What underlining means **once in a while?**

END OF TEST 6

A

1
1. <u>after</u>noon
2. <u>finger</u>nails
3. <u>over</u>head
4. <u>sea</u>shell

2
1. directly
2. imagined
3. crackling
4. fading
5. nodded
6. scraped

3
1. buckle
2. scales
3. unpleasant
4. neither
5. orange
6. task

4
1. gusts
2. settles
3. turtle
4. ugh
5. beauty
6. foam

5
1. chilled
2. damage
3. cough
4. fever
5. signal

B Figuring Out the Time of Day

Linda and Kathy do not have any clocks, so they cannot tell exactly what time it is. But they can figure out if it is morning, noon, afternoon, evening, or night. To figure out the time, they use facts about the sun.

Here are those facts:

- The sun always comes up in the east. That's called sunrise.
- The sun always goes down in the west. That's called sunset.
- When the sun is coming up in the east, it is morning.
- When the sun is right overhead, it is noon.
- When the sun sets in the west, it is evening.

The picture below shows the sun at different times of day. The arrows show which way the sun is moving.

Touch sun A. That is the first sun Linda and Kathy see in the morning. It is in the east.

Touch sun B. That sun is higher in the east. They see that sun later in the morning.

Touch sun C. That sun is right overhead. When they see this sun, they know it's around noon.

Touch sun D. That sun is moving down in the west. It is an afternoon sun.

Sun E is the last sun they see. That sun is in the west.

If you know where the sun is, you can figure out directions. If you face the sun that you see early in the morning, in which direction are you facing?

If you face the sun that you see at the end of the day, in which direction are you facing?

C The Girls Have Fish for Dinner

The girls had made a fire. Now there was a nice warm campfire burning behind the big rock.

Linda and Kathy had made the fire when the sun was almost directly overhead. They kept the fire going until late afternoon. They did that by putting sticks on it from time to time. The wind blew and the fire made crackling sounds. When the sun was setting in the west, the girls made the fire much bigger by putting some large dry branches on it. They needed a bigger fire to cook their dinner. Then the sisters began the unpleasant task of cleaning the fish.

"Ugh," Kathy said. "I don't want to do this."

"Me neither," Linda said. "But we've got to."

"I don't know how," Kathy said.

"We've got to scrape the scales off the outside of the fish. Then we have to take out the insides."

"Ugh," Kathy said. "I'll scrape the scales, but you'll have to do the insides."

"Okay," Linda said. Kathy used a seashell to scale the fish. She pressed a sharp end of the seashell against the fish and then scraped from the tail of the fish toward the head.

The scales popped off the fish. They were like little fingernails that you could see through. The scales stuck to everything. By the time Kathy had scaled two fish, her hair was covered with scales. So was her face. "Ugh," she said.

Linda made a knife from her belt buckle. She made the buckle sharp by rubbing it against a rock. She tied the buckle to a stick. She then used her knife to cut the fish open. She took out their insides and pulled out most of their bones.

• • •

There are very few places more beautiful than an island in the Pacific Ocean. And there are very few times of day more beautiful than sunset. The sun settles into the west, moving behind clouds that become filled with red and orange and yellow. The ocean looks dark, and the white foam and spray look gray in the fading light. The birds are quiet, and the breeze is sometimes warm and sometimes cool, as it gusts and stops and then gusts again.

That's how it was when Linda and Kathy ate their dinner that evening. They cooked their dinner in a large turtle shell that Kathy had found on the beach. They cooked some green plants with the fish. They drank fresh water and ate the fish and plants.

"This is about the most beautiful place in the world," Kathy said.

Linda nodded and looked out over the ocean toward the sunset. For a moment she felt the beauty of the sunset. Then she imagined that there were ships out there somewhere. Then she wondered how long it would be

before one of those ships would find Kathy and her. Suddenly Linda felt cold and unhappy.

MORE NEXT TIME

D Number your paper from 1 through 26.

The picture shows the sun at different times of day.

1. Write the letter of the sun you see early in the morning.
2. Write the letter of the sun you see at noon.
3. Write the letter of the sun you see at sunset.
4. Write the letter of the sun that shows when the girls made the fire.
5. Write the letter of the sun that shows when the girls finished dinner.

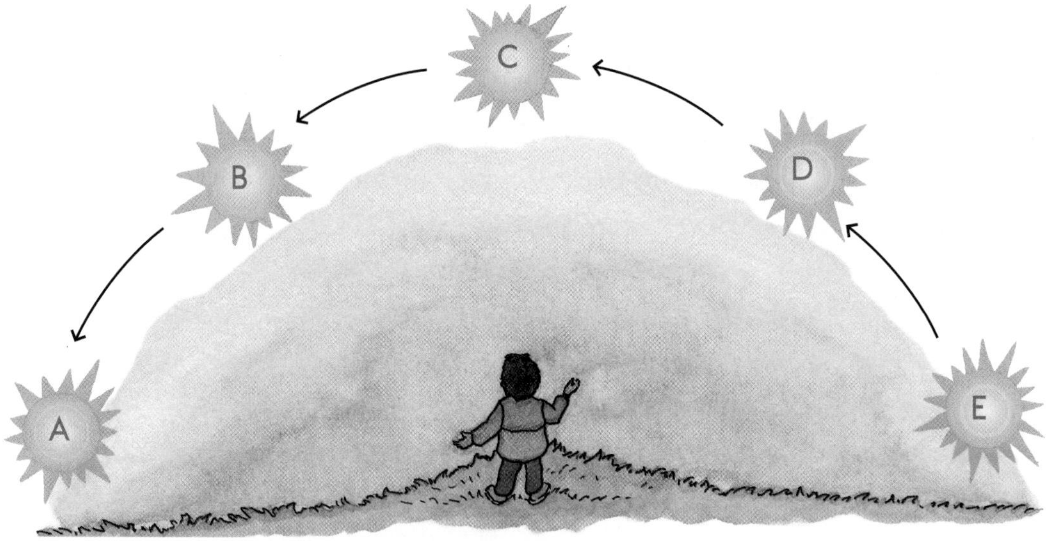

Skill Items

They constructed an enormous machine.

6. What word means **built?**
7. What word means **very large?**
8. What word names something that helps people do work?

Review Items

9. Linda and Kathy made a ___ to help them pull the fish net from the water.
10. What did the girls use for a handle?
11. The girls hammered the handle to the end of ___.
12. The girls got nails from ___.
13. They tied one end of the vine to the log and the other end of the vine to the ___.
14. When the fish were in the net, how did the girls get the net out of the water?
15. Would it be easier to catch a fly on a hot day or a cold day?
16. Would a fly move faster or slower on a cold day?

17. A plane that flies from Italy to New York City goes in which direction?
18. Where are the gas tanks on a big jet?

19. What is the temperature of the water in each jar?
20. Write the letter of each jar that is filled with ocean water.
21. Jar B is not filled with ocean water. How do you know?

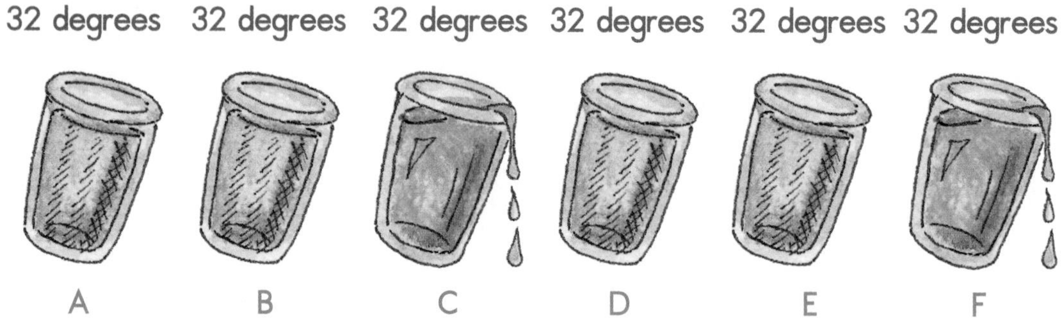

22. A mile is around ____ feet.

Jar A is filled with fresh water. Jar B is filled with ocean water.

23. Which jar is heavier?
24. Which jar will freeze at 32 degrees?
25. Will the other jar freeze when it is **more than 32 degrees** or **less than 32 degrees?**

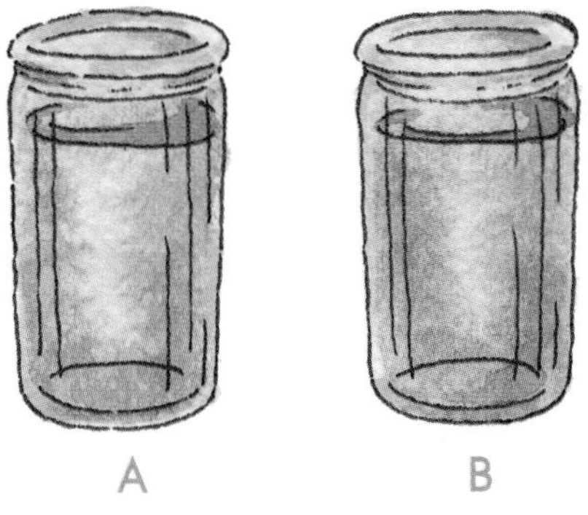

26. Write the letters of the 8 places that are in the United States.

a. Denver
b. Texas
c. Turkey
d. San Francisco
e. Ohio
f. Chicago
g. China
h. Italy
i. Lake Michigan
j. Japan
k. New York City
l. California

62

A

1	2	3
1. amazing	1. damage	1. forehead
2. cough	2. edge	2. normal
3. Greece	3. image	3. signal
4. rescue	4. ledge	4. fifteenth
5. important	5. imagine	5. harbor
6. comparison	6. orange	6. survive

4	5
1. chilled	1. fever
2. shoulders	2. woven
3. mumbled	3. built
4. occasionally	4. waving
5. highest	5. sliver
6. reporters	6. shaking

B Facts About Fevers

Your normal temperature is about 98 degrees. That's the temperature inside your body when you are healthy. Here are facts about fevers:

- When you have a fever, you are sick and your temperature goes up.

- Most fevers don't go over 101 degrees.
- A very high fever of more than 104 degrees may damage a person's brain.
- When people have high fevers, they may see things and hear things that are not real.

C Signaling for Help

Fourteen days had passed since the girls reached the island. Linda and Kathy were tired of fish and coconuts and bananas. They were waiting for a ship to come by. But for two weeks, no ship came.

Then on the fifteenth day Linda and Kathy heard something. It was an airplane. They ran out onto the beach and looked into the sky. Where was it?

They looked and listened for a long time. The sound of the plane got louder and louder, but still they couldn't see it. Then, all at once, it came over the trees. It was not very high. There it was, speeding over the beach.

The girls ran down the beach, waving their arms. They yelled, "Here we are. Here we are." They ran after the plane, but it went on, over the ocean. "Here we are. Here we are," they called.

They watched the plane get smaller and smaller. "Come back. Come back!" Kathy yelled. The girls watched the plane until they couldn't see it anymore.

"Maybe it will come back," Kathy said.

The girls looked at the sky for at least an hour. Then Kathy started to cry. "We'll never get off this island."

"Don't talk like that," Linda said. "We will get off this island. That plane didn't see us because we didn't give the plane much to see. So we'll make things that any plane or ship will see. We'll start right now by getting some rocks—lots of them."

The girls carried rock after rock onto the beach and put each rock in place. Soon the rocks formed the letters H-E-L. Linda and Kathy got more rocks. Now the rocks formed H-E-L-P. The word was over 20 feet long.

When they had finished, Kathy said, "A plane should be able to see that."

Linda said, "Right, but a ship won't. We have to make another signal for ships."

The girls went to the highest hill in the jungle. They built a fire on the hill. Then they went back into the jungle to get lots and lots of green leaves.

Linda said, "We'll keep a big pile of leaves next to the fire. We'll keep the fire going all the time. When we see a ship, we'll dump the green leaves on the fire. The leaves will make a lot of smoke."

The girls kept the fire going for four days. On the fourth day, Kathy had a fever. Linda felt Kathy's forehead. It felt much hotter than a normal temperature. In fact, Linda thought that Kathy's temperature was over 101 degrees.

During the day Kathy slept on the hill near the fire. Occasionally, she woke up. Once, she mumbled something in her sleep about "the ship, the ship." The girls had woven some mats from leaves and vines. When the sun began to set in the west, Linda covered Kathy with one of these mats. She did that so Kathy wouldn't become too chilled by the cool air.

Just as the evening sky was turning bright yellow and orange, Kathy sat up. "A ship," she said. Her eyes were wide. She pointed to the south. "A ship. I see a ship."

"Take it easy," Linda said, putting her hands on Kathy's shoulders.

"No, no," Kathy shouted. "There's a ship." Her body was shaking.

MORE NEXT TIME

D Number your paper from 1 through 24.

Skill Items

Write the word from the box that means the same thing as the underlined part of each sentence.

supported	attached	jungle	contest
image	startled	rushed	fever

1. The picture was faded.
2. The gloves were connected to the jacket.
3. He was suddenly surprised by the loud noise.

4. Compare object A and object B. Remember, first tell how they are the same. Then tell how they're different.

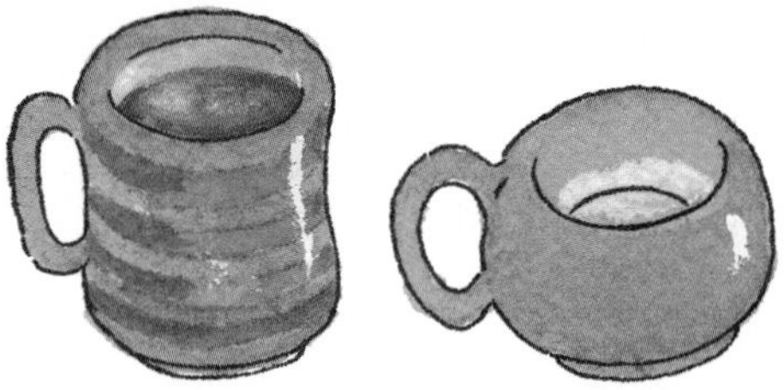

Object A Object B

Use the words in the box to write complete sentences.

attached	constructed	occasional		steady
machine	normal	hauled	foul	force

5. The ___ ___ smell was ___.
6. They ___ an enormous ___.

Review Items

7. How far is it from New York City to San Francisco?
   - 5 hundred miles
   - 25 hundred miles
   - 5 thousand miles
8. How far is it from San Francisco to Japan?
   - 5 hundred miles
   - 25 hundred miles
   - 5 thousand miles
9. What ocean do you cross to get from San Francisco to Japan?

10. How many legs does an insect have?
11. How many legs does a fly have?
12. How many legs does a bee have?
13. How many legs does a spider have?
14. How many parts does a spider's body have?
15. How many parts does a fly's body have?

16. Write the letter of the sun you see at noon.
17. Write the letter of the sun you see at sunset.
18. Write the letter of the sun you see early in the morning.
19. Write the letter of the sun that shows when Linda and Kathy finished dinner.

Look at the skin around each hair. Make an arrow like this ↑ if the hair is moving up. Make an arrow like this ↓ if the hair is moving down.

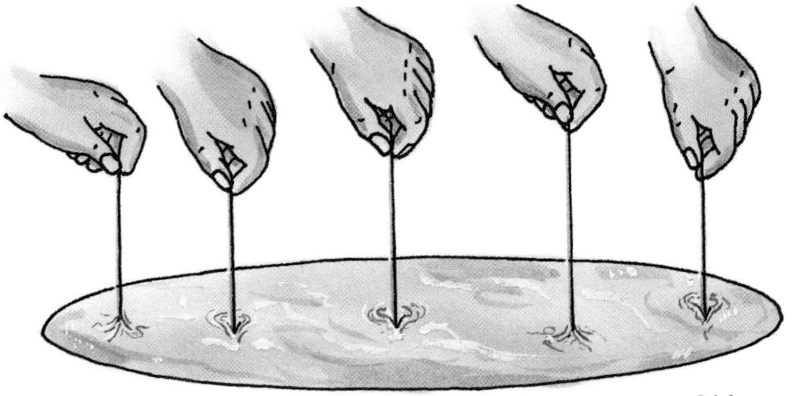

20. 21. 22. 23. 24.

63

A

1

1. war
2. protect
3. shield
4. soldier
5. calendar
6. electric

2

1. rescued
2. excited
3. lowered
4. survived
5. ordered
6. coughed

3

1. important
2. tugboat
3. newspaper
4. notice

4

1. S. S. Mason
2. S. S. Milton
3. dull
4. amazing
5. Reeves

5

1. sliver
2. fairly
3. reporters
4. harbor
5. Troy
6. ago

B

Landing a Ship

Landing a ship is a lot like landing an airplane.

- Airplanes land in airports. Ships land in harbors.
- Airplanes load and unload at gates. Ships load and unload at docks.
- Sometimes a little truck pulls an airplane to the gate. Sometimes a little boat pulls a large ship to the dock.

The boat that pulls the ship is called a tugboat. The picture shows a tugboat pulling an ocean liner into a busy harbor in Japan. Another tugboat is helping turn the ship. Along the shore are more docks with ships parked at them.

C The Girls Are Rescued

Linda didn't really believe that there was a ship in sight. But she slowly turned her head and looked south. She saw dark water and more dark water and a sliver of white. It was a ship—a ship with the sun shining on one side of it. "A ship," Linda said out loud.

Kathy raised her arms and waved. "Hello," she hollered.

"They must be two miles away," Linda said. "They won't be able to hear us. We've got to make a smoke signal."

The girls dumped all the green leaves on the fire. After a few moments, large billows of smoke rolled into the air.

The sliver on the ocean seemed to be getting larger. "More smoke," Kathy hollered. The girls threw heaps of grass on the fire. The fire coughed out bigger and bigger billows.

The ship was an ocean liner like the one that Linda and Kathy had been on. Now Linda could see people standing on the deck.

"It's stopping!" Kathy yelled. "The ship is stopping!" Linda and her sister ran down the hill. Linda fell and cut her leg. But she didn't notice it. Linda got up and ran as fast as she could until she reached the shore. She waved her arms.

A little boat was slowly lowered down the side of the great ocean liner. The little boat started toward the shore. Linda was crying for the first time since the ship went down almost three weeks before. "We're going home," Linda said. "We're going home."

The little boat came up to the beach. The girls ran into the ocean to meet the boat. One of the three men in the boat said, "I'm Captain Reeves from the ship S. S. Milton."

Linda said, "I'm Linda Jones and this is my sister Kathy. We were on the ship S. S. Mason when it sank."

Linda looked at Kathy and smiled. Then she remembered something. "Kathy's sick," Linda said.

The captain felt Kathy's forehead and ordered the men in the boat to take her to the ship. Linda and the captain stayed on the island so that Linda could show how she and her sister survived for almost three weeks.

It was getting fairly dark when Linda showed the captain their simple machine. "Amazing," the captain said. Linda also showed the signal for airplanes that was on the beach.

"Amazing," the captain said again. "You're a very smart girl."

• • •

Linda felt very proud and very excited. Linda and her sister were stars on the S. S. Milton. Everybody wanted to talk to them and ask them questions or go swimming with them. The girls ate at the captain's table. Only very important people eat at the captain's table.

Kathy felt better the day after the girls left the island. The girls traveled on the S. S. Milton for one week. When a tugboat finally pulled the ship into the harbor in Japan, many small boats crowded around the S. S. Milton. The girls' father met them at the dock. There were newspaper reporters in the crowd, too. The reporters asked the girls many questions.

Then their father drove them to their new house in Japan. It was a very pretty house on a small hill with a large tree in the front yard. Linda's father said, "You've done so many things lately that you may find it dull living here."

Linda hugged her father. "No, Daddy, it won't be dull," she said. "I'm just glad to be here."

Kathy said, "Me, too."

THE END

D **Number your paper from 1 through 18.**

1. Airplanes land at airports. Ships land at _____.
   • gates • harbors • airports
2. Airplanes are pulled by little trucks. Ships are pulled by little _____.
3. Airplanes unload at gates. Ships unload at _____.
   • gates • docks • harbors

Skill Items

Here's a rule: **Fish are cold-blooded.**

4. A whale is not a fish. So what does the rule tell you about a whale?
5. A shark is a fish. So what does the rule tell you about a shark?
6. A snapper is a fish. So what does the rule tell you about a snapper?

Review Items

7. Which object is the hottest?
8. What is the temperature of that object?
9. Which object is the coldest?
10. What is the temperature of that object?

11. Write the letter of every line that is one inch long.
12. Write the letter of every line that is one centimeter long.

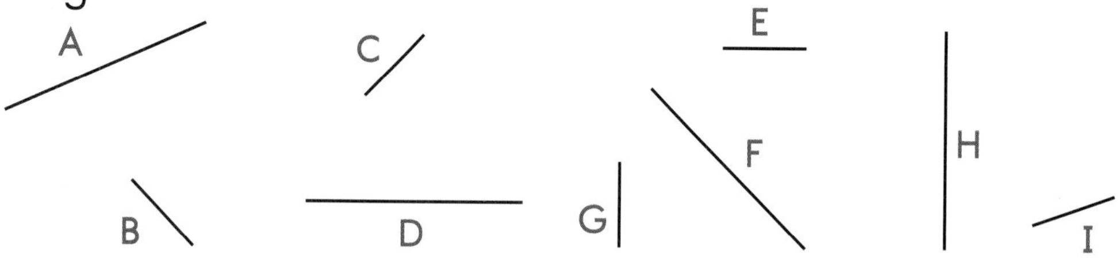

13. Palm trees cannot live in places that get ______.
14. What are the branches of palm trees called?
15. Name 2 things that grow on different palm trees.
16. All machines make it easier for someone to ______.

The arrow by the handle shows which way it turns.

17. Which arrow shows the way the log moves?
18. Which arrow shows the way the vine moves?

END OF LESSON 63 INDEPENDENT WORK

SPECIAL PROJECTS

PROJECT 1

Make a model of the machine that Linda and Kathy used to pull the fish net out of the water.

- For the tree trunk, use the cardboard tube from inside a roll of paper towels.
- For the handle, use a short pencil. Make a little hole in the tube and push the pencil through the hole.
- To hold the machine in place, use long pencils. Tie each pair of pencils together with rubber bands and stick the ends of the pencils in clay.
- For the vine, use string or make a thin vine from grass or other plants.
- For the net, use cheesecloth or make a net with string.
- For fish, make plastic cutouts or use small fish toys.

After you make your machine, you can show people how it works. Put the fish in a pan and fill the pan with water. Then put the net behind the fish and turn the handle to pull the fish from the water.

PROJECT 2

Make up more verses for the song below.

We were on a big ship, that sank in the sea.
We floated to an island, my sister and me.

64

A

1

1. weapon
2. succeed
3. sword
4. elephant
5. equipment

2

1. weapons
2. ladders
3. tanks
4. spears
5. shields

3

1. starve
2. war
3. ago
4. Greece
5. protect

4

1. battles
2. army
3. bows
4. calendar
5. suppose

5

1. dump
2. Troy
3. electric
4. soldiers

B Greece and Troy

In the next lesson, you will read a story that tells about a war between Troy and Greece. You can find Troy and Greece on the map of the world. The place that was called Troy is now part of Turkey. The country of Greece is between Italy and Turkey. Italy is shaped like a boot, and it looks like it is ready to step on Greece.

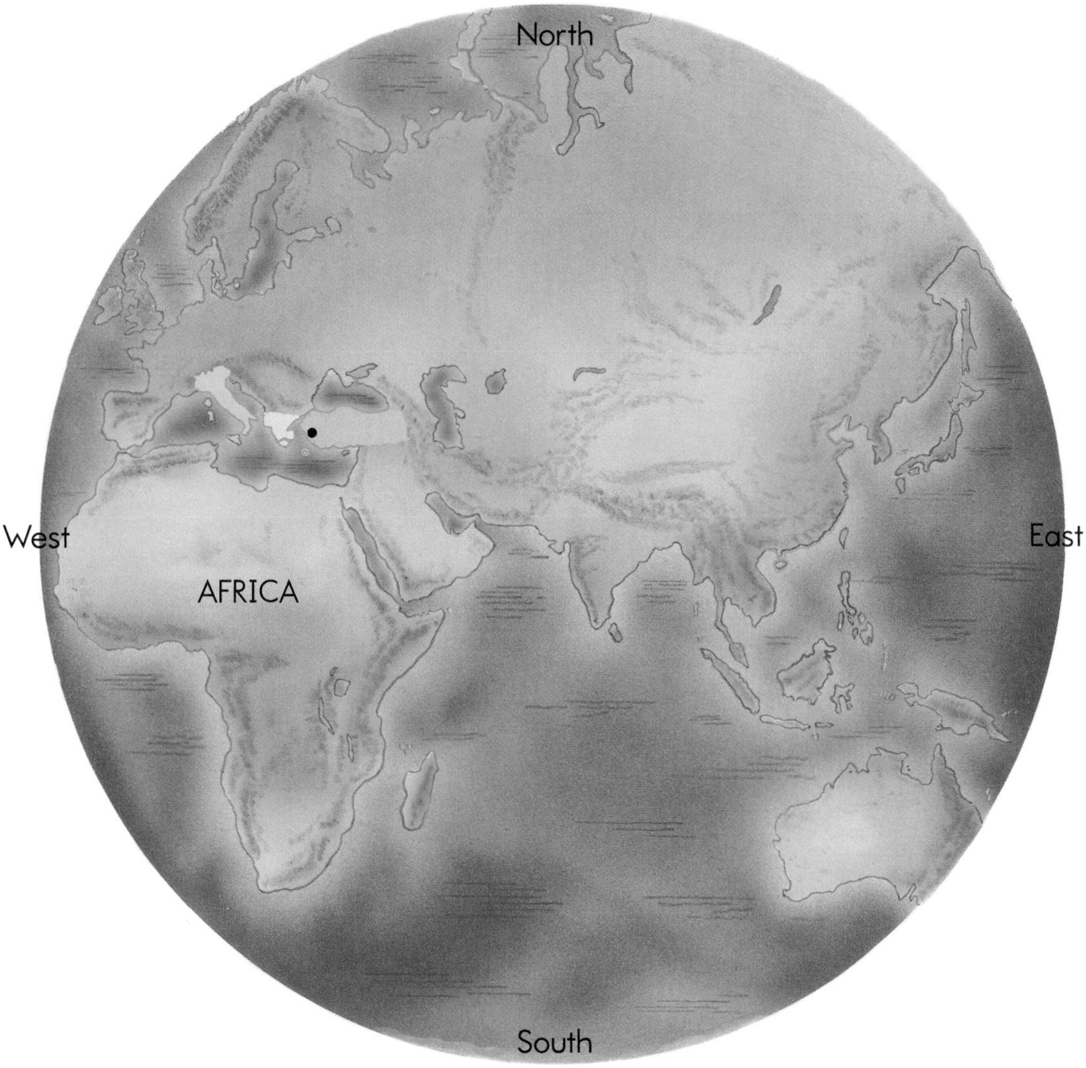

The map below makes it easier to see Troy and Greece. The war took place at Troy. The story that you'll read tells why that war took place.

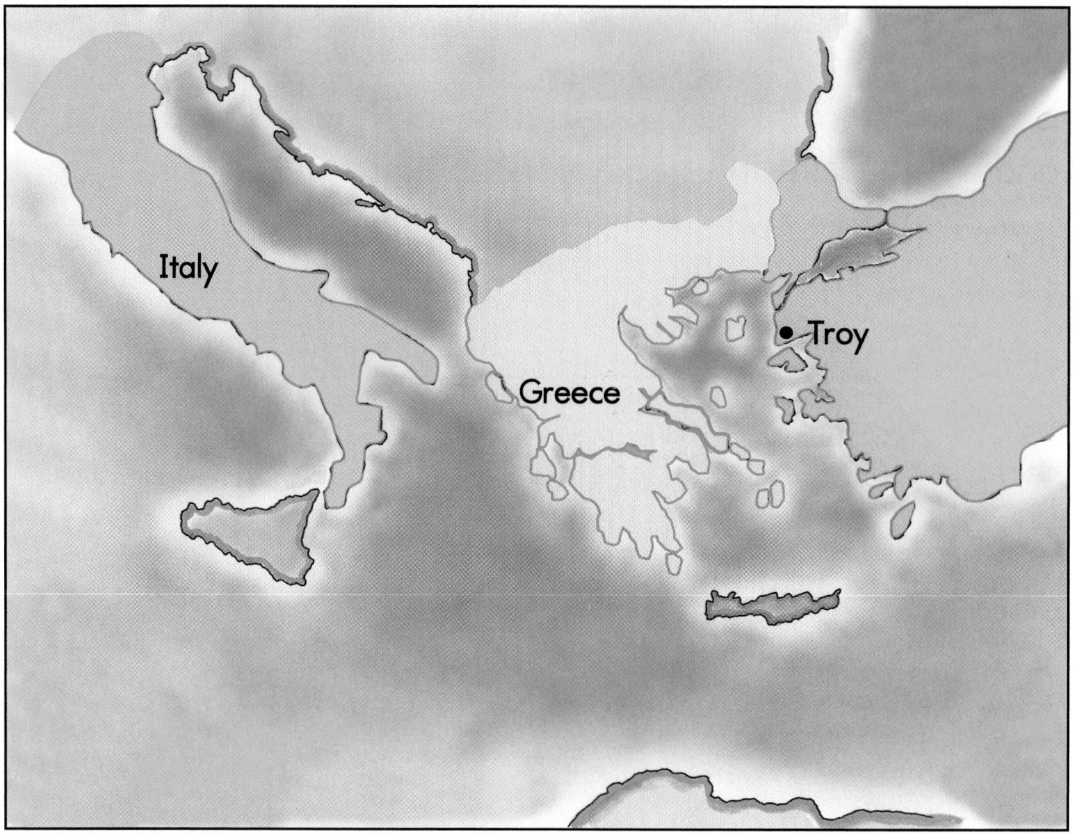

C Learning About a Time Line

You're going to read a story about something that took place a long time ago. To understand how long ago the story happened, you have to understand how a calendar works.

If the year is now 1999, the year 1 hundred years ago was 1899. If the year is now 1945, the year 1 hundred years ago was 1845.

Here's a rule about years: **The numbers get smaller as you go back in time.**

What are the first two numbers in the year 1970? If you go back 1 hundred years, the first two numbers would be 18. So the year 1 hundred years before 1970 is 1870.

What are the first two numbers in the year 1679? If you go back 1 hundred years, the first two numbers wouldn't be 16. They would be 15. So what year is 1 hundred years before 1679?

What are the first two numbers in the year 1965? If you go back 1 hundred years, what are the first two numbers? If you go back another 1 hundred years, what are the first two numbers? If you go back another 1 hundred years, what are the first two numbers?

So what year is 3 hundred years before 1965? Start with the year 1780. If you went back 2 hundred years, what are the first numbers? Say the year that is 2 hundred years before 1780.

What year is it now?

What year was it 1 hundred years ago?

What year were you born?

What year was it 1 hundred years before the year you were born?

The arrow in the picture on page 123 shows a time line. Here's the rule about the time line: **Things that happen right now are at the top of the time line.**

Things that happened a long time ago are near the bottom of the time line.

Touch the dot that says **now.** What year should go on that dot? Now touch dot B. That dot shows when you were born. That dot is very close to the top dot because you were born only a few years ago. What year goes on dot B?

Now touch dot C. That dot shows that the first airplane was made in 1903. That was about 1 hundred years ago.

Touch dot D. That dot shows the year 1 hundred years ago. What year was that?

Touch dot E. That dot shows the year 2 hundred years ago. What year was that?

Dot F shows the year that the United States became a country. What year was that?

Touch dot G. That dot shows the year 3 hundred years ago. What year was that?

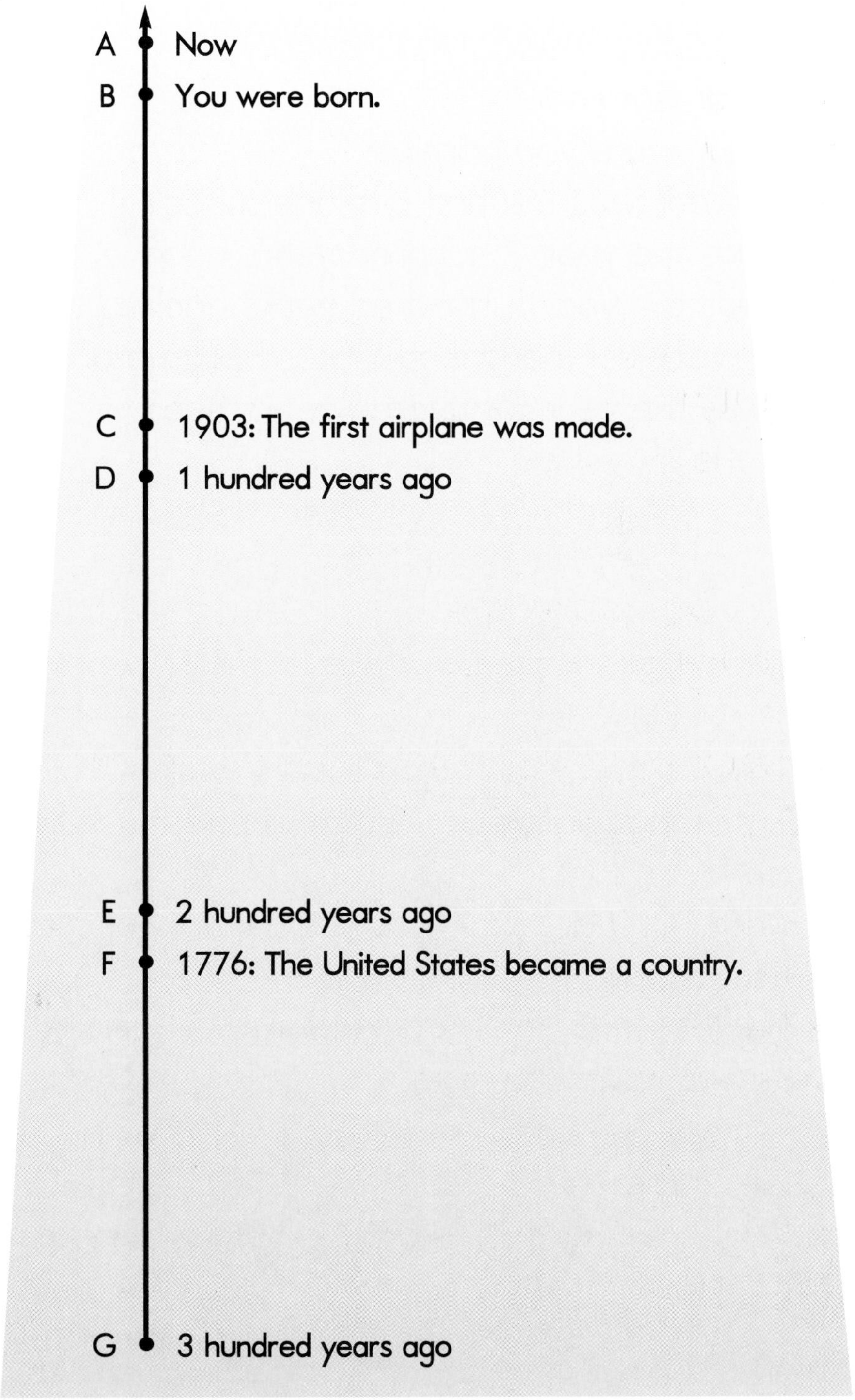
A Now
B You were born.
C 1903: The first airplane was made.
D 1 hundred years ago
E 2 hundred years ago
F 1776: The United States became a country.
G 3 hundred years ago

See how many of the dates you can remember without looking at the time line.

What year is it now?

What year were you born?

In what year was the first airplane made?

What was the year 1 hundred years ago?

What was the year 2 hundred years ago?

In what year did the United States become a country?

What was the year 3 hundred years ago?

D Number your paper from 1 through 24.

Skill Items

She survived until she was rescued.

1. What word means **saved from danger?**
2. What word means **managed to stay alive?**

Review Items

3. What does ocean water taste like?
4. If you drank lots of ocean water you would get ___.

5. Which arrow shows the way Linda's hand will move?
6. Which arrow shows the way the crate will move?

E ←

G →

Jar A is filled with fresh water. Jar B is filled with ocean water.

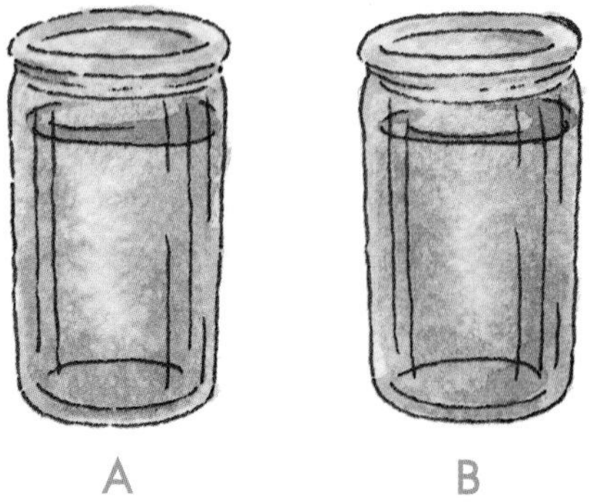

7. Which jar is heavier?
8. Which jar will freeze at 32 degrees?
9. Will the other jar freeze **above 32 degrees** or **below 32 degrees?**

10. Write the letter of each place that is in the United States.

a. New York City
b. California
c. Italy
d. San Francisco
e. Turkey
f. Alaska
g. Texas
h. Denver
i. Lake Michigan
j. Chicago
k. Japan
l. China
m. Ohio

11. Write the letter of each water strider.

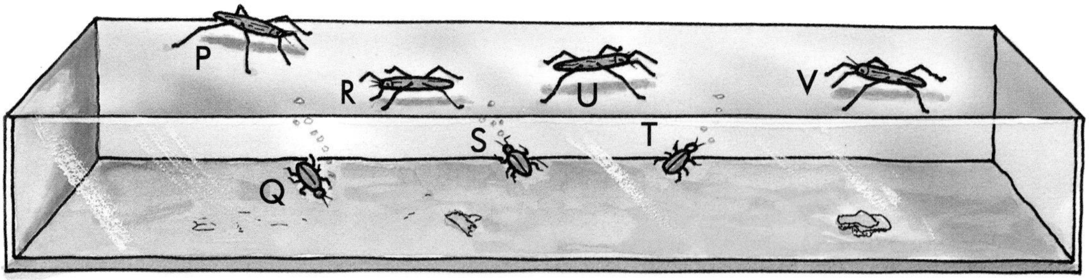

12. What part does the **A** show?
13. What part does the **B** show?
14. What part does the **C** show?
15. What part does the **D** show?

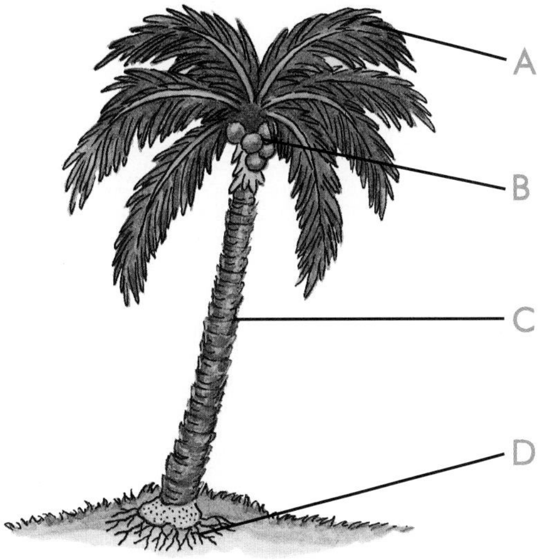

16. How many shells does a coconut have?
17. What is the juice inside a coconut called?
18. All machines make it easier for someone to ____.

19. Write the letter that shows a tugboat.
20. Write two letters that show ships.
21. Write two letters that show docks.

22. Airplanes land at airports. Ships land at ___.
23. Airplanes are pulled by little trucks. Ships are pulled by ___.
24. Airplanes unload at gates. Ships unload at ___.

A

1

1. Jesus Christ
2. equipment
3. elephant
4. protected

2

1. bows
2. swords
3. soldiers
4. battles
5. tanks

3

1. weapons
2. war
3. army
4. starve
5. ladders

4

1. spears
2. queen
3. Troy
4. shields
5. Helen

B

The City of Troy

The story that you're going to read took place a long time ago. It didn't take place one hundred years ago or two hundred years ago or three hundred years ago. It took place about 3 thousand years ago. It took place long before airplanes or cars were made. It took place long before the United States became a country.

The story took place 3 thousand years ago in a city called Troy. Herman flew right over Troy and Greece on his way to Italy. Troy was in the country that is now Turkey.

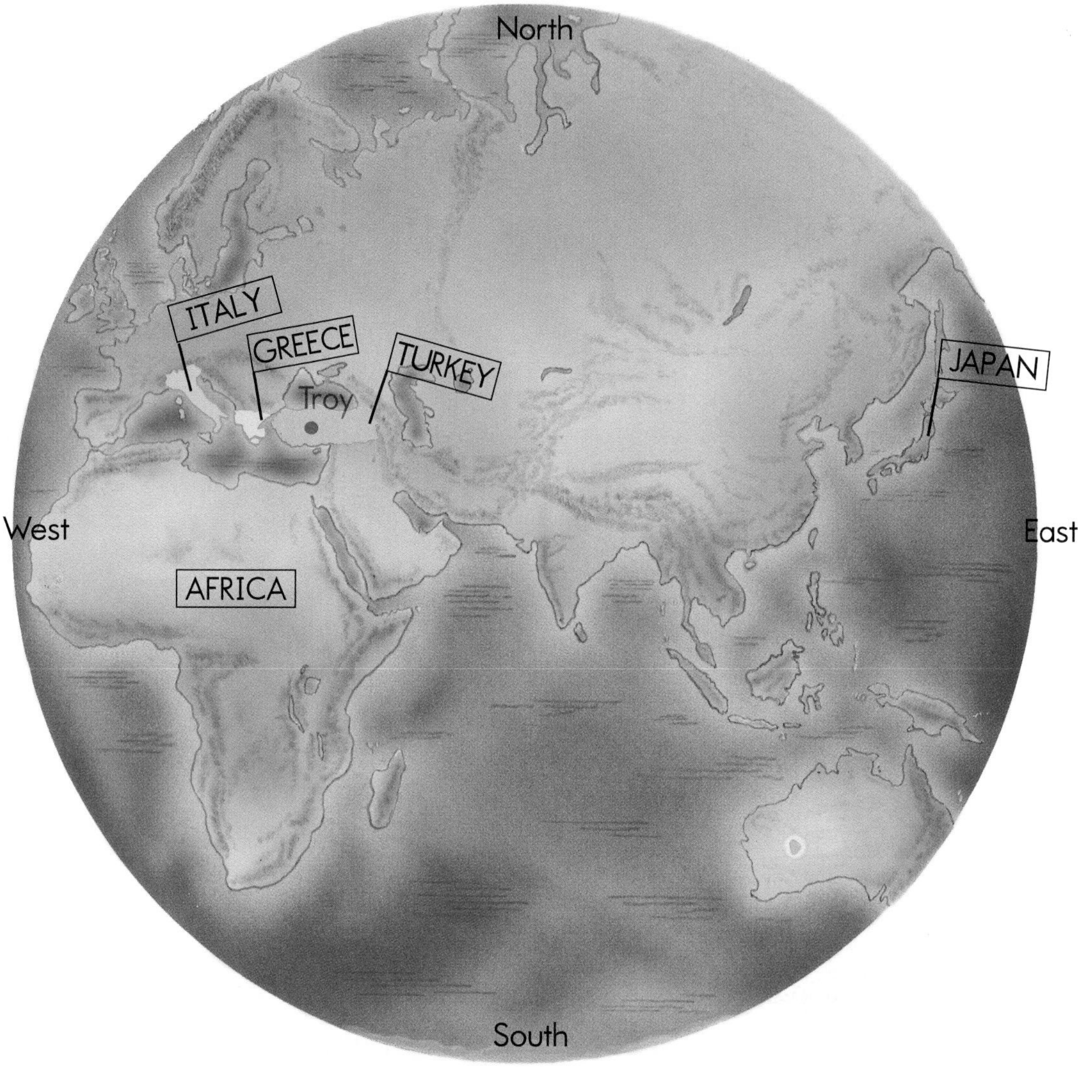

Troy was different from any city you have ever seen because there were no cars or buses in Troy. There were no telephones or televisions. There were no electric lights or refrigerators. The people in Troy had never seen any of these things because these things had not been made yet.

There were no street lights or trains. There were no planes and no guns. Although the people who lived in Troy did not have guns, they had battles and wars. They used bows and arrows and spears in these wars.

The city of Troy had a great wall around it. The wall was so high that you could not jump over it and you could not climb over it unless you had a very tall ladder. When the people inside Troy went in and out of the city, they went through a great gate that was as tall as the wall. When the people inside Troy did not want someone to

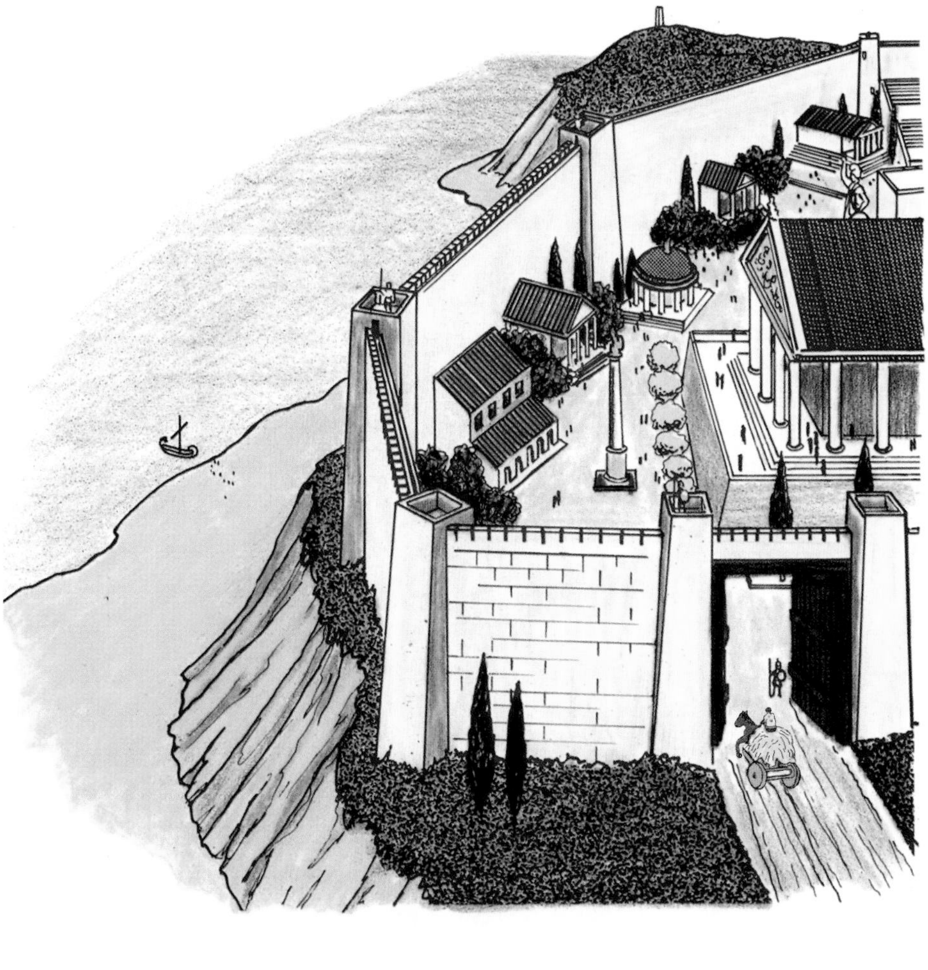

come inside the city, they closed the great gate. This gate was so strong that an elephant could not knock it down. In fact, it was so strong that ten elephants could not knock it down. Here's the rule about Troy: When the gate was closed, you could not get into the city.

Sometimes Troy went to war with another city. An army would come to Troy. This army did not have jets and tanks. This army did not have cars and great guns. But this army did have soldiers—lots of soldiers. And the soldiers had horses and ladders. The soldiers had shovels. The soldiers had swords and shields.

The picture shows some of the weapons the soldiers had.

The soldier is holding a sword in one hand. The soldier is holding a shield with the other hand. The shield is used to protect the soldier against swords and spears.

A spear is standing next to the soldier. You use a spear by throwing it.

A bow and some arrows are lying on the ground.

In back of the soldier are a ladder and a shovel. That ladder is used to help the soldier climb high walls. The shovel helps the soldier dig under walls.

The army would try to get inside the city by using these plans:

1. The army would try to get over the wall.
2. The army would try to dig under the wall.
3. The army would try to knock down the gate using great tree trunks on wheels.
4. The army would not let anybody out of the city so that the people inside would get very hungry.

For every plan that the army had, the people in Troy had a plan.

1. When the army would put ladders against the wall, the people of Troy would go to the top of the wall and push the ladders away.
2. When the army would dig holes under the wall, the people of Troy would dump boiling water into the holes.
3. When the army would try to knock down the gate, the people of Troy would shoot the soldiers with arrows and dump boiling water on them.

4. The army could not starve the people of Troy because the people of Troy had lots of food and water inside the wall.

In the next story, you will read about a great war that took place in Troy. This war lasted a long, long time because the army could not get inside the wall.

MORE NEXT TIME

C Number your paper from 1 through 26.

Skill Items

Use the words in the box to write complete sentences.

imagined	rescued	disappeared	machine
contructed	image	survived	twice

1. They ____ an enormous ____.
2. She ____ until she was ____.

Review Items

3. Write the letter of each island on the map.
4. **T** is not an island. Tell why.

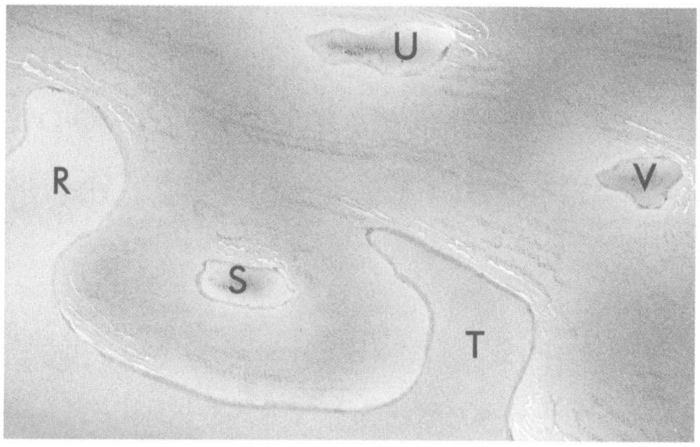

5. Palm trees cannot live in places that get ___.
6. What are the branches of palm trees called?
7. Name two things that grow on different palm trees.

8. What part does the **A** show?
9. What part does the **B** show?
10. What part does the **C** show?
11. What part does the **D** show?

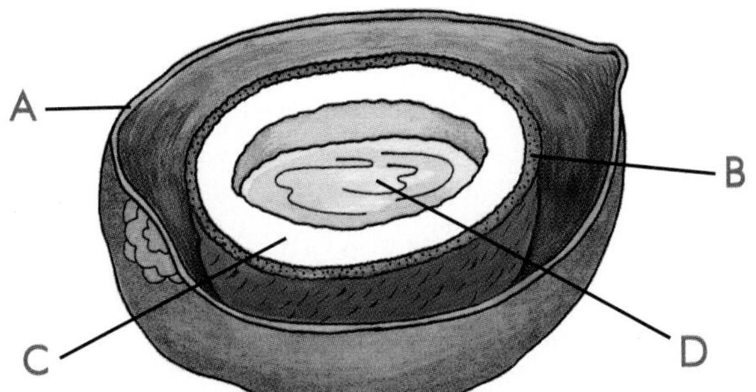

12. The temperature inside your body is about ___ degrees when you are healthy.
13. Most fevers don't go over ___ degrees.
14. When people have very high fevers, how do they feel?
15. They may see and hear things that are not ___.

16. Which letter shows where San Francisco is?
17. Which letter shows where Japan is?
18. Which letter shows where the Pacific Ocean is?

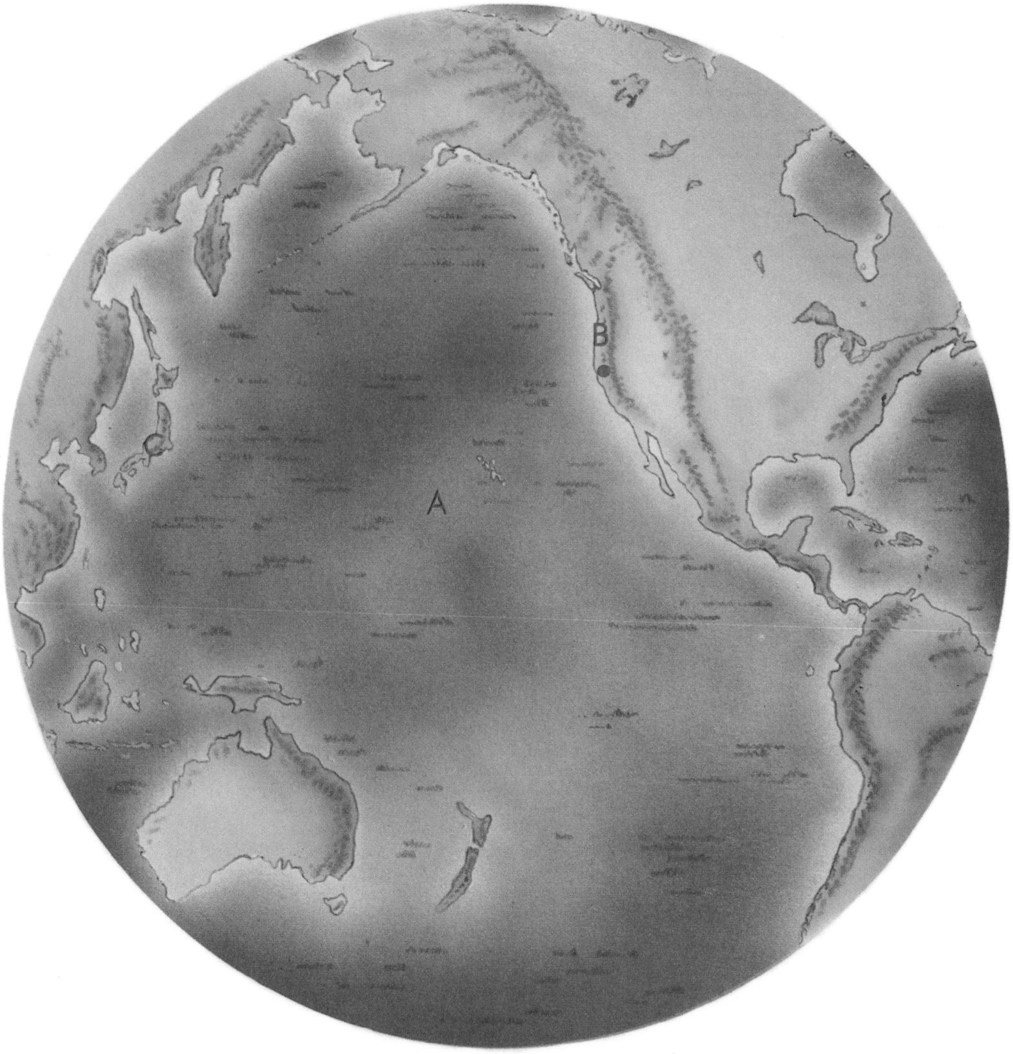

19. The place that is called Troy is now part of what country?
    - Greece
    - Turkey
    - Italy
20. What year is it now?
21. In what year were you born?
22. In what year was the first airplane made?
23. What was the year 1 hundred years ago?
24. What was the year 2 hundred years ago?
25. In what year did the United States become a country?
26. What was the year 3 hundred years ago?

66

A

1	2
1. Jesus Christ	1. succeeded
2. Greece	2. supposed
3. queen	3. quiet
4. Greek	4. quietly
5. hammer	5. Helen
6. hammered	

B

When the Story of Troy Took Place

Time line A shows how long ago the story of Troy took place. You know how the time line works. Which things are at the top of the time line? Which things are near the bottom of the time line?

Touch dot A. That's the year now. What year is that?

Touch dot B. That's the year 1 hundred years ago. What year was that?

Touch dot C. That's the year 2 hundred years ago. What year was that?

Touch the dot that shows 1 thousand years ago.

Touch the dot that shows 2 thousand years ago. That was around the time that Jesus Christ was alive.

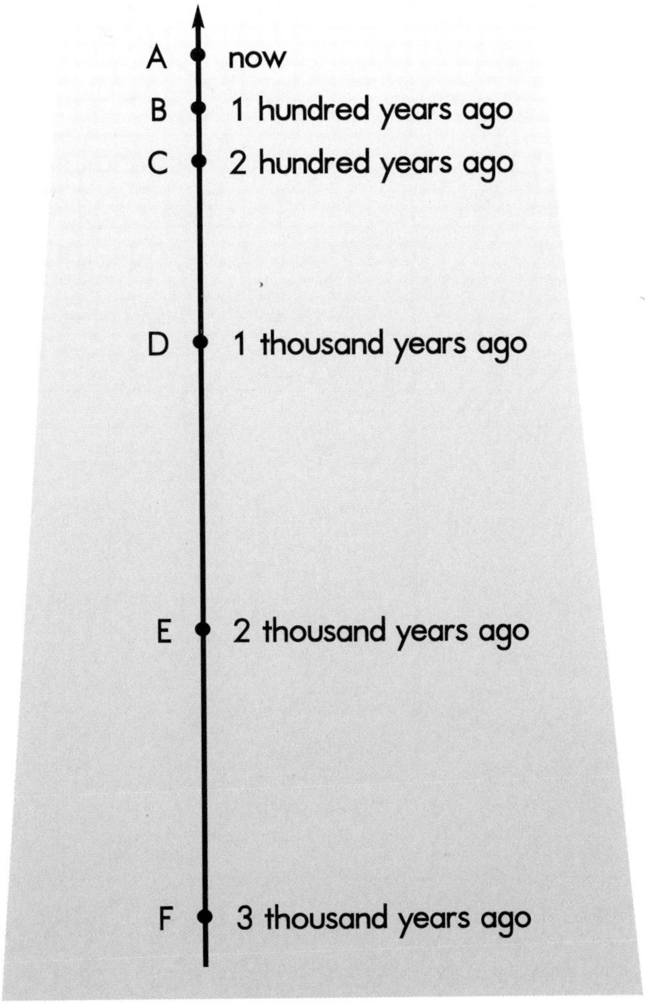

TIME LINE A

We have to go back 1 thousand more years before we reach the time that the story of Troy took place.

Touch dot F. What time does that dot show?

What happened 3 thousand years ago?

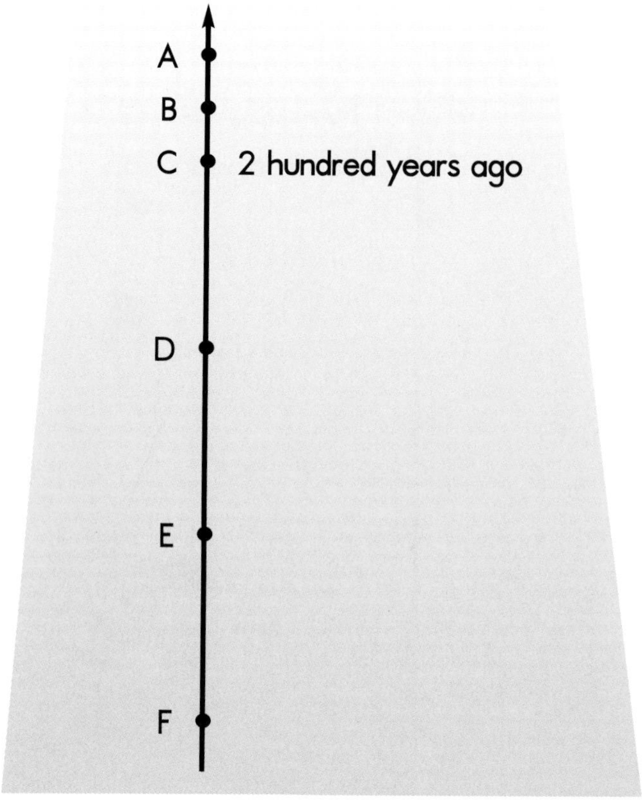

TIME LINE B

Look at time line B. It has the same dots as the other time line. See if you can touch the right dot for each time.

Touch the dot that shows 2 thousand years ago.
Touch the dot that shows 2 hundred years ago.
Touch the dot that shows 3 thousand years ago.
Touch the dot that shows 1 hundred years ago.
About how long ago did Jesus Christ live?
How long ago did the story of Troy take place?

C A Great War at Troy

There are stories about a great war that took place at Troy. Some of the stories are make-believe and some are real.

These stories say that the war took place because a man from Troy fell in love with a woman from Greece. The man from Troy was the son of the king. The woman from Greece was named Helen. She was supposed to be the most beautiful woman in the world. And she was a queen of a city in Greece. When Helen fell in love, she left her city and went to Troy. The people of her city wanted their queen back, but she wouldn't come back.

So part of Greece went to war with Troy. To reach Troy, the soldiers had to cross part of an ocean. A thousand ships sailed to Troy. The army that sailed in those ships was the largest army ever seen. When the ships reached Troy, the army poured from the ships—soldiers, horses, shields, swords, shovels, and food. The army set up camp outside the great wall of Troy. There were men and tents from the wall all the way to the sea. And along the shore of the sea were ships and ships and more ships.

Soon the battle began. Soldiers from Greece rode on horses around the ★ great wall. Soldiers of Troy shot at them with bows and arrows. Soldiers from Greece rushed to the wall with ladders and tried to climb over the wall. They did not succeed.

The army tried to dig under the wall. Men dug and dug, but they did not succeed.

The army cut down great tree trunks and put wheels on them. Soldiers pushed the tree trunks toward the gate, but they did not knock the gate down.

The army tried to starve the people inside Troy, but that didn't work either.

The war went on for month after month and year after year. The same things happened day after day. The army tried to get inside the city, but the people of Troy kept the army out.

The war went on for ten years. For ten years, the army of Greece failed. The men in that army got older and tired of the war. They said, "If only we could get a few men inside the wall, they could open the huge gate and let the rest of the army inside."

That was the plan. Four men inside the wall could open the gate. Three men inside the wall could open the gate. But for ten years, the army of Greece was not able to get one soldier inside the wall.

MORE NEXT TIME

D Number your paper from 1 through 21.

Review Items

1. Write 2 letters that show decks.
2. Write 2 letters that show bulkheads.
3. Which letter shows where the stern is?
4. Which letter shows where the bow is?

5. What is the temperature of the water in each jar?
6. Write the letter of each jar that is filled with ocean water.
7. Jar A is not filled with ocean water. How do you know?

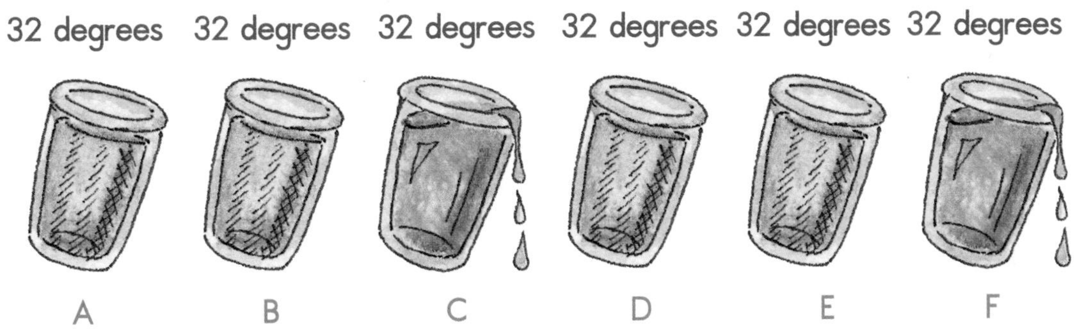

8. You would have the least amount of power if you pushed against one of the handles. Which handle is that?
9. Which handle would give you the most power?

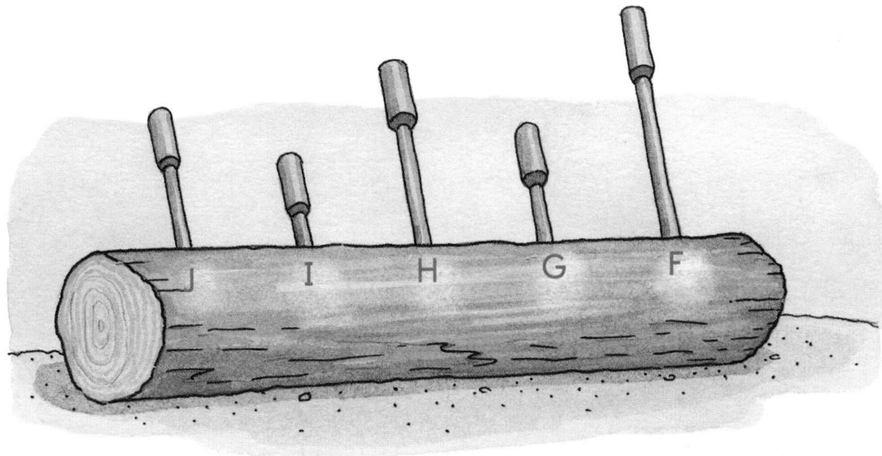

The arrow by the handle shows which way it turns.

10. Which arrow shows the way the log moves?
11. Which arrow shows the way the vine moves?

12. When did the story of Troy take place?
    - 1 thousand years ago
    - 1 hundred years ago
    - 3 thousand years ago
13. Why didn't the people of Troy have cars?
    - Cars were too much trouble.
    - There were no cars yet.
    - They didn't like cars.
14. The people of Troy got in and out of the city through the great ____.
15. Write the letters of the 4 kinds of weapons that soldiers used when they had battles with Troy.

    a. rockets b. planes c. spears d. guns
    e. swords f. bows g. arrows h. tanks

16. Write the letter of the sun you see at sunset.
17. Write the letter of the sun you see at noon.
18. Write the letter of the sun you see early in the morning.

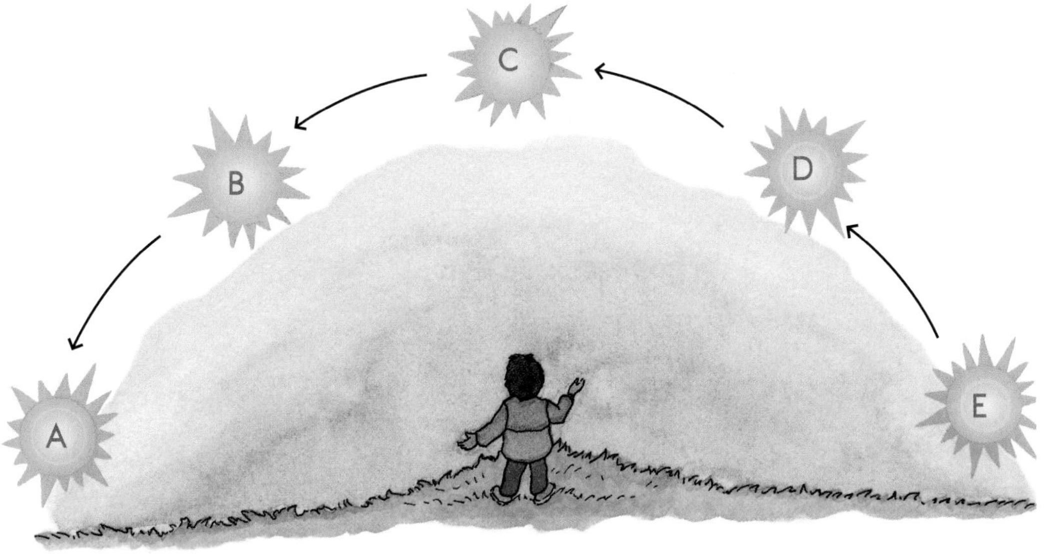

19. Airplanes land at airports. Ships land at ___.
20. Airplanes are pulled by little trucks. Ships are pulled by ___.
21. Airplanes unload at gates. Ships unload at ___.

67

A

1	2	3
1. student	1. <u>pea</u>nuts	1. failed
2. donkey	2. <u>how</u>ever	2. quietly
3. directly	3. <u>blind</u>fold	3. Greeks
4. talent	4. <u>play</u>ground	4. sawed
5. lawyer		5. trackers

4	5	6
1. gift	1. blink	1. study
2. sense	2. amaze	2. lazy
3. Bertha	3. amazement	3. lazier
4. sailed	4. lemon	4. normal
5. post	5. hammered	5. normally
	6. chart	

B The Great Wooden Horse

For ten years, the army of Greece tried to get inside the wall of Troy, but for ten years the soldiers failed. The army kept using the same four plans over and over, and the plans failed again and again. But the army kept on trying to get a few men inside the wall.

During the tenth year of the war somebody had an idea for a new plan. The army started to work on this plan.

Soldiers cut down great trees. Soldiers hammered and sawed wood. They were making something from wood. But what was it?

The people inside Troy watched from the wall. As the days went by, they saw what it was. It was a great horse—a great wooden horse. And it was huge. It stood very tall, and it had wooden wheels.

"What are they going to do?" the people in Troy asked each other.

One night after the horse was finished the soldiers of Greece rolled the huge wooden horse in front of the gate. Then the soldiers left. They got in the ships, and the ships sailed from the shore.

"The war must be over," the people of Troy said.

The people of Troy looked outside, but they could see no Greek soldiers. There were no tents, no ships, and no horses. Everything was quiet.

"Maybe the horse is a gift," they said to each other. "Maybe the Greeks left this gift to tell us that we won the war."

Slowly, the soldiers of Troy went outside the gate. They looked all around the city to see if the Greek army was trying to trick them, but no Greeks could be seen.

Suddenly, the people of Troy began to cheer and shout. For ten years they had been at war. "The war is over," they shouted. "We have won the war."

The huge gate opened wide, and the people of Troy rolled the enormous wooden horse inside. ★ When the horse was inside, the people closed the gate. Then they yelled, "Let's have a party." So they did. They ate and laughed and sang songs and danced until late at night. Then they went to sleep, very happy.

That is when something very strange happened. Part of the great horse started to move. That part was a door. Slowly the door on the horse opened. One man came out of the door. Then another man and another man came out of the door. These men were soldiers from Greece. The horse was not a gift. It was a trick. And the trick had worked.

The ships had not gone back to Greece. They had sailed until they could not be seen by the people of Troy.

They waited until the sun went down. While the people of Troy were dancing and singing, the ships sailed back to the shore. And when the people of Troy went to sleep very happy, the soldiers from Greece moved quietly toward the great gate. For ten years, they had tried to get a few men inside the wall, and now they had done it.

The men who had been inside the horse slid down a rope. They ran to the huge gate. Slowly, they pushed the gate open.

Now, the people of Troy were starting to wake up. But it was too late. Hundreds and hundreds of soldiers from Greece came through the gate. Before the soldiers of

Troy could get their swords and spears, the war was over. The army of Greece had won.

The story of the wooden horse may be make-believe. But we know that there was a great war between Greece and Troy. And the story of Troy tells us something that is important. If you can't solve a problem one way, try something else.

The army of Greece kept trying to get inside the wall by using their old tricks. Then they tried something else. It worked.

THE END

C Number your paper from 1 through 19.

Skill Items

The soldiers protected their equipment.

1. What word names men and women in the army?
2. What word means **large machines and tools?**
3. What word tells how they made sure nothing could hurt their equipment?

Review Items

4. Name a state in the United States that is bigger than Italy.
5. Italy is shaped something like a ____.

6. What place does the **W** show?
7. What place does the **X** show?
8. What place does the **Y** show?
9. What place does the **Z** show?

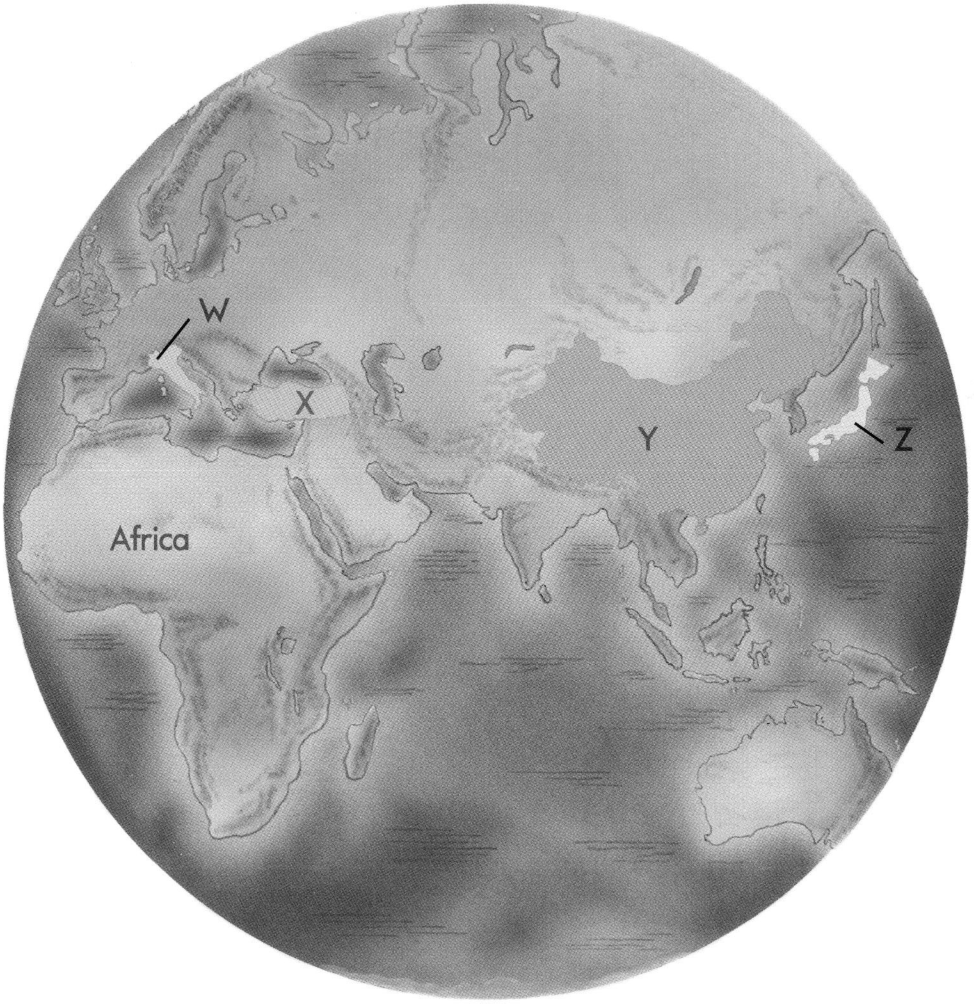

10. Greece went to war with Troy because of a woman named ______.
11. The woman from Greece was important because she was a ______.
12. The woman from Greece went away with a man from ______.
13. How many ships sailed to Troy?
14. How long did the war go on?

15. If the Greek army could get a few men inside the wall of Troy, those men could ______.
16. When the Greek army put ladders against the wall of Troy, what did the people of Troy do?
17. When the Greek army dug holes under the wall, what did the people of Troy do?
18. When the Greek army tried to knock down the gate, what did the people of Troy do?
19. Why couldn't the Greek army starve the people of Troy?

SPECIAL PROJECT

Put on a play that shows the end of the war between Greece and Troy.

First plan how you will show the horse, the walls of Troy, and the gate.

Figure out what the characters will say when they see the ships leaving and when they bring the horse inside the city.

Figure out how you'll show the party and the people who live in Troy going to sleep.

Plan the ending of the story.

Then make the things you will need for the play and act out the play.

68

A

1

1. Maria Sanchez
2. investigate
3. business
4. detective
5. company

2

1. classroom
2. horseback
3. salesman
4. playground

3

1. students
2. blinked
3. amazement
4. cheating
5. blindfolded
6. normally

4

1. however
2. trackers
3. Bertha
4. donkey
5. talent

5

1. peel
2. report
3. lawyers
4. typing
5. peanuts

6

1. peek
2. spun
3. post
4. sense
5. mowed

B

Bertha Has a Great Sense of Smell

If you looked at Bertha, you wouldn't notice anything strange about her. She was tall for a fifteen-year-old girl, but there's nothing strange about that. However, she was the only person in her high school who could do one thing. In fact, she was the only human being in the whole world who could do it.

Bertha could smell. She could use her nose to tell where things were, what they were, and who they were.

Hound dogs can smell the way Bertha could. You give the dog something the person had worn, and the hound dog sniffs the trail that person left. But the best hound dog in the world would seem to have no nose at all compared to Bertha.

Let's say that you tried to sneak up behind Bertha when she was studying. Before you could get within ten meters of her she would say, "Hi." She would know that you were there. She would know who you were. She would know exactly where you were standing. And she would know all these things through her sense of smell.

Last summer, a bunch of her friends were at a party, and they were playing Pin the Tail on the Donkey. To play that game, they put up a picture of a donkey without a tail. Then they put a blindfold on you. They spin you around, give you a donkey's tail with a pin on one end, and let you try to stick the pin on the picture of the donkey. Two people had a turn before Bertha. One pinned the tail on a post. Another one pinned the tail on the wall that was farthest from the donkey. Now it was Bertha's turn. They blindfolded her, spun her around, and handed her a tail. She walked over to the picture of the donkey and pinned the tail exactly on the rear end.

Everybody thought that Bertha had been peeking. So they put a heavy blindfold on her, and she tried it again. She pinned the tail on the exact spot.

When her friends said that she must be cheating, she faced the wall and said, "I'll show you something."

While she faced the wall and the others stood behind her, she started to tell what each person was doing. "Vern is standing next to the post. Fran is showing Judy something that's in her purse. Rodney is to my right. He has his hands folded behind his head."

Everybody looked at her in amazement. "How do you do that?" they asked. She explained that she did it with her sense of smell.

One day, the school tester called Bertha in for some tests. He had heard stories about her, and he wanted to see how smart she was and how well she could see and hear.

First he tested her eyes. After she read the letters on a wall chart, he tested her sense of smell. He said, "I'm going to give you cans that have tiny holes in the top. Sniff each can, and see if you can tell what's inside."

The first can had lemon in it. Before he took the can from his case, Bertha said, "It's part of a lemon. It's mostly the peel with some juice. The lemon was grown in Texas. It's a thick-skinned lemon."

The tester blinked four times and looked at Bertha and then looked at the can. Before he could pick up the next can she said, "That's a rose. It's a very dark pink flower that was picked about three days ago."

After the test, there were many stories about Bertha and her sense of smell.

Bertha was sorry that she had let people know about her talent. She didn't like it when her teachers whispered about her. And she didn't like it when her friends treated her as if she was strange. Bertha wanted to be like everybody else. But during that summer when she was fifteen years old, things changed. She was really glad that she had her sense of smell. In the next story, you'll find out why.

MORE NEXT TIME

C Number your paper from 1 through 15.

Skill Items

Use the words in the box to write complete sentences.

failed	beauty	protected	peeked	equipment
rescued	imagined	secret	survived	soldiers

1. She ____ until she was ____.
2. The ____ ____ their ____.

Review Items

3. Tom is 4 miles high. Jack is 20 miles high. Who is colder?
4. Tell why.
5. A plane that flies from Italy to New York City goes in which direction?
6. When did the story of Troy take place?
   - 1 thousand years ago
   - 3 thousand years ago
   - 1 hundred years ago
7. During the war with Troy, what did the Greek army build to help them get inside Troy?
8. What was inside this object?
9. What did they do after they came out of the object?
10. Who won the war, Troy or Greece?

The picture shows objects caught in a whirlpool. The path is shown for object A.

11. Will the path for object B go around **more times** or **fewer times?**
12. Which path will go around the fewest times, the path for A, B, or C?

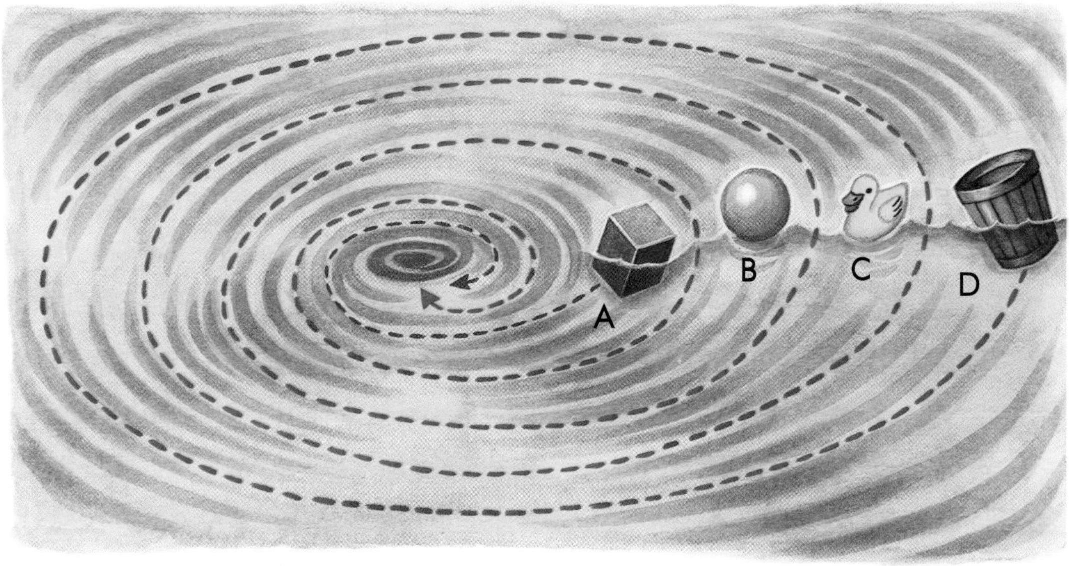

13. Airplanes land at airports. Ships land at ____.
14. Airplanes are pulled by little trucks. Ships are pulled by ____.
15. Airplanes unload at gates. Ships unload at ____.

69

A

1

1. refinery
2. honest
3. insist
4. clue
5. several
6. approach

2

1. horseback
2. classrooms
3. pipeline
4. motorcycle
5. salesperson

3

1. shrugged
2. kidding
3. investigator
4. typing
5. heater
6. watering

4

1. company
2. detective
3. business
4. businesses
5. office

5

1. Maria Sanchez
2. lazy
3. lazier
4. computer
5. crude
6. screen

6

1. well
2. creek
3. report
4. crime
5. law
6. study

B

Maria Gets a Job as an Investigator

The weeks just before the summer vacation went very slowly for Bertha. It seemed that summer would never come.

The classrooms got very hot during the last week of school. But suddenly school was out for the summer, and suddenly Bertha didn't have anything to do. She didn't have to go to class. She didn't have to get up as early in the morning. She didn't have to study. For a couple of days, she didn't do much of anything. She just felt empty. She went to the pool, visited with her friend Tina, and went horseback riding. She ate more peanuts than she normally ate, and she felt a lot lazier than she normally did.

About a week after summer vacation had begun, she was sitting on her front steps trying to think of something new to do. She noticed that her new neighbor was walking to her van. The neighbor's name was Maria Sanchez. "Where are you going?" Bertha asked.

Maria replied, "I'm going to start my new job today."

Maria walked toward Bertha. Bertha stood up and said, "What is your new job?"

"I am an investigator." Maria smiled and looked very proud of herself, but Bertha didn't know what an investigator does. So she asked, "What does an investigator do?"

"An investigator investigates," Maria replied, and she laughed. "I have a job with a state office. I investigate businesses that do not follow the law."

Bertha wasn't sure what that meant. She shrugged. Maria laughed. Then she said, "Here's how it works. Let's say that you buy a car. Let's say the salesperson lies about the car. When you find out you were cheated, you call the state and tell what happened. Then I go out and investigate. When I investigate, I try to find out what really did happen, and I try to find out if the salesperson broke any laws."

"Wow," Bertha said, "that sounds like a lot of fun. I wish I was going with you."

But Bertha did not go with her, at least not on that day. Maria got in her van and drove off to work. And Bertha didn't see her for two days. But on Friday, Bertha was coming back from the pool, and there was Maria, sitting on her porch. She had a little table set up, and she was typing something on her computer. Bertha didn't want to bother her, but she wanted to find out what Maria was working on.

"I can't figure this one out," Maria said, "and I have to finish my report today. I don't think I'm a very good investigator." She shook her head and looked back at her computer screen.

Bertha asked, "Can you tell me what you're writing?"

"Sure," Maria said. "Somebody told us that a large oil company is breaking the law. The person said that the company is taking water from a creek that runs next to the company's land. The company is supposed to take water from deep wells that are on the company's land."

Maria showed Bertha a map. The yellow part of the map was the land owned by the oil company. The creek that Maria was investigating was east of the oil company's land.

Bertha looked at the map and then laughed. "When you talked about an oil company, I thought you were talking about a little gas station. This is a place that makes gasoline."

"Yes," Maria said. "They take the oil that is pumped from the ground, and they change it into gasoline."

Maria tapped the place on the map that was marked with an X. "This is the place where the problem is," Maria

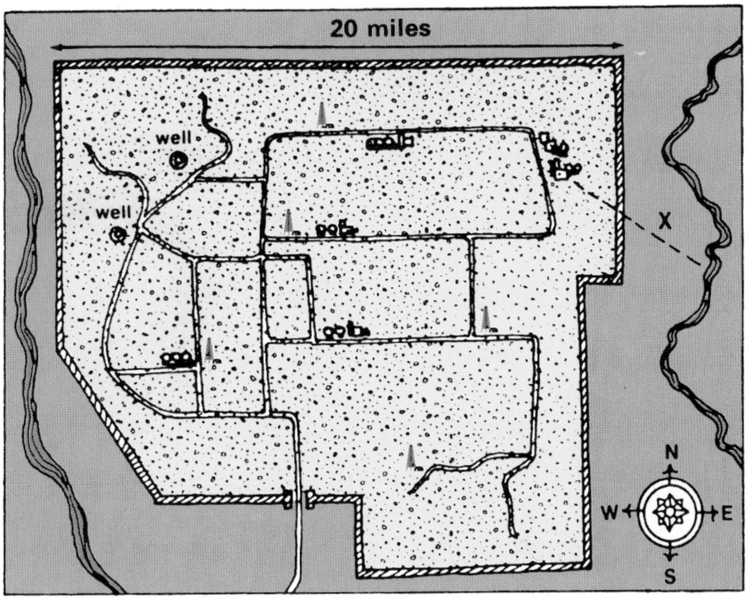

said. "The dotted line shows an old pipe that goes from the creek to the oil plant. The people who run the oil company tell me that they don't use this pipe to take water from the creek. They say they haven't used the pipe in ten years." Maria shook her head. "I don't believe them, but I can't prove that they are taking water from the creek."

Bertha said, "I think I can help you."

MORE NEXT TIME

C Number your paper from 1 through 24.

Review Items

Some of the lines below are one inch long and some are one centimeter long.

1. Write the letter of every line that is one centimeter long.
2. Write the letter of every line that is one inch long.

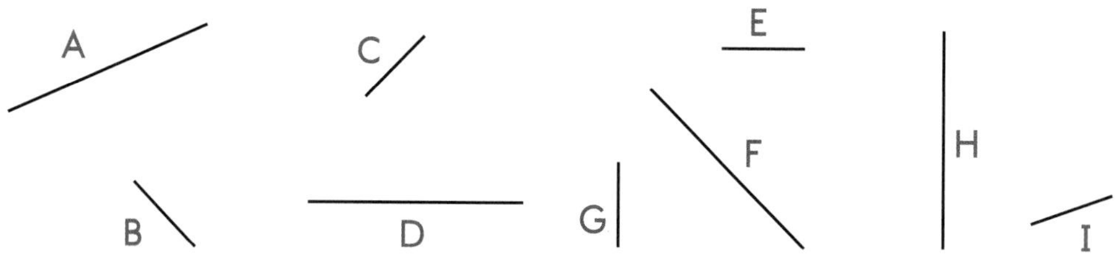

3. A mile is a little more than _____ feet.
    - 1 thousand • 5 hundred • 5 thousand
4. Does dew form in the middle of the day?
5. Dew forms when the air gets _____.
    - cooler • windy • warmer
6. When we weigh very small things, the unit we use is _____.

Each statement tells about how far something goes or how fast something goes. Write **how far** or **how fast** for each item.

7. She walked 4 miles.
8. She walked 4 miles per hour.
9. The plane was flying 300 miles per hour.
10. The plane was 300 miles from Denver.

11. How fast is truck **A** going?
12. How fast is truck **B** going?
13. Which truck is going faster?

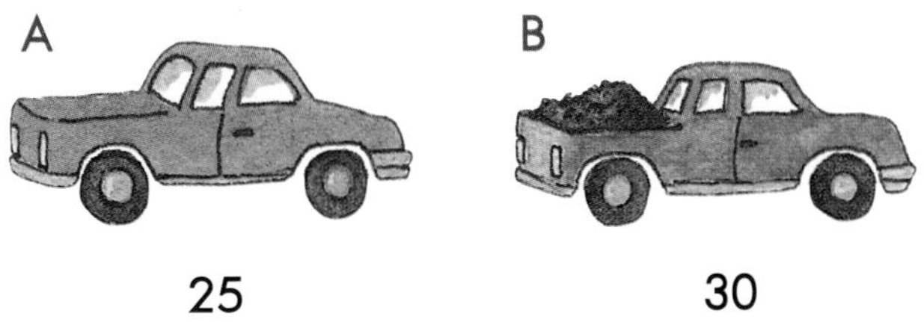

14. How many parts does the body of an insect have?
15. How many legs does an insect have?

16. How many legs does a spider have?
17. How many parts does a spider's body have?
18. What's the boiling temperature of water?

19. Write the name of the city that's on the east coast.
20. Write the name of the city that's on the west coast.
21. Which letter shows where Denver is?
22. Which letter shows where Chicago is?

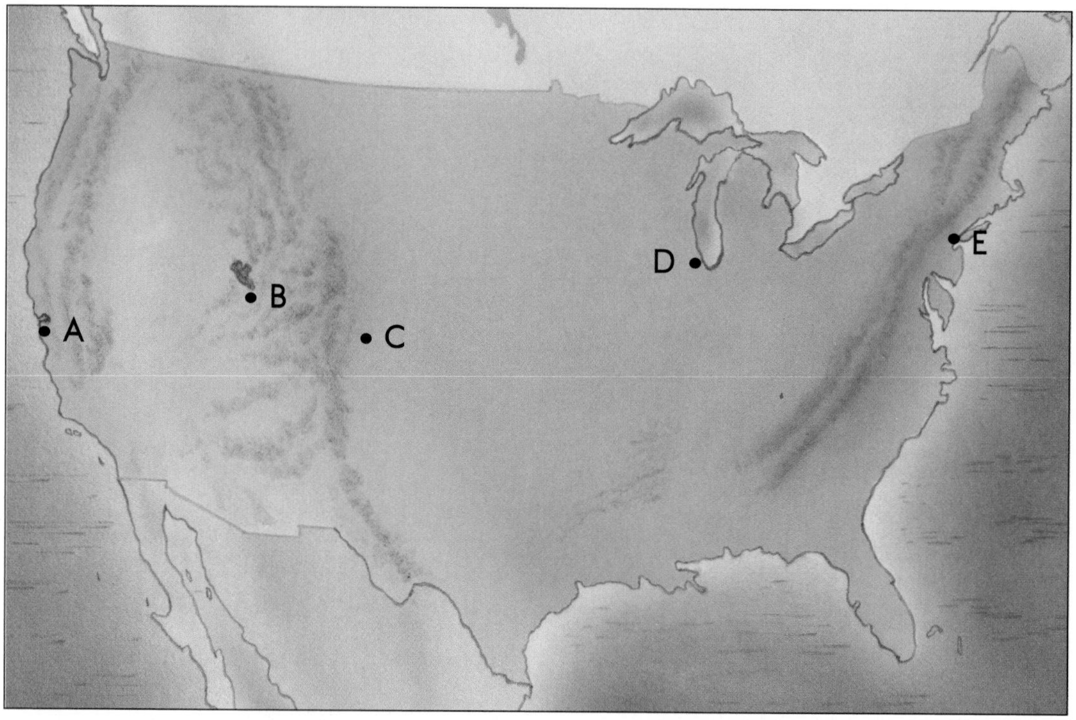

23. Why didn't the people of Troy have cars?
    - They didn't like cars.
    - There were no cars yet.
    - Cars were too much trouble.
24. The people of Troy got in and out of the city through the great ▭.

TEST 7

Number your paper from 1 through 36.

1. Write the letter of the sun you see early in the morning.
2. Write the letter of the sun you see at sunset.
3. Write the letter of the sun you see at noon.

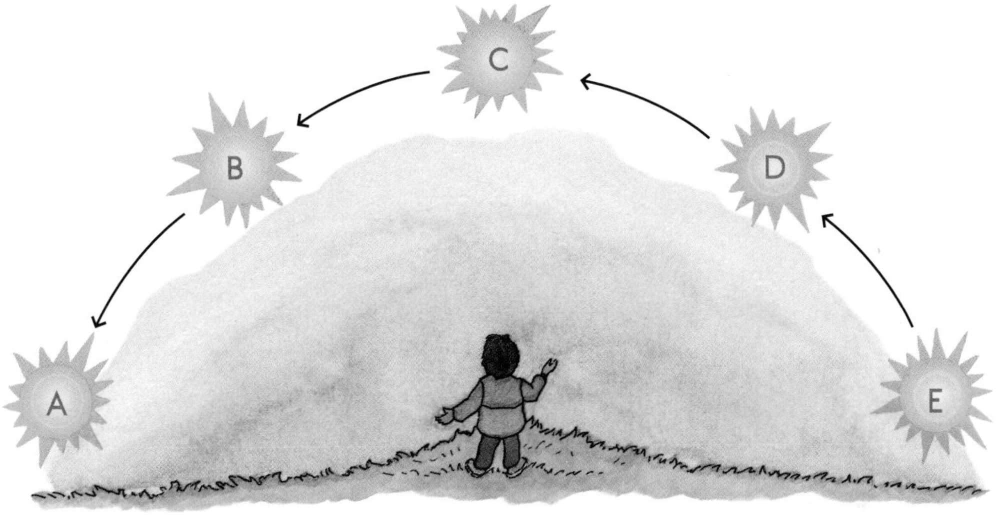

4. The temperature inside your body is about _____ degrees when you are healthy.
5. Most fevers don't go over _____ degrees.
6. Airplanes land at airports. Ships land at _____.
7. Airplanes are pulled by little trucks. Ships are pulled by _____.
8. Airplanes unload at gates. Ships unload at _____.

9. Which letter shows where Troy used to be?
10. Which letter shows where Greece is?
11. Which letter shows where Italy is?

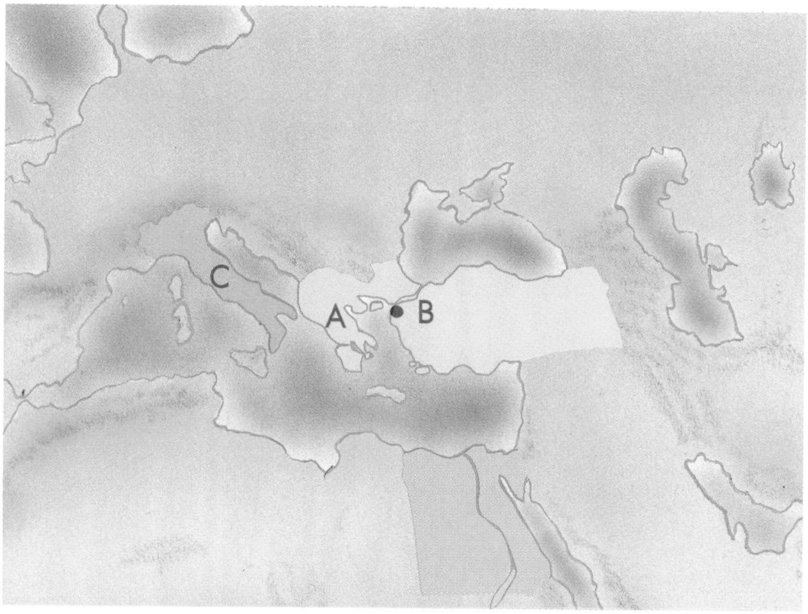

12. In what year was the first airplane made?
13. In what year were you born?
14. What year is it now?
15. In what year did the United States become a country?
16. What was the year 2 hundred years ago?
17. What was the year 1 hundred years ago?
18. What was the year 3 hundred years ago?
19. When did the story of Troy take place?
    - 1 thousand years ago
    - 1 hundred years ago
    - 3 thousand years ago

20. Greece went to war with Troy because of a woman named ____.
21. The woman from Greece was important because she was a ____.
22. The woman from Greece went away with a man from ____.
23. How many ships sailed to Troy?
24. How long did the war go on?

25. If the Greek army could get a few men inside the wall of Troy, those men could ____.
26. During the war with Troy, what did the Greek army build to help them get inside Troy?
27. What was inside this object?
28. What did they do after they came out of the object?
29. Who won the war, Troy or Greece?

Skill Items

30. Compare Linda and Kathy. Remember, first tell how they're the same. Then tell how they're different.

For each item, write the underlined word from the sentences in the box.

They <u>constructed</u> an <u>enormous</u> <u>machine</u>.
She <u>survived</u> until she was <u>rescued</u>.
The <u>soldiers</u> <u>protected</u> their <u>equipment</u>.

31. What word means **saved from danger?**
32. What word means **very large?**
33. What word means **large machines and tools?**
34. What word names something that helps people do work?
35. What word means **managed to stay alive?**
36. What word means **built?**

END OF TEST 7

A

1
1. Mr. Daniels
2. recognize
3. elevator
4. medicine
5. guess
6. dozen

2
1. silently
2. watering
3. heater
4. approached
5. fairly

3
1. clues
2. doctors
3. offices
4. drugs
5. typists
6. lawyers

4
1. cock your head
2. equipment
3. motorcycle
4. refinery
5. friendly
6. unfriendly

5
1. explain
2. insist
3. honest
4. crude
5. fifth

6
1. narrow
2. prison
3. polite
4. several
5. pipeline

B

Oil Wells

A well is a deep hole in the ground. The well has pipe in it so the hole stays open.

There are different types of wells.

- Some wells are fresh-water wells. These wells pump fresh water from under the ground.

• Some wells are oil wells. These wells pump crude oil from under the ground.

Picture 1 shows a machine that is drilling a hole for a well.

If the machine keeps drilling, what type of liquid will it reach first?

If the machine keeps drilling past the fresh water, what kind of liquid will it reach next?

If the machine keeps drilling, what will it reach after the oil?

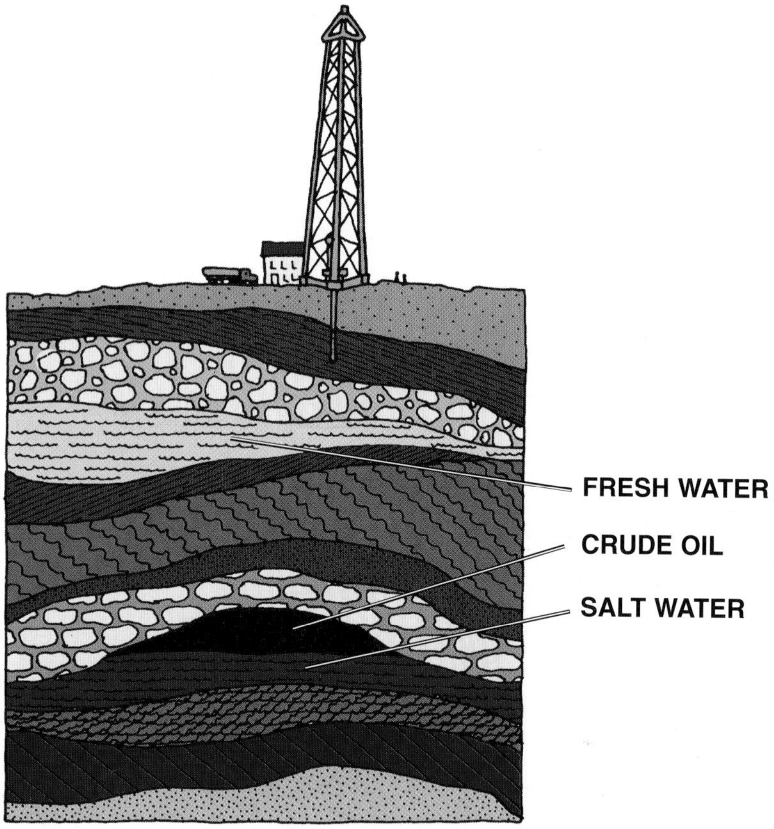

PICTURE 1

If the well is an oil well, it pumps crude oil from the ground. Crude oil is a dark liquid that can be changed to make things like gasoline, motor oil, and plastic.

The crude oil is pumped from the well. Then it goes into a pipeline. The pipeline goes along the ground and carries the crude oil many miles to a refinery.

The refinery is a large place with strange-looking equipment and large tanks for holding oil.

The refinery changes crude oil into gasoline and other things.

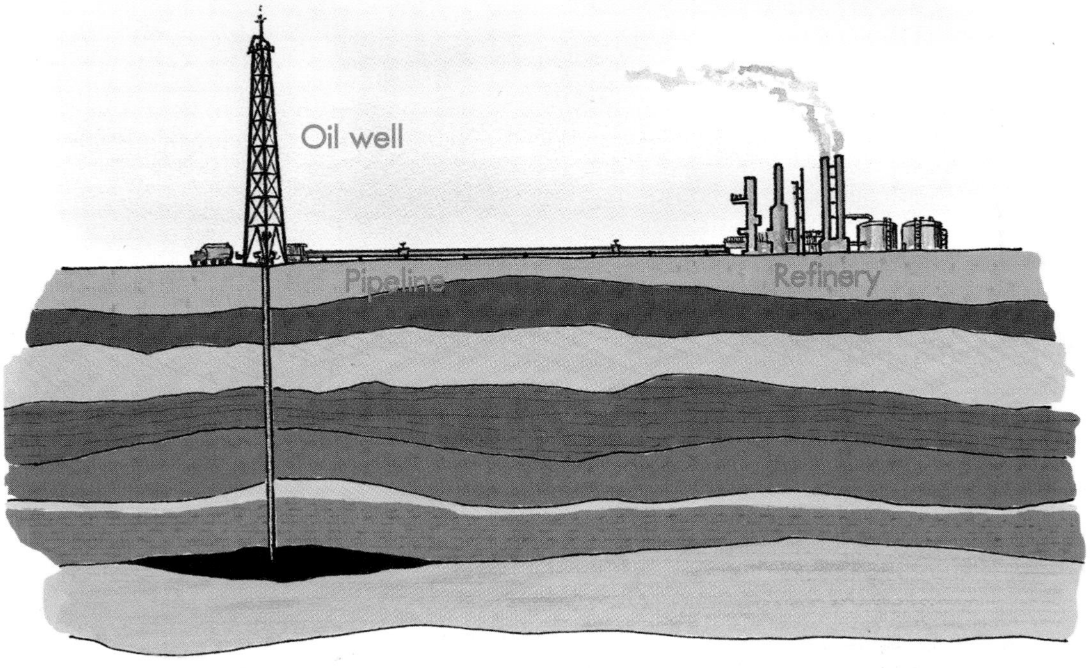

PICTURE 2

C Maria Tests Bertha's Talent

Bertha had a plan for helping Maria figure out where the water came from. You probably know what her plan was. Although Bertha didn't know too much about oil wells and refineries, she did know that she could smell the difference between water taken from the creek and water taken from water wells.

Bertha was sitting on Maria's porch. She said, "Maria, it's easy for me to tell if the water comes from the creek or from the well. I'll just smell it."

Maria looked slowly at Bertha and made a face. "What are you talking about?"

Bertha said, "Take me with you and I'll tell you where the water comes from."

Maria made another face. "How will you know where it comes from?"

"I told you. I'll smell it," Bertha said. Then she explained her talent. "I can tell about anything by smelling it. Honest I can."

Maria cocked her head and looked at Bertha. "What is this, a joke?" Maria asked.

Bertha said, "Give me a test. Get glasses of water from different places. I'll tell you where you got each glass of water." At first Maria didn't want to do it. "This is crazy," she kept saying. But Bertha kept insisting on the test. Finally Maria went into her house and came back with three glasses of water. She said, "You can't feel them, or you may get some clues about where I got them."

Bertha said, "I don't have to feel them. The one on the left is from your water heater. The middle glass is from a watering can or something like that. That water has been sitting out for a couple of days. The water in the last glass came from a water jug or something in your refrigerator. It's been in the refrigerator for a long time, and it probably doesn't taste very good."

"I don't believe this," Maria said, and she tasted the water from the last glass. She made a face. "Oh, you're right. It's bad."

Suddenly Maria laughed, turned around, and looked at Bertha. She said, "I don't believe this." Then she said, "I don't believe this," three or four more times. "You're amazing. You are amazing. You are the most amazing person I have ever seen."

She kept talking very fast. She told about some of the amazing things that she had seen—a cow with two heads and a building over 3 hundred meters high. Finally, she said, "I once saw a man jump a motorcycle over twenty cars and that was amazing, but you are five times as amazing."

"Can I go with you?" Bertha asked.

"Yes, yes, yes, yes, yes," Maria said. "This will be great."

MORE NEXT TIME

D Number your paper from 1 through 19.

Skill Items

Lawyers with talent normally succeed.

1. What word means the opposite of **fail?**
2. What word names people who help us when we have questions about the law?
3. What word means **usually?**
4. What word refers to the special skills a person has?

Review Items

5. You can see drops of water on grass early in the morning. What are those called?

6. Which letter shows the coconut milk?
7. Which letter shows the inner shell?
8. Which letter shows the coconut meat?
9. Which letter shows the outer shell?

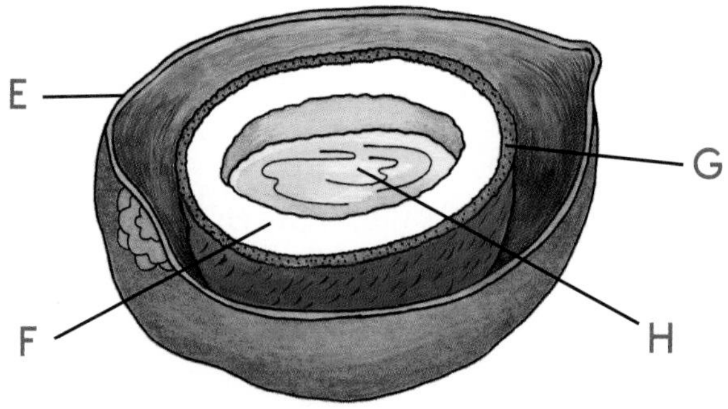

10. All machines make it easier for someone to ______.

11. You would have the most power if you pushed against one of the handles. Which handle is that?
12. Which handle would give you the least amount of power?

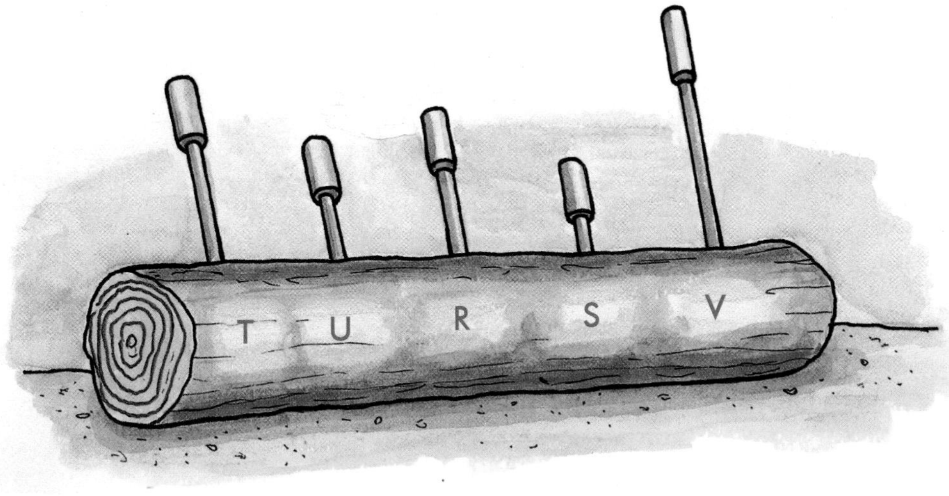

13. When people have very high fevers, how do they feel?
14. They may see and hear things that are not ______.

15. Write the letter that shows a tugboat.
16. Write two letters that show ships.
17. Write two letters that show docks.

18. The place that is called Troy is now part of what country?
    - Greece
    - Italy
    - Turkey
19. Write the letters of the 4 kinds of weapons that soldiers used when they had battles with Troy.
    a. bows
    b. swords
    c. arrows
    d. rockets
    e. spears
    f. guns
    g. planes
    h. tanks

A

1	2	3
1. doubt	1. fairly	1. Mr. Daniels
2. vehicle	2. medicine	2. unfriendly
3. ceiling	3. elevator	3. appear
4. pretend	4. uneasy	4. appeared
5. secretary	5. doctors	5. silently
6. interesting	6. several	6. approached

4	5	6
1. stretch	1. guard	1. fifth
2. fancy	2. signs	2. drugs
3. fancier	3. offices	3. speck
4. recognize	4. polite	4. narrow
5. guessed	5. prison	
6. typists	6. dozen	

B

Maria and Bertha Go to the Oil Refinery

A high fence stretched around Reef Oil Refinery. Signs on the fence warned: KEEP OUT. The fence stretched as far as Bertha could see. Bertha was sitting next to Maria in the front seat of the van as it moved down a narrow road. They had been driving for over an hour. Finally, the road turned to the right and came to a large gate. Maria drove to the gate and stopped.

A guard approached the van. He said, "What can I do for you?" Bertha noticed that the guard was wearing a gun.

Maria replied, "We're from the state. We're here to investigate a report about the water you are using."

The guard said, "One moment please. I'll check with the main office."

As the guard walked to a little building next to the gate, Bertha said, "Wow, this place is like a prison."

Maria said, "The first time I came here, I had to wait for over twenty minutes before they let me in."

Bertha watched the guard as he talked on the phone. He nodded several times and said something, but Bertha couldn't hear what he said. She knew that he was very angry, however. When people become angry, they give off a smell that is easy for Bertha to recognize.

The guard walked back to the van. He smiled and said, "Stay on the main road to building C. Mr. Daniels will meet you there." Bertha knew that the guard was still angry.

Maria drove slowly past the high fence and down a long road. Far down the road was a group of tiny specks. The specks were buildings. One of the specks was building C.

Ten minutes later, the car was close to building C. Building C was very large. Bertha looked up and counted five floors. There were large windows on the top floor.

Another guard motioned to Maria, showing her where to park. Before the van had stopped, the guard was standing next to it. "If you will follow me, I'll take you to Mr. Daniels."

The guard was polite, but he was also angry. And he didn't like Maria.

Bertha was beginning to wonder if it was a good idea for her to be with Maria. When she and Maria had talked about it on Maria's porch, the idea had seemed great. But now, Bertha was a little frightened. She felt almost like she was having a bad dream. Here she was in this strange place, miles from anything. And the people wore guns and smelled of anger.

"Right this way," the guard said and led Maria and Bertha into the building and toward the elevator.

As the elevator moved silently toward the top floor, Bertha's nose was very busy. There was a restaurant on the second floor. One of the things being served was fish. Another was roast beef. The third floor had offices on it. And there were lawyers on the third floor. Bertha could always tell lawyers' offices because their books have a strange smell. The books that doctors use have the same kind of smell, but doctors' offices also smell of medicine and drugs.

The fourth floor had a lot of typists on it. Most of them were fairly young women. Bertha could tell by the kind of clothes they wore and the make-up they used.

The fifth floor was the top floor. Bertha guessed that there weren't more than ten people on the whole floor. This floor was where the top people in the Reef Oil Refinery worked, and there was something cold and unfriendly about the fifth floor.

MORE NEXT TIME

C Number your paper from 1 through 16.

Skill Items

Use the words in the box to write complete sentences.

fail	succeed	starve	talent	faded
protected	slivers	soldiers	lawyers	equipment

1. The ______ ______ their ______.
2. ______ with ______ normally ______.

Review Items

3. Palm trees cannot live in places that get ______.
4. What are the branches of palm trees called?
5. Name **2** things that grow on different palm trees.

6. Which letter shows the trunk?
7. Which letter shows the fronds?
8. Which letter shows the coconuts?
9. Which letter shows the roots?

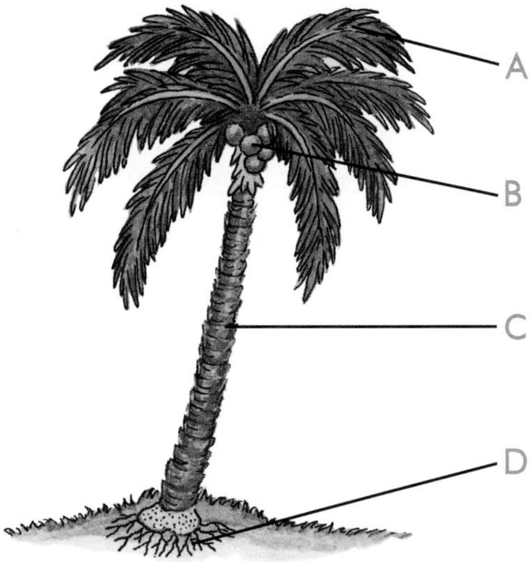

10. How many shells does a coconut have?
11. What is the juice inside a coconut called?
12. Name **2** kinds of wells.

13. Which letter shows the crude oil?
14. Which letter shows the fresh water?
15. Which letter shows the salt water?

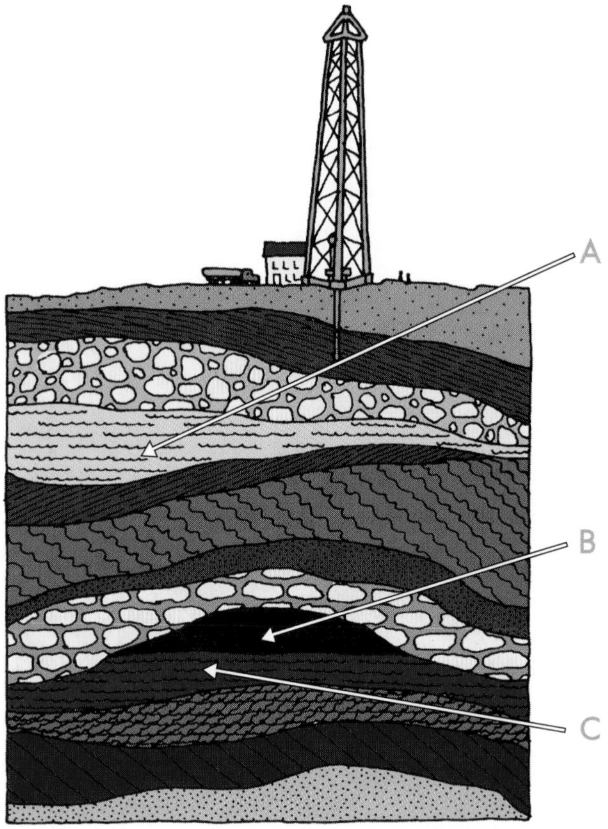

16. Gasoline comes from a liquid called ____.

A

1	2	3
1. weather	1. winked	1. pretend
2. garage	2. shrugged	2. buzzer
3. respond	3. ducked	3. bucket
4. excused	4. appeared	4. sweaty
5. demand		

4	5	6
1. beyond a doubt	1. fancier	1. stare
2. interesting	2. vehicle	2. staring
3. ceiling	3. liar	3. faint
4. secretary	4. uneasy	4. faintly

B Underlined Words

Some of the words in the story you will read today must be spoken loudly. Here's the rule about words that must be spoken louder than other words: **The words that must be spoken louder are underlined.**

Below are sentences with underlined words. Say the underlined words in a loud voice. Say the other words in a soft voice.

a. That is <u>wrong</u>.
b. You are a <u>crook</u>.
c. I am <u>not</u> a crook.
d. I'm <u>tired</u> of reading.
e. My name is <u>Sam</u>.
f. <u>My</u> name is Sam, <u>too</u>.
g. This book is <u>hard</u>.
h. If you think <u>your</u> book is hard, try reading <u>this</u> book.
i. You sure like to <u>talk</u>.

C

Maria and Bertha Meet Mr. Daniels

With a whisper, the doors of the elevator opened. And there was the fifth floor. A woman was standing in front of the elevator door. "Hello," she said, smiling. Her smile was real, and she was not angry. "I'm Mr. Daniels' secretary, Donna."

"Hi," Bertha said, feeling better to be near somebody who was not pretending to be polite.

Donna led Bertha and Maria to a very fancy office, with thick rugs and windows that went up the walls and continued across part of the ceiling.

"Would you care for orange juice or anything?" Donna asked.

"Yes, thank you," Bertha said.

Donna left the office. Bertha said, "What a huge office."

"Yeah," Maria said. "This place makes me feel funny."

For a few moments Bertha stood in the middle of the room, feeling very small.

Donna appeared again. "Here you are," Donna said, holding a large glass of orange juice.

"Oh, thanks," Bertha said.

Just then a buzzer sounded from a desk in the far corner of the office. "That's Mr. Daniels," Donna said, and walked very quickly to her desk. "Yes, Mr. Daniels?" she said into a speaker.

"You may send them in."

Before Bertha knew it, she and Maria were being led into an office that was even larger and fancier than the one they had been in. Bertha was very busy, looking, listening, and sniffing.

"I'm Mr. Daniels," a voice said. The smell told Bertha that he was very angry. But his face was smiling as he approached Maria and Bertha.

"Hi," Bertha said. She realized that she was still holding her juice. She almost spilled it as she reached to shake hands with Mr. Daniels. He was a tall man, wearing a gray suit. His head was almost bald, but he didn't look very old. His hand was sweaty.

He looked at Maria. "Now then, Miss Sanchez," Mr. Daniels said in a smooth voice. He continued, "What brings you back to visit us? I thought we had answered all your questions about the water."

Maria said, "I have some more questions. This time I brought along Bertha, who may give us the answers. She can tell beyond a doubt where the water comes from."

Mr. Daniels' face seemed to become hard. "I don't like this," he said. His anger was beginning to show in his face, which was turning redder. "We do a lot of work with the state, and we have always tried to be good to people from the state." His voice was quite loud.

"I'm sorry," Maria said. "I'm an investigator, and I have to do my job."

"Then <u>do</u> it," Mr. Daniels said sharply. Mr. Daniels walked from the office.

Before Bertha could ask, "What do we do now?" Donna came into the room. Bertha could tell that she felt very uneasy. "I'm to take you to building 9," she said. "You will see the water in that building."

"Is that where they use the water?" Maria asked.

"I think so," Donna said. She was lying. When people lie, they give off a special smell.

MORE NEXT TIME

D Number your paper from 1 through 17.

Review Items

1. Which arrow shows the way Linda's hand will move?
2. Which arrow shows the way the crate will move?

3. Write the letter of each island on the map.
4. **L** is not an island. Tell why.

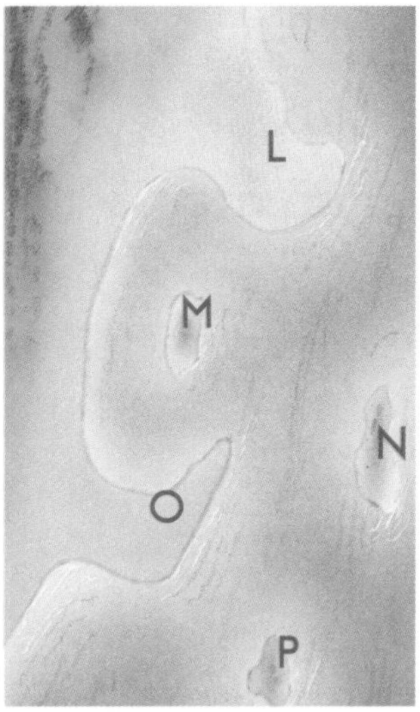

5. Which letter shows the crude oil?
6. Which letter shows the refinery?
7. Which letter shows the pipeline?

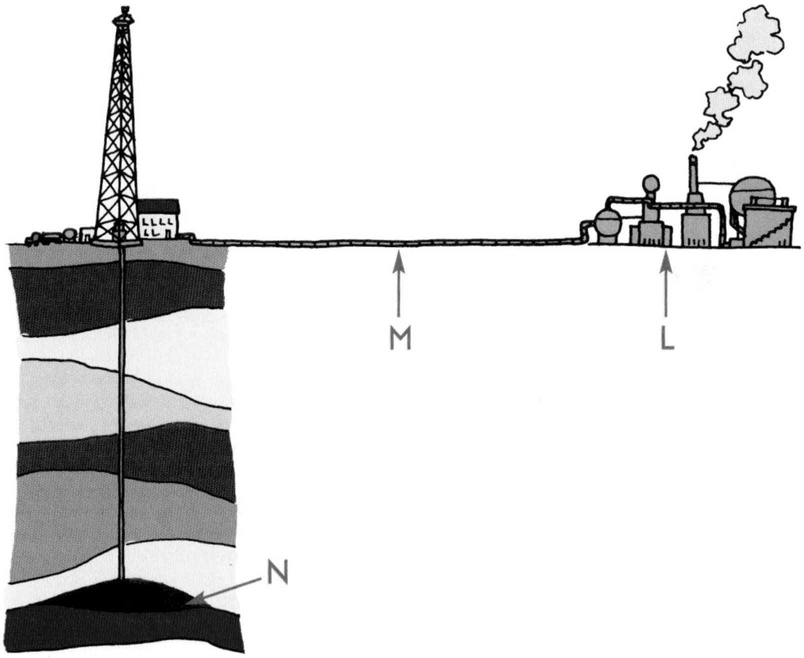

8. Which arrow shows the direction the crude oil is moving at A?
9. Which arrow shows the direction the crude oil is moving at B?

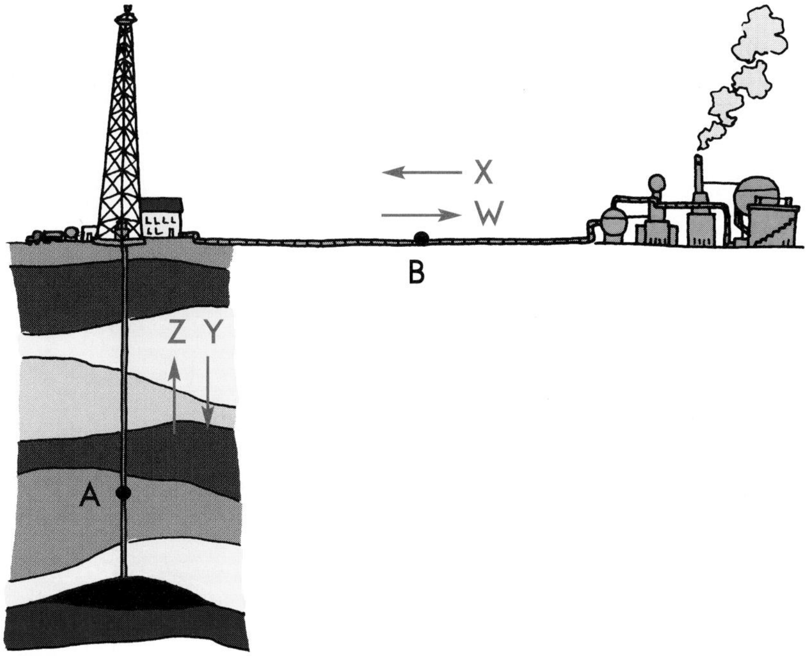

10. When a pot of water gets colder, which way does the temperature go?
11. A sidewalk gets hotter. So what do you know about the temperature of the sidewalk?
12. What does ocean water taste like?
13. If you drank lots of ocean water you would get ____.

14. Which object is the hottest?
15. What is the temperature of that object?
16. Which object is the coldest?
17. What is the temperature of that object?

A
45 degrees

B
90 degrees

C
60 degrees

A

1

1. chief
2. arrange
3. factory
4. practice
5. adventure
6. comfortable

2

1. excused
2. staring
3. faintly
4. winked
5. vehicles
6. ducked

3

1. complain
2. complaint
3. garage
4. weather
5. bucket

4

1. liar
2. swoop
3. clover
4. respond
5. demand

B Bertha Tests Some Water

The drive to building 9 was probably three miles. Bertha was riding with Donna in Donna's car and Maria was following them in the van. On the way to building 9, Donna tried to be friendly. She talked about the weather and about what she planned to do next month when she went on her vacation. But Bertha's nose told her that Donna felt very uneasy.

Building 9 looked like a giant garage. More than a dozen trucks and cars were parked inside. Workers were working on three of the vehicles.

As Bertha left Donna's car, Donna said, "I've got to go back to my desk. Big Ted will take care of you. He's the head of this garage."

Big Ted was one of the biggest people Bertha had ever seen. The top of Bertha's head came up to Big Ted's chest. "You want water, you've got water," Big Ted announced in an unfriendly way. He turned around, picked up a bucket full of water and placed it on the floor in front of Maria.

Some water spilled over the side of the bucket. "Water, water," Big Ted said smiling. "You want it, we've got it." He turned around and winked at one of the other men.

Bertha said, "Where did you get this water?"

Big Ted said, "From the refinery, of course."

Bertha said, "And how did the water get to the refinery?"

"From a well," Ted responded without smiling.

"Not so," Bertha said. "This water came from that truck over there." She pointed to a tank truck that had the words REEF OIL REFINERY painted on it. "And that truck got the water from a place that must be 20 miles south of here. It's from a stream that leads to the ocean. It did not come from a well."

"Hey," Ted shouted. "Who is this kid?" He bent down so that his face almost touched Bertha's. "Are you calling me a liar?"

Bertha swallowed. Some of the men who had been working on the vehicles were staring. Bertha looked down. Her heart was pounding. With all her power she made herself say this: "I don't mean to call you a liar. I'm just telling you where the water came from."

"Don't pick on her," Maria shouted. Her voice echoed through the large garage. "She's telling the truth and you know it!"

Big Ted stared at Maria. Then he smiled. "Okay, okay," he said. "The kid looks at water and can tell where it comes from. You believe her instead of me. If that's what you want to do, I'm not going to stop you."

Ted walked to a man standing by the phone. "Call Daniels," Ted said. "Tell him to get down here right now."

Ted smiled. "If you girls will excuse me, I've got other things to do."

Ted walked away, and Bertha and Maria were once more standing all alone in the middle of the huge garage. None of the workers looked at them. Nobody talked to them.

Within ten minutes, Donna's car pulled up in front of the building. Mr. Daniels got out of the car. "What's the problem?" he said as he walked toward Maria.

"Plenty," Maria shouted. Bertha didn't know that Maria could shout that loudly. The workers stopped and began to stare again. "What kind of tricks are you trying to pull?" Maria demanded. Before Mr. Daniels could answer, she continued, "You bring us out here to a garage and show us some water that you brought in by truck. Why don't you just take us to the place where you are using the water? Let us test that water."

"Well," Mr. Daniels said, looking away from Maria, "I can't do that. I just can't . . . "

"Why not?" Maria demanded.

Mr. Daniels looked up. "You'll have to come back on another day. You cannot go to the refining buildings today."

"Just a minute," Maria said. "If you throw us out, I'm coming back with the police. I'm an investigator for the state, and you'd better remember that."

Mr. Daniels turned around and smiled faintly. He didn't say a word, but his expression was filled with hate. He ducked into Donna's car, and the car moved slowly down the road.

MORE NEXT TIME

C Number your paper from 1 through 17.

Skill Items

A dozen typists approached the stairs.

1. What word names people whose job is to type things neatly?
2. What word means **moved toward something?**
3. What word means **twelve?**

Review Items

4. Write the letter of the animal that is facing into the wind.
5. Which direction is that animal facing?
6. So what's the **name** of that wind?

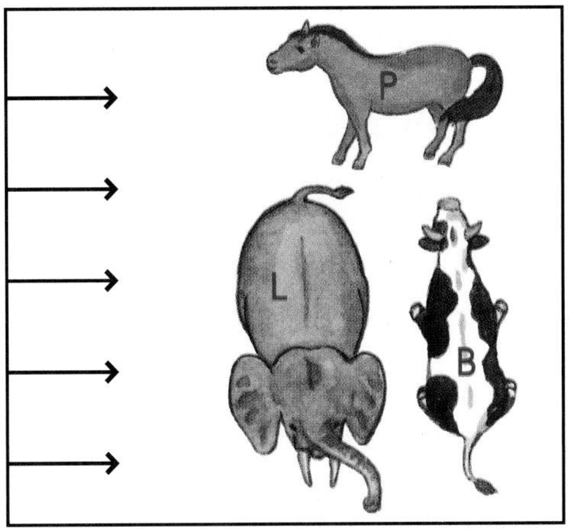

7. When an object gets hotter, the temperature goes ▒▒▒.

8. What place does the **A** show?
9. What place does the **B** show?
10. What place does the **C** show?

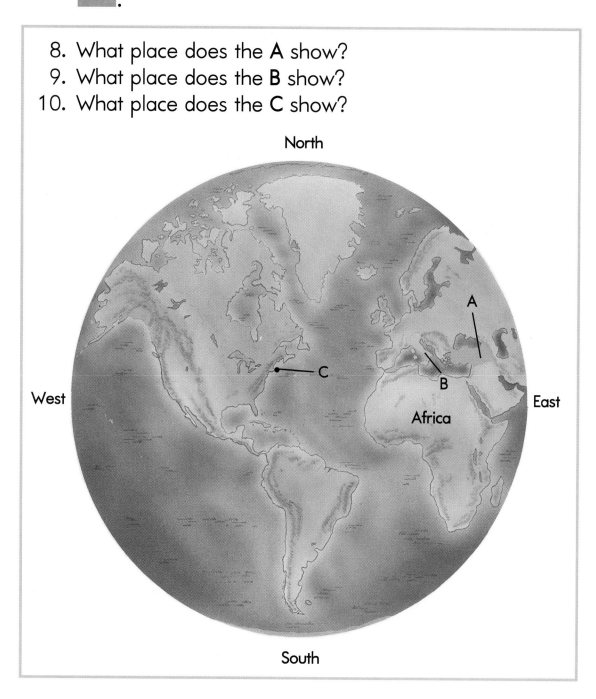

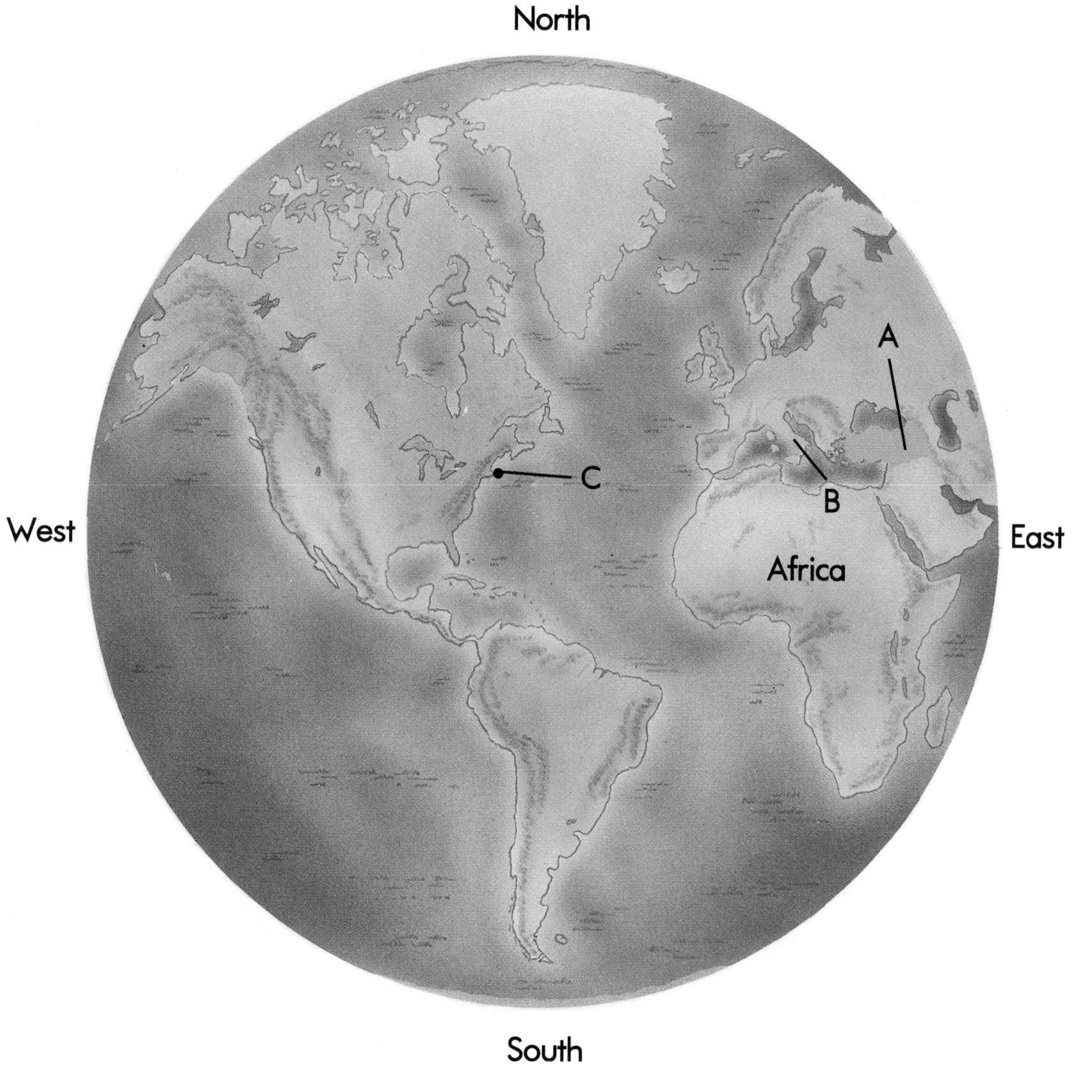

11. Write 2 letters that show bulkheads.
12. Write 2 letters that show decks.
13. Which letter shows where the bow is?
14. Which letter shows where the stern is?

15. What is the temperature of the water in each jar?
16. Write the letter of each jar that is filled with ocean water.
17. Jar E is not filled with ocean water. How do you know?

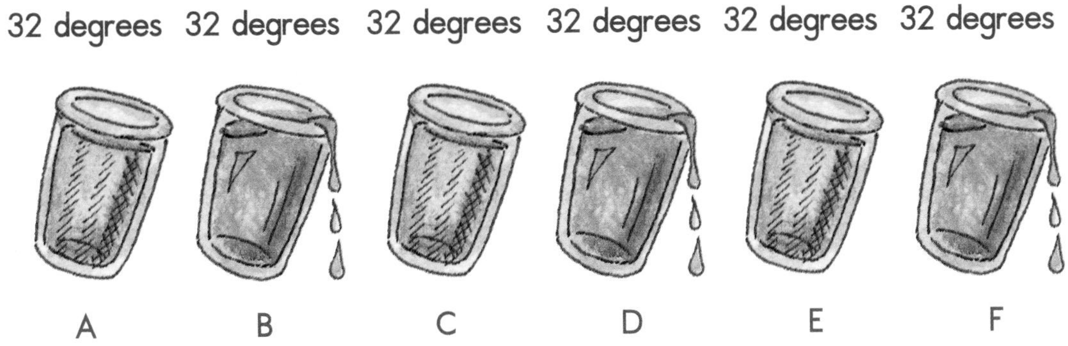

75

A

1	2	3
1. shadow	1. factories	1. adventure
2. aware	2. swooped	2. complaint
3. sticky	3. upper	3. arranged
4. dizzy	4. comfortable	4. breathe
5. chief	5. practiced	5. purple
6. clover	6. tingles	

B

Maria and Bertha Make Up a New Plan

Bertha wanted to tell everybody about her adventure, but nobody was around. Tina was swimming and Judy wasn't home. Even Bertha's mother was out of the house.

After making five phone calls, Bertha went over to Maria's house. The windows were open, and Bertha could see Maria talking on the phone. "But, Chief," she said. "I didn't <u>force</u> my way into anybody's office. . . . No, I did <u>not</u> call Daniels a crook. . . . That's a lie, Chief. I didn't say anything like that to Big Ted." At last Maria hung up the phone and walked outside, shaking her head.

"That Mr. Daniels called up my office and told a <u>lot</u> of lies," Maria said. "And the chief believes him. The chief told me that if there's one more complaint, I'll have to turn this investigation over to another investigator."

"I've got an idea," Bertha said. "Why don't you get your chief to go out there with us?"

"Oh, no," Maria said. "That will never work."

"Why not?"

"Well, for one thing, you're not a state investigator, and I'll have trouble explaining why you're going along."

"Oh, that's right," Bertha said. Bertha looked up at the sky. Three white fluffy clouds were so bright that they hurt her eyes. Three birds moved across the sky, landing in a huge tree on the next block. The smells of summer were heavy. Someone had just mowed a lawn on the next block. The grass had a lot of clover in it.

"I've got it," Bertha said suddenly. "Oh, boy." She began to do a little dance. Bertha said, "Listen to this idea. It's great. You get your chief to go with you. And I hide under a blanket in the back of your van. You just make sure that the van is near the refining building. Bring a jar of water from the refining building to the van. Tap on the back of the van, and I'll tell you where the water comes from."

"No," Maria said. "That will never w---." She stopped talking and slowly smiled. Maria said, "I'll bet it will work. I think that's a great idea." She began to laugh. "We'll get that Mr. Daniels yet."

• • •

It was dark under the blanket in Maria's van. But Bertha didn't need her eyes to know where the van was. By using her nose, she could tell when the van was at the corner of Fifth and Main, when the van went past the factories on Main, and when the van was outside the city. Bertha knew nearly as much about where she was as she would have known if she could have used her eyes.

The smell of the refinery gave Bertha an uneasy feeling. She remembered the anger that came from most of the people at the Reef Oil Refinery. Maria also felt uneasy. Bertha could tell from the smells that came from the van. Maria's chief did not feel uneasy. He gave off the smell of somebody who is sleepy.

The van came to a stop at the gate, and Bertha could hear voices. She had trouble understanding what they said, and she began to wonder how loudly she would have to talk for Maria to hear her. They probably should have practiced talking to each other when Bertha was under the blanket, but Maria had been a little late that morning so they had no time to practice.

The voice outside the van said something about Mr. Daniels. Did the voice say that Mr. Daniels would come to the gate? Bertha wasn't sure. She lifted her head and tried to hear better, but nobody was talking now.

As Maria's van waited at the gate, it began to fill with new smells, the smells of heat. The sun beat down on the van, and Bertha got hotter and hotter under the blanket. Bertha rolled over and tried to find a comfortable spot. It was getting so hot under the blanket that Bertha was starting to feel a little sick.

MORE NEXT TIME

C Number your paper from 1 through 18.

Skill Items

Use the words in the box to write complete sentences.

doctors	pretend	succeed	typists	talent
appeared	lawyers	approached	doubt	

1. ______ with ______ normally ______.
2. A dozen ______ ______ the stairs.

Review Items

3. How fast is car **A** going?
4. How fast is car **B** going?
5. Which car is going faster?

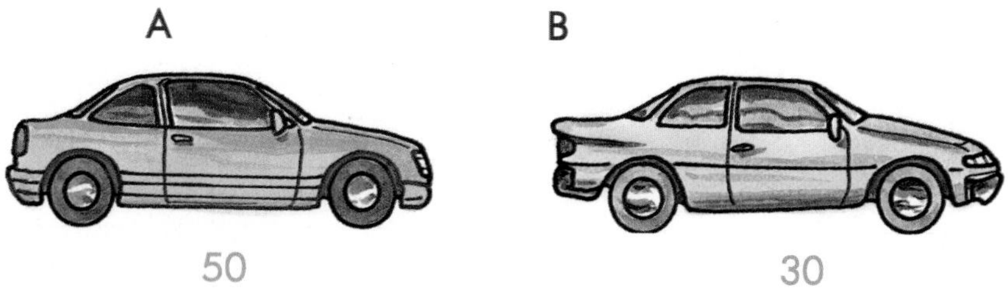

6. Which eye can see more things at the same time, a human's eye or a fly's eye?
7. The United States is a ____. • city • state • country
8. Japan is a ____.
9. How many states are in the United States?
10. Name a state in the United States that is bigger than Italy.
11. Italy is shaped something like a ____.

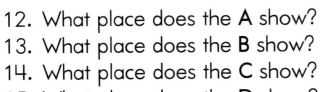

12. What place does the **A** show?
13. What place does the **B** show?
14. What place does the **C** show?
15. What place does the **D** show?

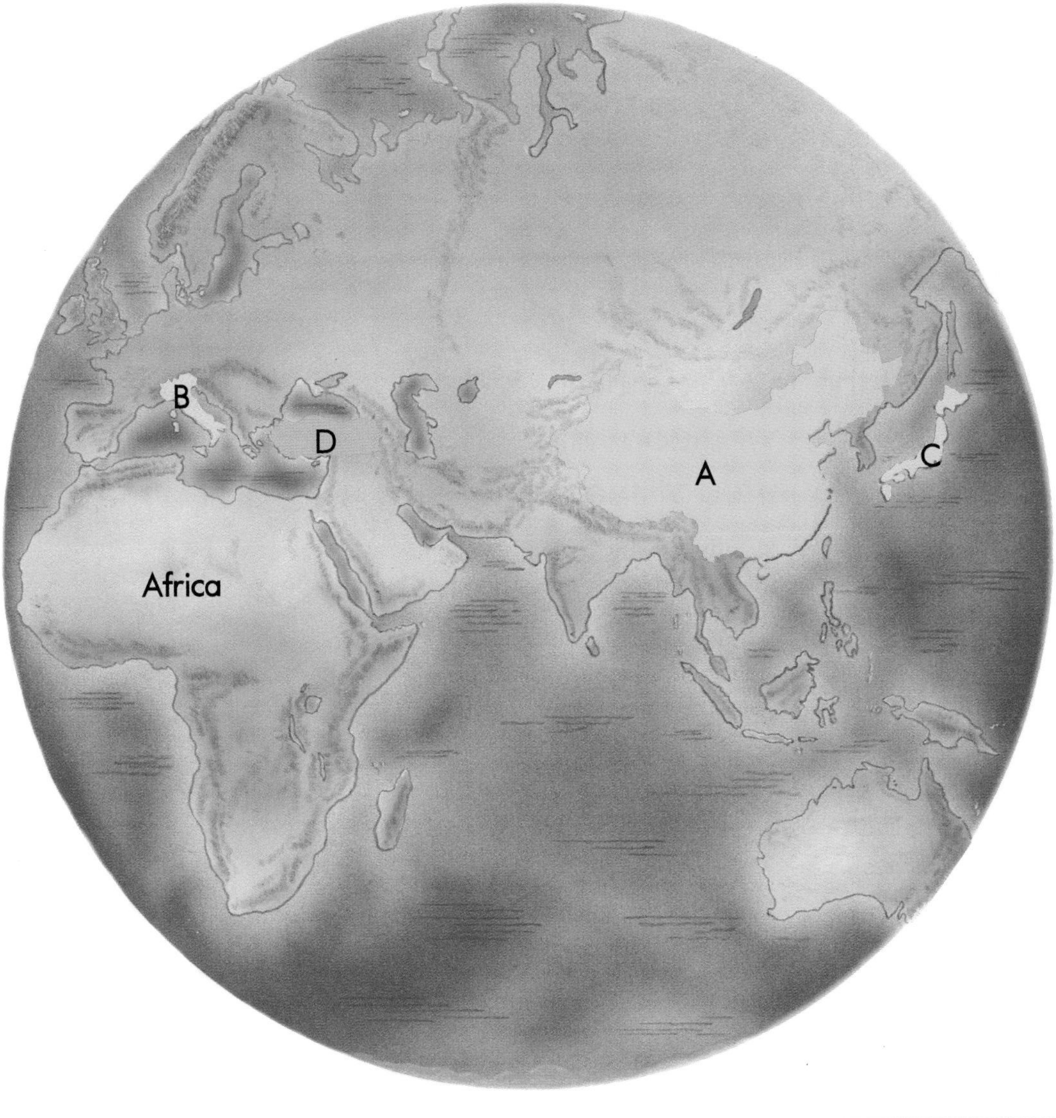

The picture shows objects caught in a whirlpool.

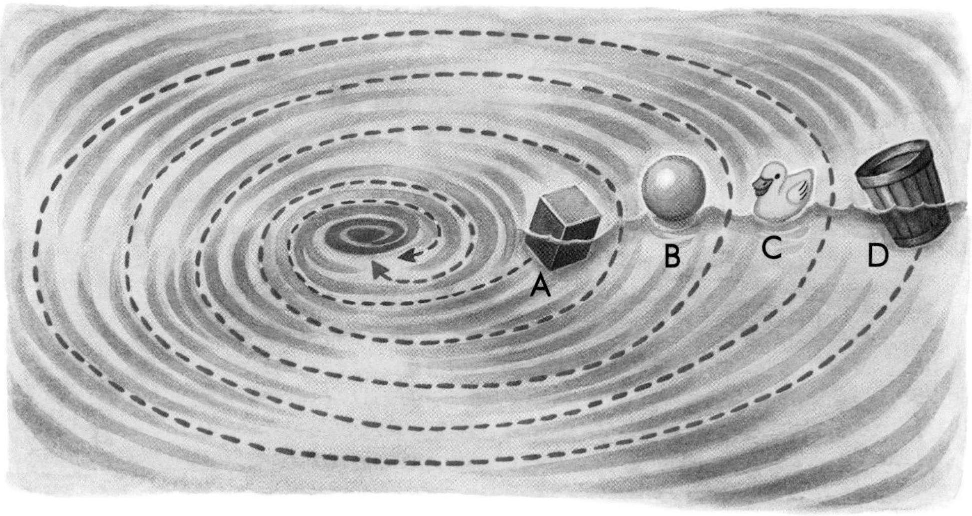

16. Write the letter of the object that will go down the hole in the whirlpool first.
17. Write the letter of the object that will go down the hole in the whirlpool next.
18. Write the letter of the object that will go down the hole in the whirlpool last.

76

A

1

1. objected
2. require
3. consultant
4. shadows
5. aware
6. half-aware

2

1. sticky
2. tingles
3. purple
4. dizzy
5. bumper

3

1. make sense
2. in a fog
3. twenty-one
4. wood
5. cottonwood

4

1. faint
2. breathe
3. upper
4. brand
5. studied
6. confused

B

Inside a Hot Van

Maria's van was waiting at the gate, and Bertha was starting to feel sick from the heat under the blanket. At last, a voice outside the van said, "Drive to building twenty-one. To get there, keep right." The voice continued to give directions. Bertha didn't hear the rest of the directions.

Bertha was starting to talk to herself. "Let's go," she said. "Let's get moving." She didn't talk loud enough for anybody to hear her. But she knew that if the van was moving, the air in the van wouldn't stay so hot. At least, she hoped that the air wouldn't stay so hot. "Let's go."

The van went to building twenty-one. Bertha could tell by the smells that building twenty-one was near many other buildings. The smell of oil was so strong that anybody could smell it. Building twenty-one was one of the buildings that refined the crude oil.

The van doors opened. Maria and the chief got out of the van. They talked to two men. Bertha knew that one of these men was Mr. Daniels. She didn't know the other man.

Suddenly, Bertha realized that Maria had parked the van in the sun. The temperature inside the van was going up. It was already so hot that Bertha couldn't stand it. The air seemed thick and hard to breathe. Now it was getting even hotter. Bertha was starting to breathe hard. Her body was wet and sticky.

The voices outside faded as Maria and the others went into building twenty-one. For a long time nothing happened, except the heat continued to pound against Bertha. Suddenly, Bertha caught the smell of Maria. She was near the van, but she wasn't alone. The man that had been with Mr. Daniels was next to Maria.

Water. Yes, there was the smell of water. Maria was holding a container of water close to the back of the van.

Bertha heard the man say something about going back inside. Maria answered in a loud voice, "I want to look at the water in the sunlight." Bertha knew that was a lie.

The water was from the creek. But Bertha couldn't say anything while the other man was around.

"Wow!" Bertha said out loud. She was starting to feel dizzy. Her hands and feet felt strange. She was starting to see purple dots that she knew were not actually there.

Then, without knowing it, she yelled out, "Near the barn." She was only half-aware that she said anything. The words didn't make any sense to her, and she didn't know what made her say them. She was in a fog made up of purple dots, tingles, and a feeling that everything was falling, falling.

• • •

The back door of the van was open, the blanket was gone, and the hot sun was beating down on Bertha. Two forms were close to her. One was Maria. Her face was very close to Bertha's. Her mouth was moving and sounds were coming from it. Bertha noticed that Maria had a little scar on her upper lip. " . . . all right? Are you all right?" Maria's voice said.

" . . . trying to do?" the man's voice said angrily. "What are you trying to do here? Who is this girl? I'm getting Mr. Daniels right now."

Bertha sat up. Maria's arms were around her. Bertha was starting to feel better. "I'm sorry," she said. "I think I fainted from the heat."

"It's all right," Maria said. "Don't try to talk. Just take it easy for a few minutes."

Three men walked quickly from building twenty-one—Mr. Daniels, the chief, and the man who had been with Maria.

That man said, "She was hiding in the van. I don't know what they are trying to do."

The three men stopped near the van. Two of their shadows fell on Bertha. Maria's chief said, "Maria, what is this all about?"

MORE NEXT TIME

C Number your paper from 1 through 17.

Skill Item

1. Compare object A and object B. Remember, first tell how they're the same. Then tell how they're different.

Object A 

Object B 

Review Items

Each statement tells about how far something goes or how fast something goes. Write **how far** or **how fast** for each item.

2. He ran 5 miles per hour.
3. He ran 5 miles.
4. The plane was 500 miles from New York City.
5. The plane was flying 500 miles per hour.

6. What part of a car tells how fast the car is moving?
7. What's the boiling temperature of water?
   - 212 miles
   - 212 degrees
   - 112 degrees

Some of the objects in the picture are insects, and some are spiders.

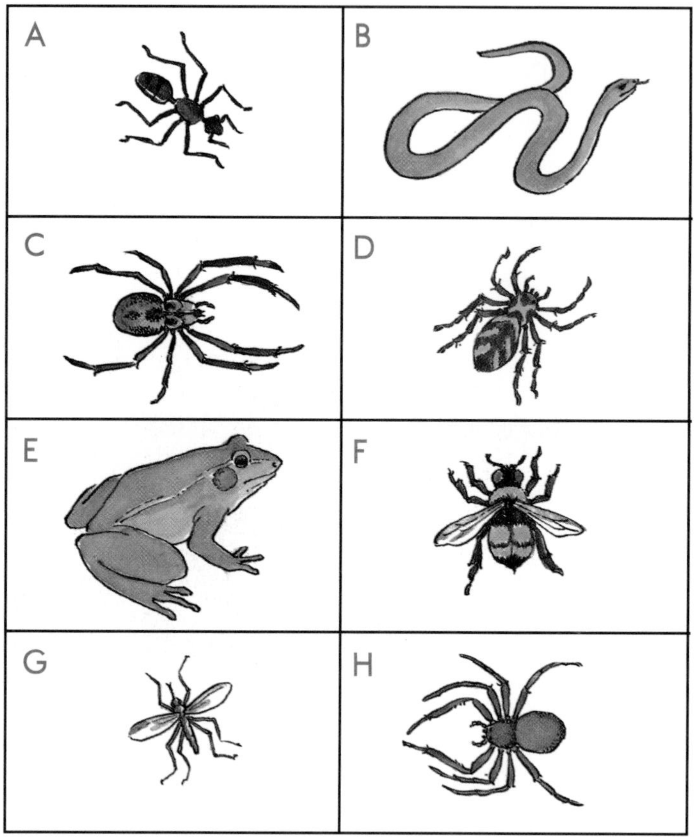

8. Write the letters of the spiders.
9. Write the letters of the insects.
10. When a glass gets colder, which way does the temperature go?
11. A street gets hotter. So what do you know about the temperature of the street?

12. What liquid does the **A** show?
13. What liquid does the **B** show?
14. What liquid does the **C** show?

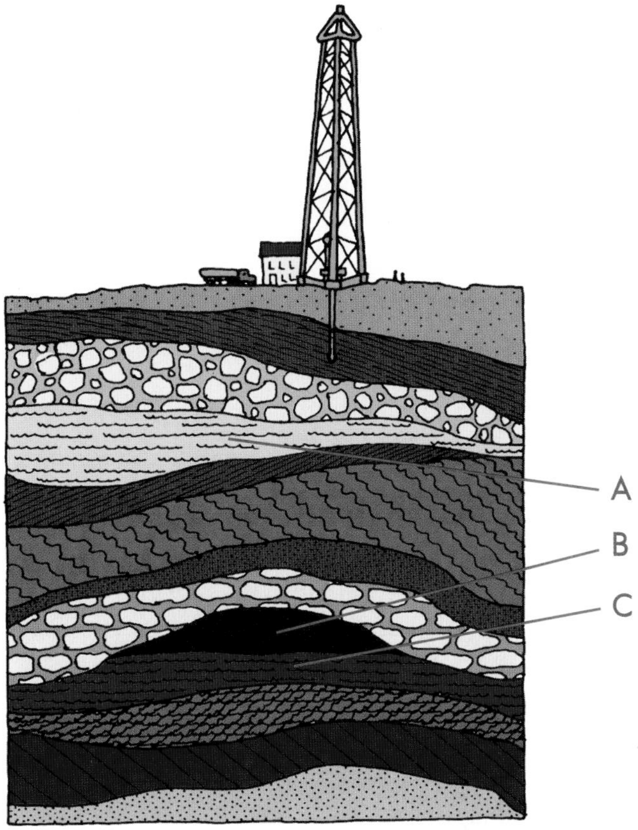

15. Which eye works like many drops, a human's eye or a fly's eye?
16. The biggest state in the United States is ____.
17. The second-biggest state in the United States is ____.

77

A

1	2
1. permitted	1. objected
2. immediately	2. bumper
3. unless	3. studied
4. cottonwood	4. confused

3	4
1. fair	1. weak
2. unfair	2. list
3. cloth	3. bench
4. cost	4. hood
5. brand	

B The Chief Listens to Bertha

Bertha was lying in the open van. Donna was next to Bertha. She was holding a cool wet cloth on Bertha's neck. She smiled at Bertha and asked, "How are you doing?"

Bertha said, "Okay."

The shadows were cool, but the sun was very bright and hot. Next to the van was a group of people. The chief asked why Bertha had come along. Maria was trying to explain. "Chief," she said, "Bertha can tell us exactly where the water comes from. I knew that you might not let her come along because she doesn't work for the state. So what I did was . . . "

Suddenly, everybody seemed to be talking at once, and their shadows moved around. For one moment Bertha would feel cool in the shadows. The next moment, she would feel the terrible heat of the sun.

Mr. Daniels was saying something about the state bringing kids out to an oil refinery. The man who was with Mr. Daniels kept asking, "What kind of trick is the state trying to pull?"

Maria kept saying, "But she can tell us where the water . . . "

"Everybody, be quiet," the chief said loudly and raised his hand. "Let Maria answer this question. How could that girl tell us where the water comes from?"

"She smells," Maria said, and everybody looked at her. There was a long moment of silence. "I mean," Maria said, "she smells with her nose. I don't mean she smells bad. She can smell things and tell what they are or where they are from."

The chief looked at Bertha. He gave off the smell of somebody who was not afraid but was a little confused. "Is that right?" he asked Bertha. "Can you really do that?"

Bertha was feeling better now. She nodded her head.

"What kinds of things can you tell about me?" he asked.

She took a deep breath. "Your socks are brand new," she said. "First time you wore them."

The chief didn't say anything. He just looked at her. He studied her face. "This is crazy," Mr. Daniels was saying. "We're trying to run a business here. We don't have time . . . "

The chief held up his hand again. Bertha said to the chief, "You live two miles south of town, near some cottonwood trees. You have a dog."

The chief smiled and shook his head. "That's amazing," he said.

"It's crazy if you ask me," Mr. Daniels said. "We're trying to run a . . . "

The chief sat down on the van's bumper. "Tell me," he said softly to Bertha, "what does your nose tell you about the water they're using here?"

"Who cares what a kid says?" Mr. Daniels objected. The chief didn't take his eyes off Bertha.

"The water comes from the creek," Bertha said. "It is not well water."

"How can she tell that?" Mr. Daniels yelled. "She's calling us liars. I'm not going to stand for that. I'm going . . . "

The chief did not take his eyes off Bertha. "Are you sure?" he asked.

"Yes," Bertha said. "I could smell tiny plants in the water. These plants need sunlight to grow. So the water can't come from a well."

Mr. Daniels was yelling louder. "When did the state start using kids to do its business? The water is from a well, not from the creek."

Suddenly the chief turned around and pointed his finger at Mr. Daniels. "You be quiet. Do you understand?" The chief turned to Maria. "Get me six jars of water—three from the well and three from the creek."

"I'll have one of my men get them," Mr. Daniels said.

"No, thanks," the chief said. "Maria will get them." Mr. Daniels' face turned red.

MORE NEXT TIME

C Number your paper from 1 through 15.

Review Items

1. Greece went to war with Troy because of a woman named ____.
2. The woman from Greece was important because she was a ____.
3. The woman from Greece went away with a man from ____.

4. Which letter shows where Troy used to be?
5. Which letter shows where Greece is?
6. Which letter shows where Italy is?

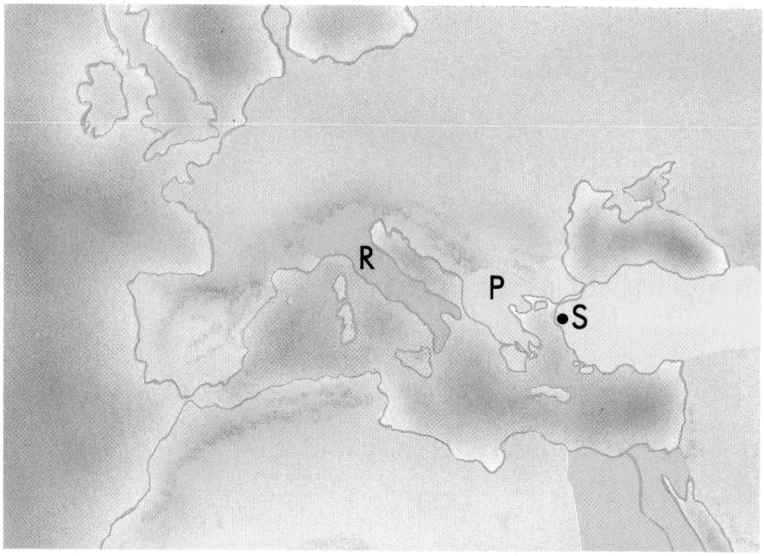

7. What place does **A** show?
8. What place does **B** show?
9. What place does **C** show?
10. What place does **D** show?

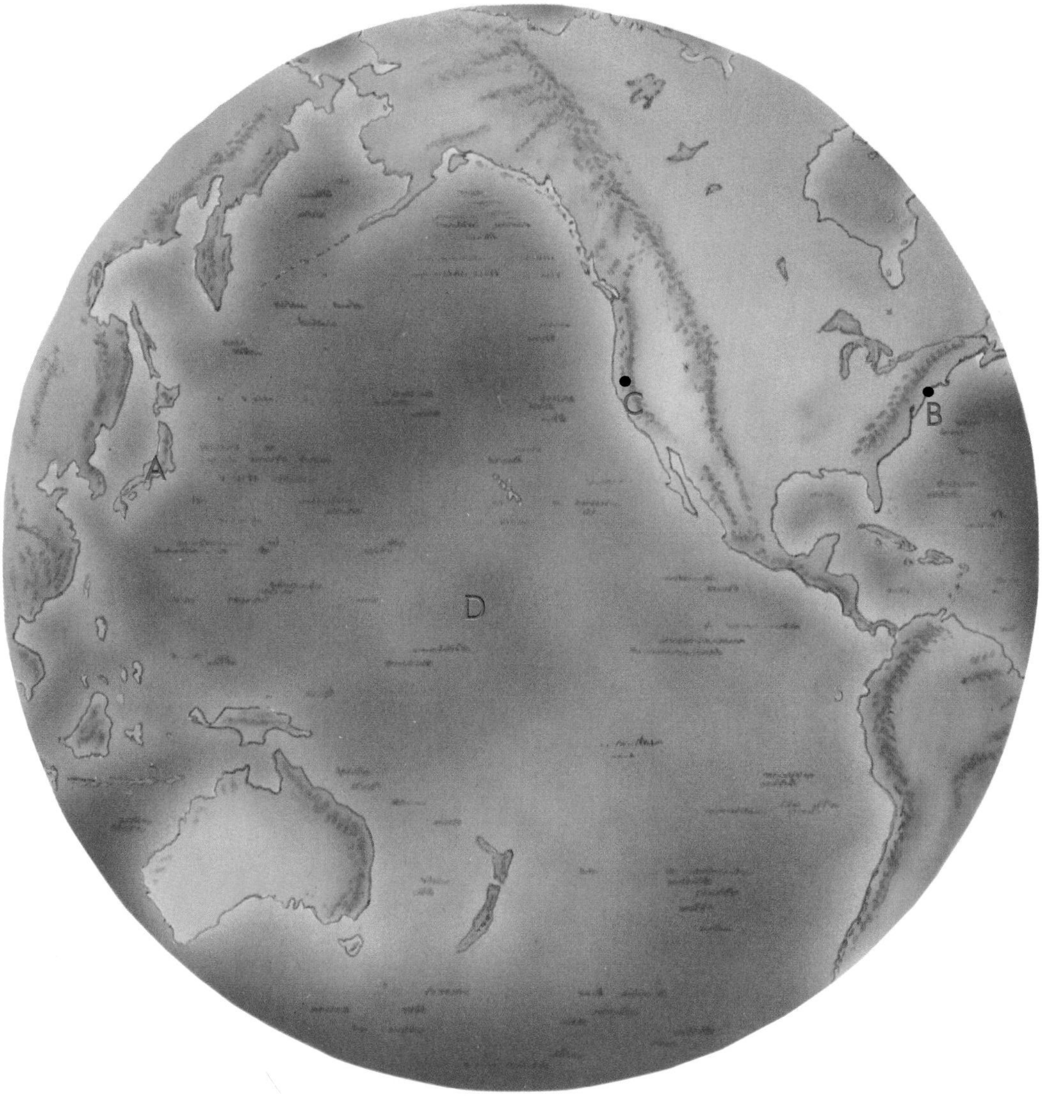

11. Which letter shows the crude oil?
12. Which letter shows the refinery?
13. Which letter shows the pipeline?

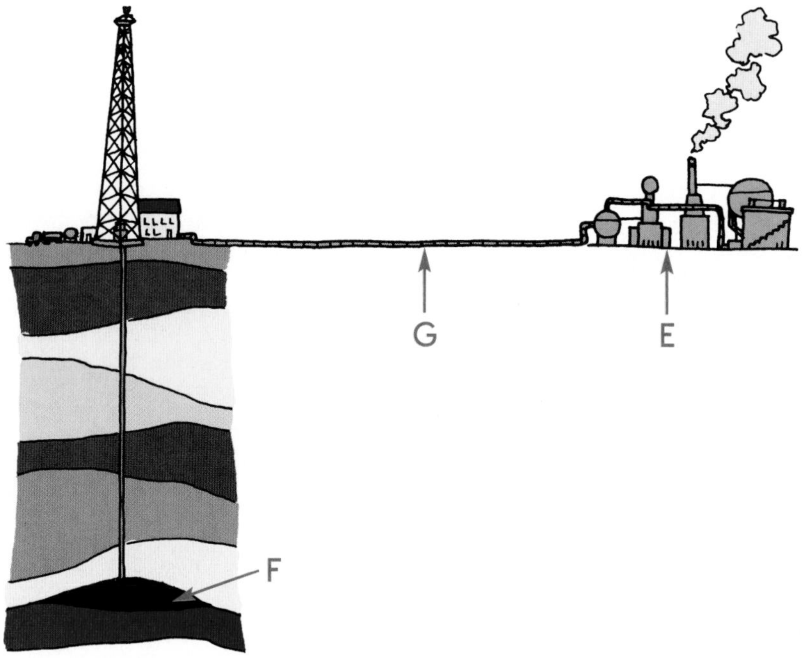

14 Which arrow shows the direction the crude oil is moving at A?

15. Which arrow shows the direction the crude oil is moving at B?

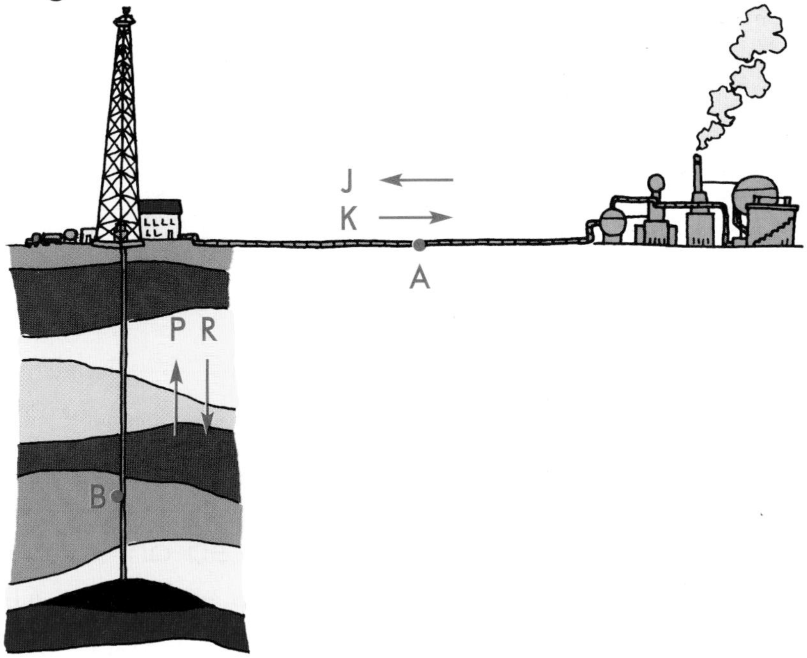

78

A

1	2	3
1. Achilles	1. fear	1. weak
2. shoulders	2. cost	2. weakness
3. permitted	3. magic	3. box
4. consultant	4. cloth	4. boxer
5. required	5. list	5. bench
6. unless	6. unfair	6. hood

B Bertha Tests the Water

Half an hour later, Bertha was seated on a long bench just outside building twenty-one of the refinery. She was blindfolded. In fact, she wore three blindfolds. The chief had stuck tape over each eye. He had then wrapped a long cloth around her head. Finally, he had placed a hood over her head. The hood came down to her shoulders. Next to her on the bench were six jars. Each was marked with a letter—A, B, C, D, E, and F.

The chief said, "This will be a good test. There is no way that she can see through the blindfolds. Even if she could see, she has no way of knowing where the water in each jar came from."

The chief continued, "She won't be permitted to touch the jars, so she won't be able to use the water temperature as a clue. The only way that she'll be able to figure out where the water came from is to use her nose."

"I think this test is <u>unfair</u>," Mr. Daniels said. "I'm calling our lawyers, right <u>now</u>."

"You call your lawyers," the chief said. "But I would like you and your men to watch what happens here. I'm going to write down what Bertha says about each jar. When she's done, I'll read where the water in each jar actually came from."

The chief picked up jar A. "I'm holding jar A in front of you," the chief said.

"Yes," Bertha replied. "And that water comes from the creek."

"You're sure about that?" the chief asked.

"I'm very sure," Bertha replied. The chief wrote, "Jar A–creek."

The chief held up the other jars one at a time. He told the letter of the jar. Then Bertha told about the water. Then the chief wrote what she said.

After she had smelled all six jars, the chief told Maria, "Now give me the list that tells where you got each jar of water."

Maria handed the list to the chief.

He read the list to himself and smiled. "It seems that Bertha made a perfect score on this test. The water in jars A, B, and D came from the creek. The water in jars C, E, and F came from the well. That is exactly what Bertha said."

"This doesn't prove *anything*," Mr. Daniels objected.

"I think it proves a *lot*," the chief replied. "Bertha showed that she can tell where these jars of water came from. If she's right about these jars, she must be right about the water in the refinery. She says that the water in the refinery is from the creek. So that water must be from the creek."

The chief said to Mr. Daniels, "You are using water from the creek. That is against the law. I order this refinery closed—immediately."

"You can't do that," Mr. Daniels shouted.

"I just did it," the chief said. "And I mean immediately."

Bertha couldn't help but smile. The chief walked up to Bertha, put an arm around her shoulder, and walked toward the van with her.

He said, "We can't use people who don't work for the state unless they are special consultants."

"Oh," Bertha said sadly.

"Special consultants must fill out a form, and we must pay them."

"Oh," Bertha said.

"In fact, we're required to pay special consultants five hundred dollars a day."

"Oh," Bertha said.

"So you'd better fill out one of those forms if you want to be a special consultant. You've already worked two full days."

Bertha didn't want to say, "Oh," again and she didn't know exactly what to say, so she just looked up at the chief and smiled. She felt that she was smiling too much, but she couldn't seem to stop.

Smile, Bertha Turner. Smile.

THE END

C Number your paper from 1 through 17.

Skill Items

The job required a consultant.

1. What word names a person who is hired for a special job?
2. What word means **needed?**

Review Items

3. When we weigh very small things, the unit we use is ______.

4. Write the letter of the ruler that will make the lowest sound.
5. Write the letter of the ruler that will make the highest sound.

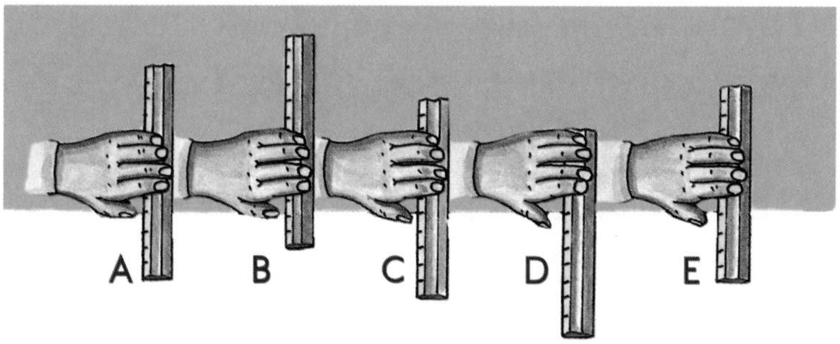

6. When we talk about miles per hour, we tell how ______ something is moving.
7. When something tries to move in one direction, something else tries to move ______.

8. Arrow X shows the direction the boy will jump. Which arrow shows the direction the block of ice will move?

9. A mile is a little more than ____ feet.
   - 1 thousand
   - 5 thousand
   - 5 hundred

10. How fast is truck **A** going?
11. How fast is truck **B** going?
12. Which truck is going faster?

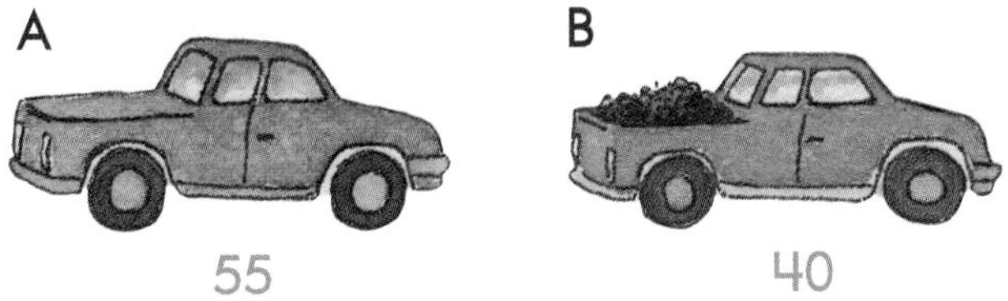

13. Airplanes land at airports. Ships land at ____.
14. Airplanes are pulled by little trucks. Ships are pulled by ____.
15. Airplanes unload at gates. Ships unload at ____.
16. Which is longer, a centimeter or a meter?
17. How many centimeters long is a meter?

SPECIAL PROJECT

Bertha's nose was as good as a dog's nose. Dogs are able to use their nose to find things that we can't find any other way.

- Dogs have been trained to use their nose to find things that people are trying to hide from the police.
- Dogs have also been trained to find a part of a person's body that has a disease that can't be found any other way. (If a dog could find a disease like cancer early enough, it could save the life of the person.)

A

1	2
1. poison	1. Achilles
2. Hector	2. feared
3. boxer	3. weakness
4. magic	4. battled

B

Learning About an Achilles Heel

Another name for a **weakness** is **Achilles heel.** Read this sentence: Her **love of candy** was her **weakness.**

Here's a sentence that means the same thing: Her **love of candy** was her **Achilles heel.**

Read this sentence: His **poor reading** was his **weakness.**

Here's a sentence that means the same thing: His **poor reading** was his **Achilles heel.**

Read this sentence: The **boxer's left hand** was his **weakness.**

Say the sentence another way.

Read this sentence: Her **bad health** was her **weakness.**

Say the sentence another way.

You may wonder why the words **Achilles heel** mean **weakness.** The story that you will read today tells why. That story took place over 3 thousand years ago. The story is about a man named Achilles who was in a great war that took place 3 thousand years ago. Which war was that?

Achilles was a great soldier in the army that was at war with Troy. What army was that?

C Achilles Heel

The story about Achilles is make-believe.

When Achilles was a baby, his mother took him to a river. The river was filled with magic water. Special people could go into this river, but only one time. Here's the rule about what would happen: **If the water touched a part of your body, nothing could hurt that part.** If the water touched your hand, nothing could hurt your hand. A knife or an arrow could not hurt your hand. If you put your leg in this magic water, what would happen to the leg?

Achilles' mother loved her baby very much. She did not want anything to hurt him. She said, "I will dip my baby in the magic river. Then nothing will be able to hurt Achilles."

But the water in the river moved very fast. Achilles' mother said, "If I let go of my baby in the water, the river will carry him away. So I must hold on to part of him." Achilles' mother thought and thought about how to hold her baby when she dipped him into the river.

At last she said, "I will hold Achilles' heel when I dip him in the magic river." So she did. Achilles' mother held on to his heel and dipped him in the magic river. The only part of Achilles that did not get wet in the magic river was his heel.

Achilles grew up to be the greatest soldier that Greece ever had. All the cities in Greece heard about Achilles, and the soldiers from these cities were afraid of him. When he was still a boy, he battled the best soldiers. They hit him with their swords, but the swords did not cut him. They shot him with arrows, but the arrows did not hurt him. When they saw that they could not kill him, they tried to run from him. But Achilles rode after them on his horse and killed them.

When the war with Troy started, Achilles was the most feared soldier in the world.

MORE NEXT TIME

D Number your paper from 1 through 14.

Write each sentence below using other words for the word **weakness.**

1. His left hand was his **weakness.**
2. Their love of money was their **weakness.**

Skill Items

Use the words in the box to write complete sentences.

friendly	approached	explained	guard	required
dozen	fairly	complaint	consultant	

3. A _____ typists _____ the stairs.
4. The job _____ a _____.

Review Items

5. When did the story of Troy take place?
   - 3 hundred years ago
   - 3 thousand years ago
   - 1 thousand years ago
6. Write the letters of the 4 kinds of weapons that soldiers used when they had battles with Troy.

   a. spears b. bows c. rockets d. tanks
   e. arrows f. planes g. swords h. guns

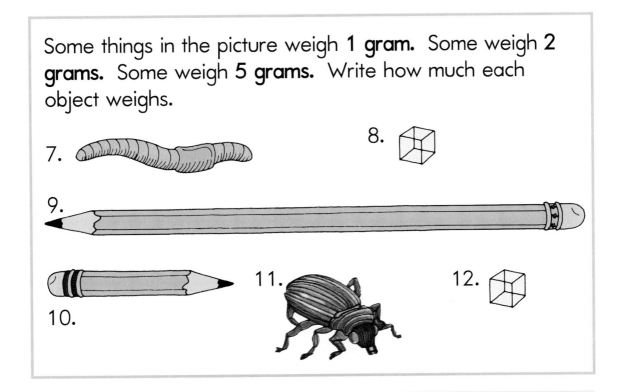

Some things in the picture weigh **1 gram.** Some weigh **2 grams.** Some weigh **5 grams.** Write how much each object weighs.

7. 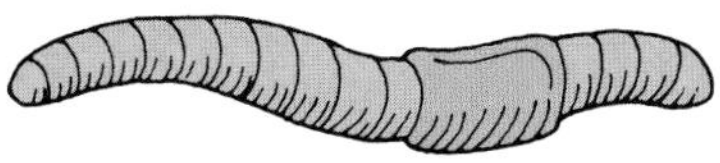

8. 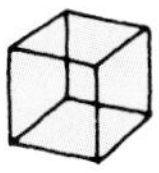

9. 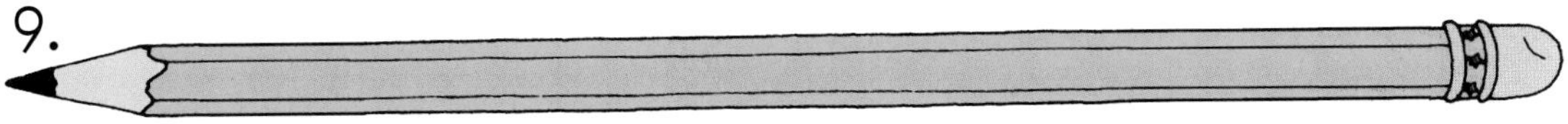

10. 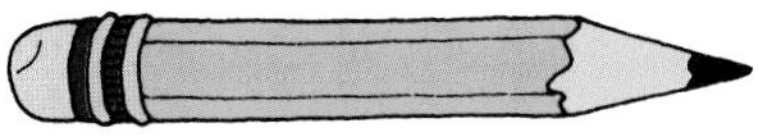

11. 

12. 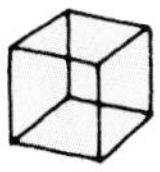

13. Which is longer, a centimeter or a meter?
14. How many centimeters long is a meter?

END OF LESSON 79 INDEPENDENT WORK

80 TEST 8

Number your paper from 1 through 19.

1. Name 2 kinds of wells.

2. What liquid does the **D** show?
3. What liquid does the **E** show?
4. What liquid does the **F** show?

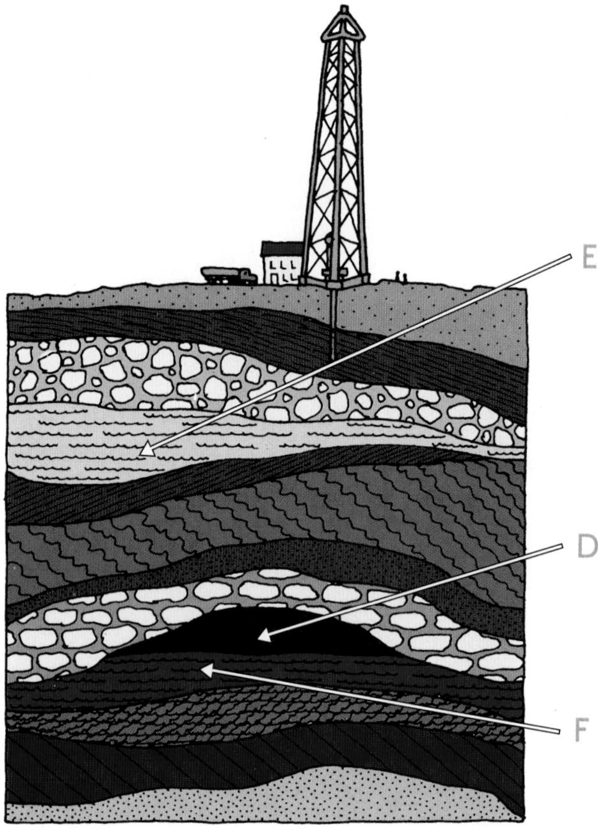

5. Which letter shows the crude oil?
6. Which letter shows the refinery?
7. Which letter shows the pipeline?

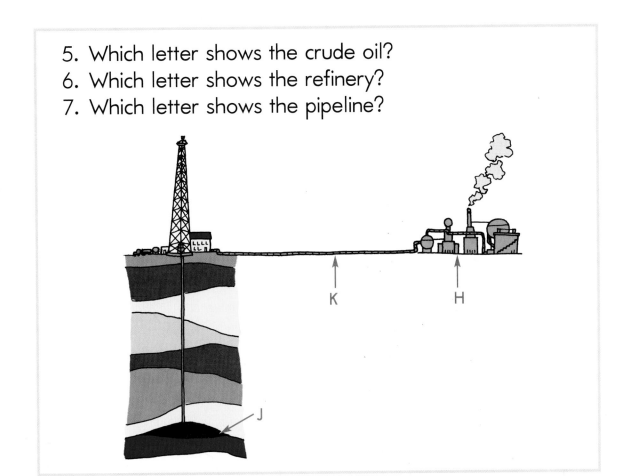

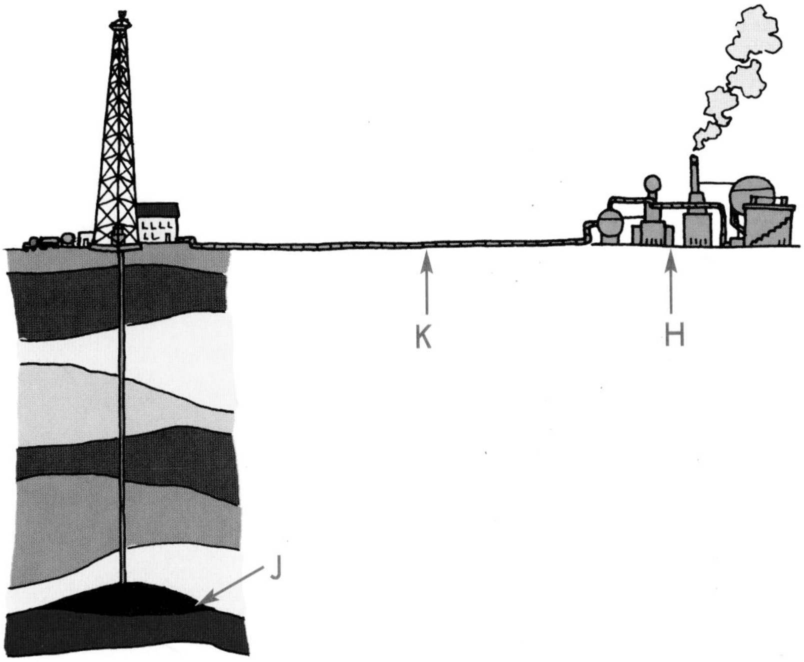

8. Which arrow shows the direction the crude oil is moving at A?
9. Which arrow shows the direction the crude oil is moving at B?

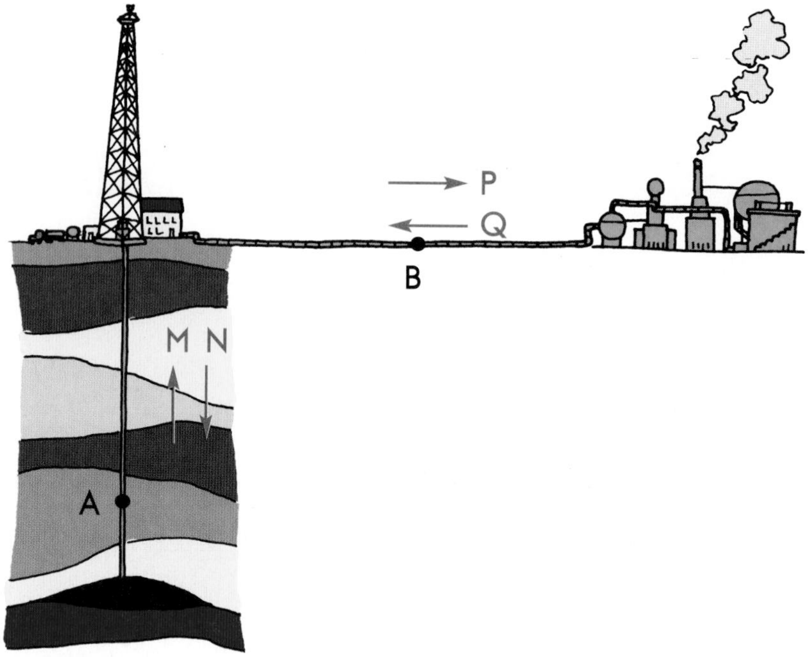

10. Gasoline comes from a liquid called _____.
11. Write the sentence using other words for the word **weakness.**

His love of money was his **weakness.**

Skill Items

For each item, write the underlined word from the sentences in the box.

Lawyers with talent normally succeed.
A dozen typists approached the stairs.
The job required a consultant.

12. What underlining means **needed?**
13. What underlining names people whose job is to type things neatly?
14. What underlining names a person who is hired for a special job?
15. What underlining names people who help us when we have questions about the law?
16. What underlining means **usually?**
17. What underlining means **twelve?**
18. What underlining means the opposite of **fail?**
19. What underlining refers to special skills?

END OF TEST 8

81

A

1	2
1. chariot	1. ashes
2. adults	2. burnt
3. buffalo	3. crushed
4. huddled	4. poisoned
5. Hector	5. eighty

B

Chariots

During the war between Greece and Troy, people didn't have the kinds of vehicles we have today. They used horses to pull their vehicles on land. Horses pulled carts. Horses also pulled small vehicles with two wheels, called chariots. Soldiers used chariots in battles. Chariots could move very fast. Maybe six horses would pull the chariot. Maybe two horses would pull it.

Sometimes two soldiers would be in a chariot. One would steer. The other would be able to use both hands to shoot arrows or hold a shield and throw spears.

Look at the vehicle in the picture. What is its name? How many wheels does it have? How many soldiers are in it? How many horses are pulling it? What is soldier A doing? What is soldier B doing?

If you look closely at the picture, you will see that the chariot has sharp knives on it. These knives turn around and around when the chariot moves. They would cut through anything that got in their way. Where are those knives?

C The Greatest Soldier

A thousand ships went to war with Troy. There were soldiers on every ship. Achilles was on one of the ships. For ten years he was in the war with Troy. The soldiers of Troy shot arrows at him and threw spears at him. But nothing hurt Achilles.

There was also a great soldier in the city of Troy. His name was Hector. The people of Troy said, "Hector is as fast as a deer. He is as strong as an elephant."

Achilles knew that Hector was the greatest soldier of Troy. Achilles had heard the stories about how fast Hector was and how strong he was.

Achilles was getting tired of hearing people say that Hector was the greatest soldier. "I am the greatest soldier," Achilles said. "And I'll prove it."

Achilles went to the wall of Troy. He yelled to the men on the wall, "Send out Hector. I will fight him. We will see who is the greatest soldier."

Soon the huge gate opened, and a man came out. He was a huge man, carrying a great spear. "I am Hector," the soldier from Troy yelled. "I will show you who is the greatest soldier."

Hector and Achilles started to fight. The men on the wall of Troy watched. The Greek soldiers watched. Hector and Achilles fought for hours. At last Achilles won the fight. Hector was dead. Achilles held up his spear and said, "I am the greatest soldier of all. Nothing can hurt me."

The soldiers of Troy shouted back at him. They could not believe that Hector had been killed. They hated Achilles. So they shouted at him and called him names.

Achilles laughed at the soldiers of Troy. Then he shouted back at them, "You would like to kill me. I will give you a chance to do that."

He took a chariot and started to ride around the wall of Troy. He stayed very close to the wall so that the soldiers of Troy could shoot arrows and throw spears. The arrows and spears bounced from his head and his chest and his legs. He laughed. "Kill me," he shouted, waving his sword at them. "Here is your chance to kill me."

By the time he was about half-way around the great wall, arrows and spears were stuck all over the chariot. One of the horses had been hit by an arrow. Spears and arrows were falling like rain on Achilles. Some of the arrows had poisoned tips. But they didn't bother Achilles. He was laughing and shaking his sword at the soldiers of Troy.

Then something strange happened. A soldier on the wall shot a poisoned arrow at Achilles. The arrow almost missed Achilles. But it hit him in the heel. Immediately, he dropped his sword. He cried out and fell from the chariot. He tried to stand up, but then he fell over. Achilles was dead. He had been killed because of his Achilles heel.

THE END

D Number your paper from 1 through 19.

1. What is the name of the vehicle in the picture?
2. How many wheels does the vehicle have?
3. What is pulling the vehicle?
4. What is soldier A doing?
5. What is soldier B doing?

Review Items

Write **W** for warm-blooded animals and **C** for cold-blooded animals.

6. ant
7. cow
8. dog
9. spider

10. Lee is 10 miles high. Jean is 15 miles high. Who is colder?
11. Tell why.

The ship in the picture is sinking. It is making currents as it sinks.

12. Write the letter of the object that will go down the whirlpool first.
13. Write the letter of the object that will go down the whirlpool last.

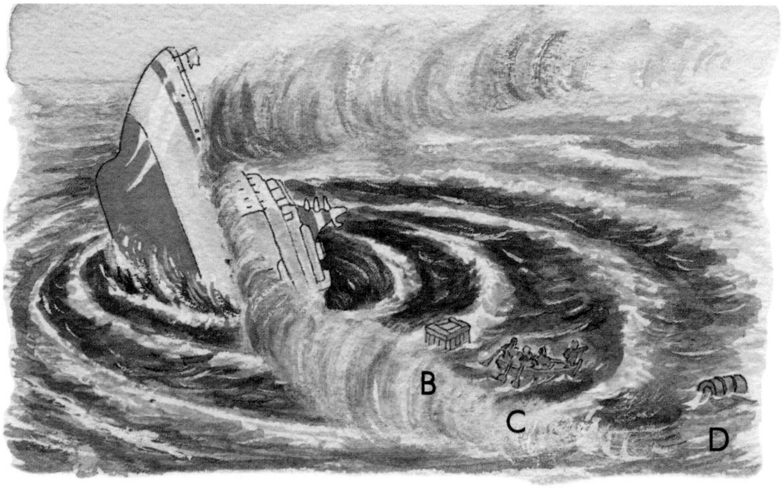

14. The temperature inside your body is about ___ degrees when you are healthy.
15. Most fevers don't go over ___ degrees.
16. The place that is called Troy is now part of what country?
    - Greece
    - Turkey
    - Italy

17. Write the letter of the sun you see at sunset.
18. Write the letter of the sun you see at noon.
19. Write the letter of the sun you see early in the morning.

SPECIAL PROJECT

Some of the stories that you have read are called **myths.** They are fiction, but they tell about famous heroes. The myth about Achilles is a Greek myth.

Here are the names of other heroes of Greek myths: Athena, Zeus, Poseidon, Hermes, Hercules, Jason. Select 2 names and find out what those characters did.

82

A

1	2	3
1. figure	1. expression	1. cave
2. early	2. adventure	2. buffalo
3. opposite	3. immediately	3. eighty
4. twelve	4. objected	4. adults
5. huddled	5. chariot	5. ashes

B

Clues from Thousands of Years Ago

Look at the time line. It goes all the way back eighty thousand years. Touch the dot on the line that shows the war between Greece and Troy.

Touch the dot that shows things that happened forty thousand years ago.

Touch the dot that shows things that happened eighty thousand years ago.

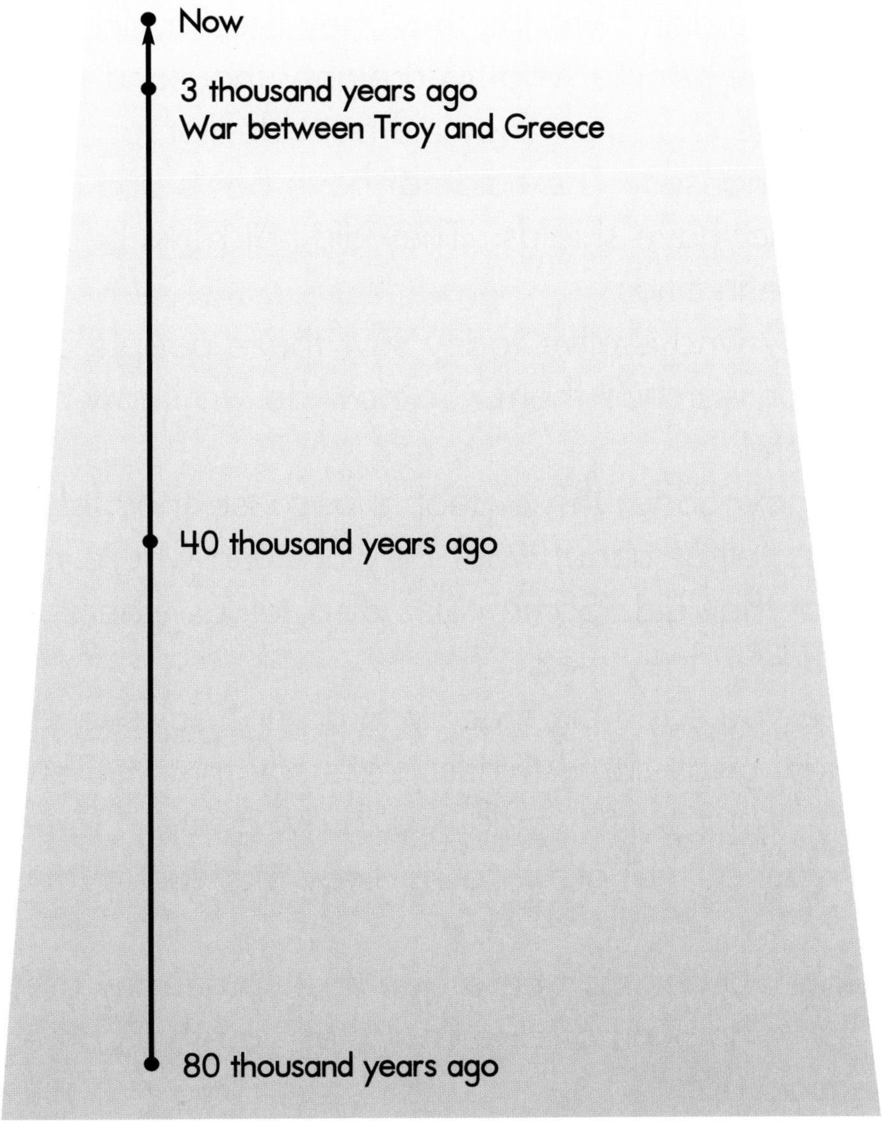
Now
3 thousand years ago
War between Troy and Greece
40 thousand years ago
80 thousand years ago

The world was very different eighty thousand years ago. People didn't live the way they lived during the war of Troy. The people who lived eighty thousand years ago did not have chariots. They did not ride horses. They did not live in houses. They did not have bows and arrows. They did not have shields. They did not have books. They did not live in cities.

Nobody who is alive today saw these people or talked to them or watched them. So how do we know anything about them?

We know about these people because they left clues. The clues tell us about what they ate and where they lived and what they did. Some clues also tell us where they died and how they died.

When you eat a big meal, you do not eat everything. You throw away some things. Let's say that you eat chicken. What parts would you throw away? Some parts of the chicken that are thrown away may last a long, long time.

Chicken bones may be a clue that somebody ate chicken. What kind of clue could tell you that somebody ate a coconut?

What kind of clue could tell you that somebody ate part of a very large animal?

So one of the best places to look for clues about people and how they lived is their garbage pile.

Some garbage piles left by people who lived eighty thousand years ago are in caves. If we find garbage piles in caves, we have a clue about where the people ate. Where did they eat?

The bones in these garbage piles do not have marks from the teeth of dogs. What does that tell us about the people who lived eighty thousand years ago?

The garbage piles of people who lived only eight thousand years ago are different. Some bones in these garbage piles have marks from dogs' teeth. What does that tell us about these people?

Sometimes garbage piles tell us about how animals were killed. Let's say that we found bones of a large animal like a buffalo. Let's say that these bones were broken in many places. An animal like a buffalo might get many broken bones falling from a high place. Maybe the people who hunted these large animals chased them to a cliff and then made them run off the cliff.

Another thing we can tell from the garbage is how the people who lived in caves fixed their food. If they made fires, some clues would be left behind. Can you think of some?

Let's say we do not find any rocks with smoke and heat marks on them. And we do not find any ashes. And we do not find any burn marks on bones. These clues tell us something about how the people ate their food.

If we look at a garbage pile in a cave that people have used for hundreds of years, we can tell how things changed. We can tell if the people began to eat different things. Let's say we find that some of the garbage in a pile was not cooked. These things are near the bottom of the garbage pile. Let's say the things near the top of the pile were cooked. By looking at the pile, we can tell that people who lived in the cave first did not cook their food. They ate things raw. The people who lived in the same cave many, many years later began to cook food. In the next story, you'll learn the rule for getting clues from a pile.

MORE NEXT TIME

C Number your paper from 1 through 17.

Review Items

1. Write the letter of each place that is in the United States.

   a. Denver
   b. Turkey
   c. Chicago
   d. China
   e. Alaska
   f. Italy
   g. Lake Michigan
   h. Japan
   i. New York City
   j. Texas
   k. San Francisco
   l. Ohio
   m. California

2. Write the letter of the animal that is facing into the wind.
3. Which direction is that animal facing?
4. So what's the **name** of that wind?

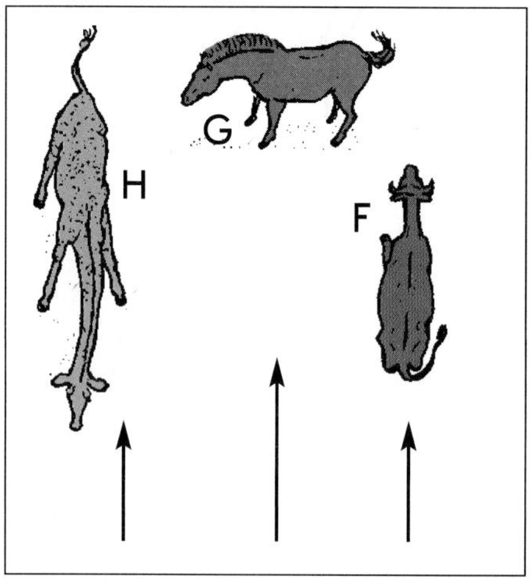

5. What is the temperature of the water in each jar?
6. Write the letter of each jar that is filled with ocean water.
7. Jar C is not filled with ocean water. How do you know?

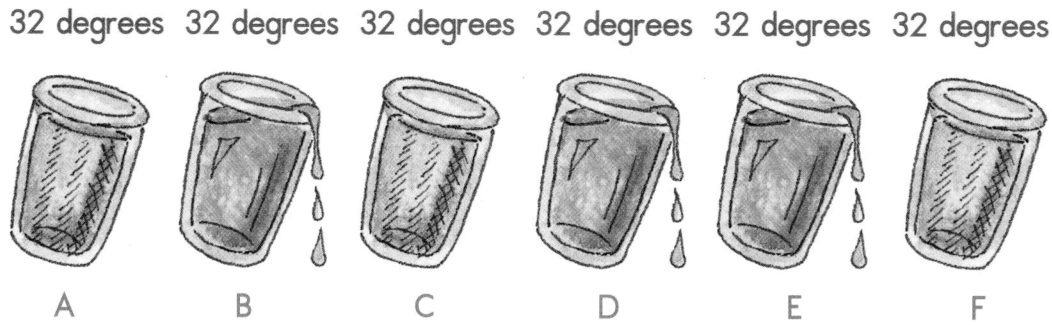

8. Which letter shows where Troy used to be?
9. Which letter shows where Greece is?
10. Which letter shows where Italy is?

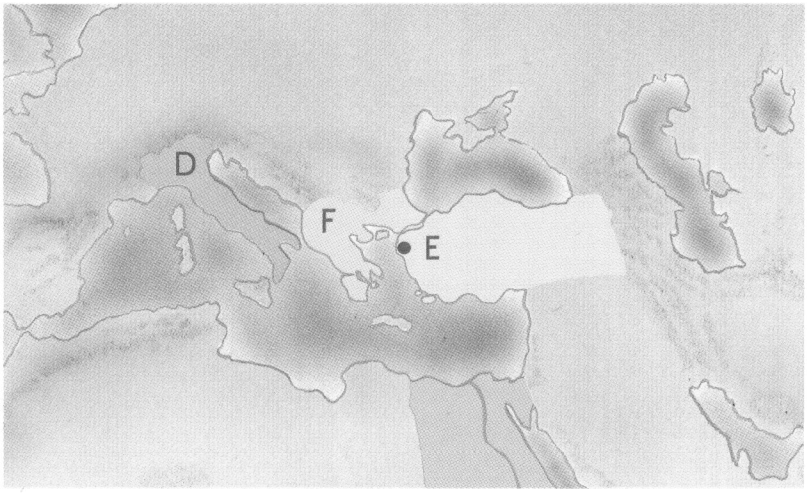

11. What is the name of the vehicle in the picture?
12. How many wheels does the vehicle have?
13. What is pulling the vehicle?
14. What is soldier X doing?
15. What is soldier Y doing?

16. You would have the least amount of power if you pushed against one of the handles. Which handle is that?
17. Which handle would give you the most power?

A

1	2
1. lightning	1. figuring
2. imitate	2. blinding
3. thunder	3. huddling
4. earlier	4. carrying
5. changed	5. pouring

3	4
1. crouch	1. glow
2. twelve	2. swoop
3. crouches	3. animal
4. together	4. stare

B

Digging into Piles

A garbage pile gives us clues about what happened earlier and what happened later. Here's the rule about garbage piles and all other piles: **Things closer to the bottom of the pile went into the pile earlier. Things closer to the top of the pile went into the pile later.**

What does the rule tell about things closer to the bottom of the pile?

What does the rule tell about things closer to the top of the pile?

Look at picture 1. It shows a pile of garbage in a hole of a cave. Touch the thing labeled A and the thing labeled R.

The thing labeled R is part of a fish. The thing labeled A is a snail's shell. The thing closer to the bottom of the pile went into the pile earlier. Which thing is that?

The thing closer to the top of the pile went in later. Which thing is that?

So the people who lived in the cave threw the fish into the garbage pile before they threw the snail into the pile.

Touch the thing labeled S and the thing labeled B.

What does the rule tell about things closer to the bottom of the pile?

What does the rule tell about things closer to the top of the pile?

Which letter is closer to the bottom of the pile, S or B?

So what do you know about thing S?

What do you know about thing B?

Touch thing A and thing S.

Which thing went into the pile earlier, A or S? How do you know?

We always use the rule about piles for figuring out which things happened earlier and which things happened later.

Let's say that we come into the cave and start digging into the pile that we've just been looking at. When we start digging, the first thing we'll pick up is big bone M. Name the next thing we'll pick up.

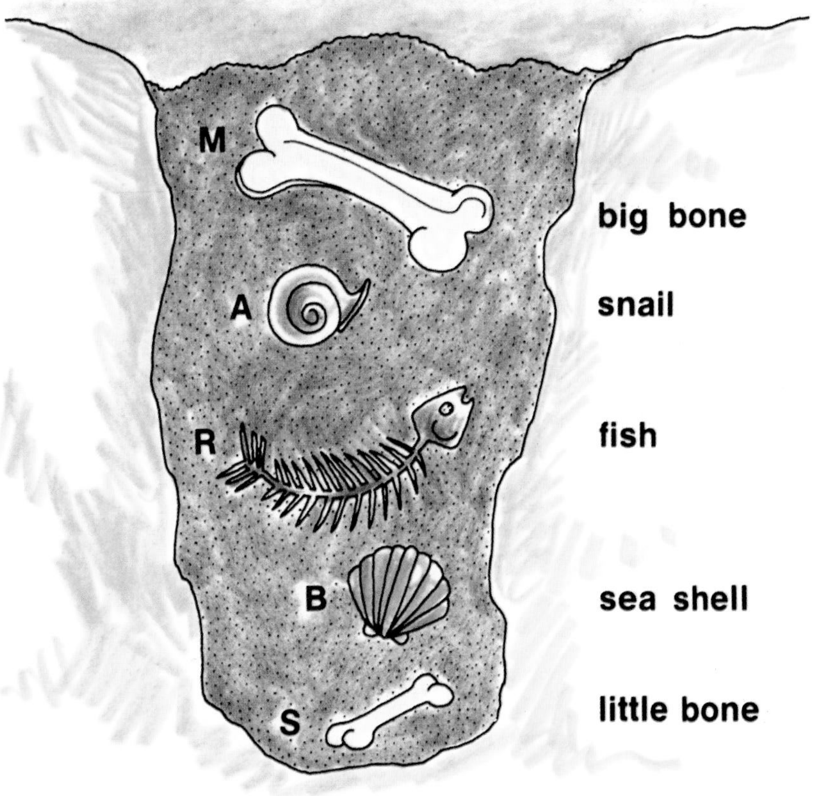

PICTURE 1

Which of those things is closer to the bottom of the pile, M or A?

So which thing went into the pile earlier?

We've picked up thing M and thing A. What's the next thing we'll pick up?

Which is closest to the bottom of the pile, M, A or R?

If thing R is closest to the bottom of the pile, what else do we know about R?

What's the next thing we'll pick up?

What's the letter of the last thing we'll come to?

So S went into the pile before any of the other objects.

A pile is like a time line. The things closer to the top are the things that happened later. The things closer to the bottom are the things that happened earlier.

Look at picture 2. It shows a hole dug near a beach. There are small stones at the top of the hole and mud at the bottom of the hole. What things are closest to the top of the pile? Those are the last things to go into the pile.

Touch the time line next to the picture. Name the last thing that went into the pile.

Name the thing that went in just before the small stones.

What went into the pile just before the sand?

What went into the pile just before the shells?

What was the first thing that went into the pile?

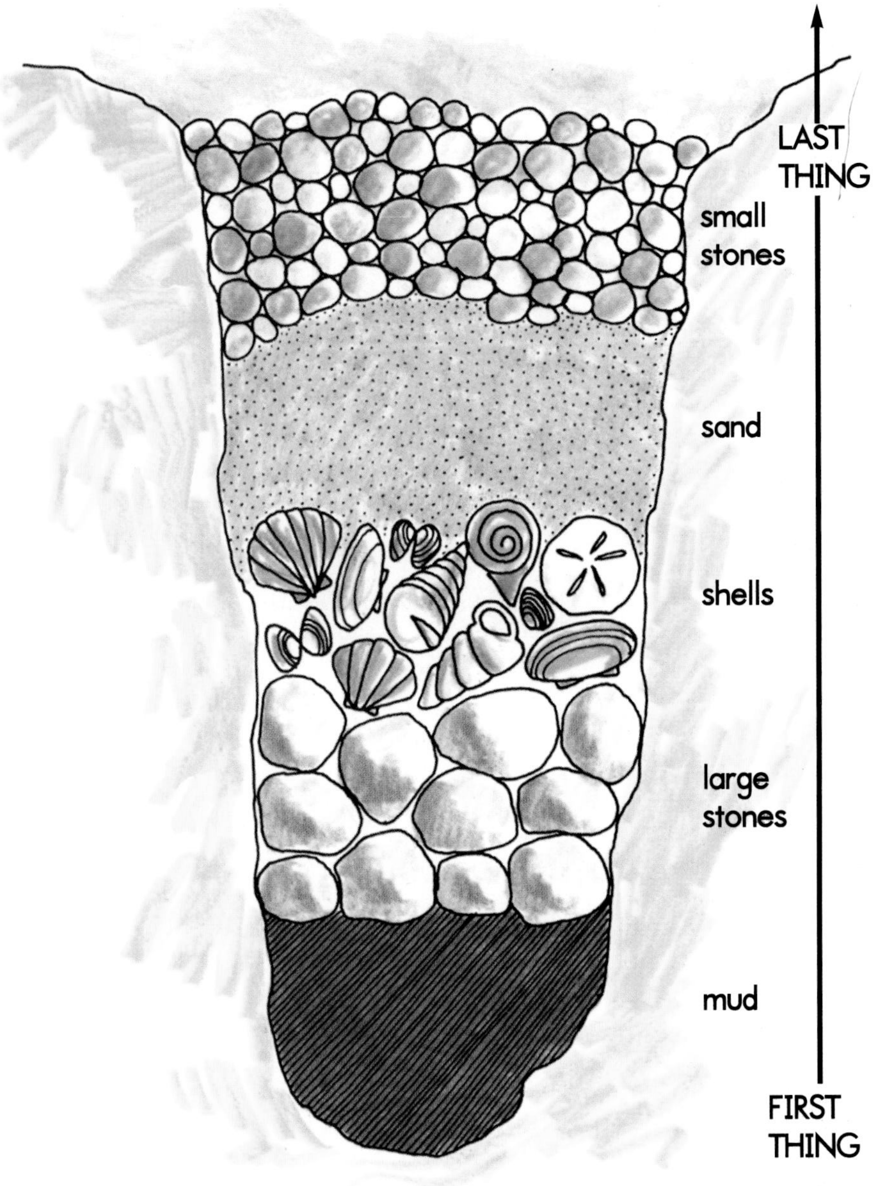

LAST
THING
small
stones
sand
shells
large
stones
mud
FIRST
THING

PICTURE 2

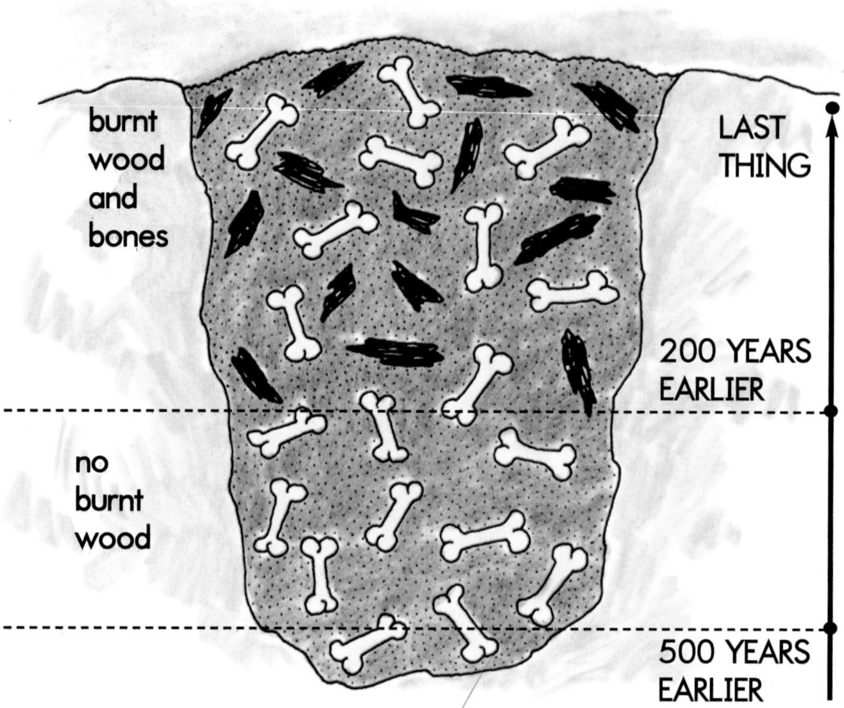

PICTURE 3

Picture 3 shows what we find when we look at the piles of garbage in the caves used for five hundred years.

Touch the dot that shows 500 years earlier. The time line shows that the first things went into the pile five hundred years before the last things went in. For five hundred years, people threw garbage into this pile. What kind of things went into the pile 500 years earlier?

There are no bits of burnt wood near the bottom of the pile. So we know that people in the cave did not always cook their food. The people who lived later used fire. Touch the dot that shows 200 years earlier. Burnt wood started to go into the pile at this time.

MORE NEXT TIME

C Number your paper from 1 through 21.

Skill Items

The adults huddled around the fire.

1. What word tells that the adults crowded together?
2. What word means **grown-ups?**

Review Items

Jar A is filled with ocean water. Jar B is filled with fresh water.

3. Which jar is heavier?
4. Which jar will freeze at 32 degrees?
5. Will the other jar freeze **above 32 degrees** or **below 32 degrees?**

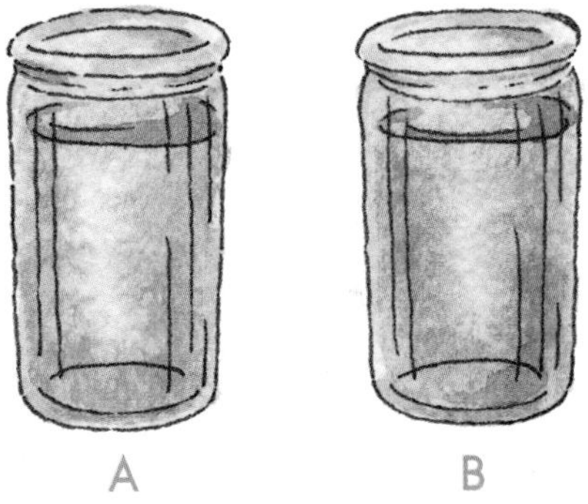

6. During the war with Troy, what did the Greek army build to help them get inside Troy?
7. What was inside this object?
8. What did they do after they came out of the object?
9. Who won the war, Troy or Greece?

10. What part does the **A** show?
11. What part does the **B** show?
12. What part does the **C** show?
13. What part does the **D** show?

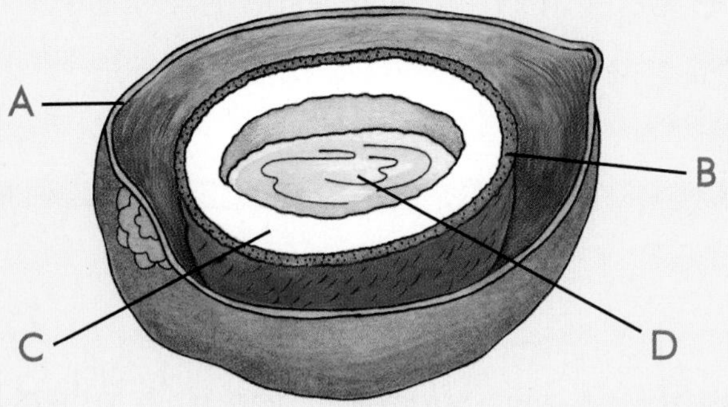

14. When people have very high fevers, how do they feel?
15. They may see and hear things that are not ______.
16. People who lived 80 thousand years ago did not have many things that we have today. Write the letters of 4 things they did not have.

a. bones	b. trees	c. computers	d. food
e. rocks	f. stoves	g. cars	h. movies

17. Name 2 clues that tell us that dogs may have lived with people 8 thousand years ago.
18. Name one clue that tells us how people may have hunted large animals like buffalo.

19. Write the letter that shows a tugboat.
20. Write two letters that show ships.
21. Write two letters that show docks.

84

A

1
1. tusks
2. crouches
3. imitates
4. stares
5. outlines
6. glows

2
1. pouring
2. blinding
3. lightning
4. huddling
5. figuring

3
1. direction
2. thunder
3. important
4. suddenly
5. hollow
6. interested

4
1. fire dies down
2. moment
3. tomorrow
4. earlier
5. overhead

5
1. paint
2. heat
3. earth
4. changed
5. swoop

B

Fire and Heat

Here's a rule about fire: **Fire likes to move up.** Picture A shows a man holding a burning stick with the burning end down. The fire will move up and burn the man.

Picture B shows a man holding a burning stick with the burning end up. The fire will burn up and the man will not get burned.

Remember the fact about fire. Fire likes to move up, so the heat moves up.

PICTURE A PICTURE B

C The Cave People Discover Fire

We don't know how the cave people learned about fire, but some people think it happened during a storm in the late fall.

A group of people live in a cave. They are inside. Outside, it is starting to rain—a cold rain. Heavy clouds are low over the trees.

CRASH, BOOM. That's the sound of thunder.

One of the children runs to the back of the cave and tries to hide. BOOM. Another great blast of thunder, and a cool wind, carrying a light spray of water. BOOOOOOM. That blast of thunder was very close. The clouds overhead are very dark. Two men and a woman sit near the mouth of the cave and look outside. Everybody else has moved to the back of the cave. Two of the people are holding their hands over their ears.

A silent flash of lightning as bright as the sun cuts through the sky. A moment later another roar of thunder. BOOOM.

Another blinding flash, just outside the cave. The lightning works like a knife and cuts a path down the trunk of a tree. The lightning throws pieces of bark into the air. BOOOOOOOOOOOOM. The sound is so loud that the people near the front of the cave hold their hands over their ears. The lightning has thrown a small branch right in front of the cave. There are flames coming from one end of the branch. That branch is burning. Fire. The people have seen lightning fires before, but never so close. The people watch the fire for a moment. Then one of the men reaches out and tries to grab it.

The man licks his fingers, and the others watch the fire.

Soon, all the people gather close to the fire. One of the children touches the part of the branch that is not on fire. Slowly, the child picks up the branch and holds it so the burning part is down. The child drops the branch inside the cave and runs away from the fire. A man picks up the branch and holds it so the burning end is up. He smiles. The others smile. They like the fire.

The man holding the burning branch waves it over his head. A girl picks up a stick and waves it over her head. The man shakes his branch. The girl imitates the man.

The man smiles and points his stick at the girl's stick. The girl points her stick at the man's stick. The ends touch. When the girl pulls her stick away, the end is on fire.

For a moment she stares at her stick with wide eyes. Then she smiles. Then everybody in the cave smiles and laughs. They pick up sticks and branches that are inside the cave and hold one end of them in the fire. For a while everybody laughs and runs around with burning sticks and branches. A woman drops her stick onto a pile of sticks and large branches near the back of the cave. Soon, there is a large fire in the cave, and it is hot inside the cave.

The people move outside the cave and stand in the rain, looking inside at the fire.

Smoke is pouring from the cave, and the inside of the cave is very hot.

They stand there in the rain for a long time, until the fire dies down. Now the fire is a deep red glow that is very hot. There are no high flames coming from the fire. There is very little smoke. But there is still a lot of heat.

Suddenly, a cold north wind swoops over the hills and hits the people. Winter is near, and soon there will be days and days of cold. Slowly, the people walk inside the warm cave. They feel heat coming from the fire, but they don't look forward to the cold winter days that are coming.

The people know the rules about the fire now: **If you put things in the fire, those things will get hot. And the fire makes the cave warm.**

A man walks to the mouth of the cave. He waves at the wind and then laughs at the wind. The children imitate him. The cave is warm.

THE END

D Number your paper from 1 through 26.

Story Items

1. The people who lived 80 thousand years ago did not live like we do. Where did the people live?
2. The adults who lived in the cave didn't like winter because it was too ___.
   - slow
   - cold
   - hot
3. Let's say that Jack stands up. What would you do to imitate Jack?
4. Let's say that Jean hops on one foot. What would you do to imitate Jean?
5. During a storm, which comes first, lightning or thunder?
6. What happened when the child in the story held the burning branch with the burning part pointed down?
7. A man held the burning branch with the burning part pointed ___.
8. Did the man get burned?
9. How did the people in the cave feel about the fire?

The cave people learned two rules about fire.

10. If you put things in the fire, those things will get ___.
11. The fire makes the cave ___.

Skill Items

12. Compare a house and a cave. Remember, first tell how they're the same. Then tell how they're different.

Use the words in the box to write complete sentences.

realized	adventure	skeletons	permitted	consultant
continued	required	expression	adults	huddled

13. The job ____ a ____.
14. The ____ ____ around the fire.

Review Items

15. Arrow B shows the direction the girl will jump. Which arrow shows the direction the boat will move?

16. What does ocean water taste like?
17. If you drank lots of ocean water you would get ______.
18. How many shells does a coconut have?
19. What is the juice inside a coconut called?
20. What year is it now?
21. In what year were you born?
22. In what year was the first airplane made?
23. What was the year 1 hundred years ago?
24. In what year did the United States become a country?
25. Things closer to the bottom of the pile went into the pile ______.
26. Things closer to the top of the pile went into the pile ______.

A

1

1. quarter
2. muscle
3. rough
4. Mongolian

2

1. <u>cow</u>boys
2. <u>base</u>ball
3. <u>basket</u>ball
4. <u>day</u>dream
5. <u>out</u>line
6. <u>race</u>horse

3

1. draft
2. grade
3. draw
4. graders
5. drawn

4

1. pony
2. straw
3. paint
4. earth
5. hollow
6. tusks

B

Cave Pictures

The piles of garbage inside caves give us clues. The piles tell us what the people who lived in the caves ate. The piles also tell us that earlier cave people didn't cook their food. The piles aren't the only clues inside the caves.

The people made pictures on the walls of their caves. They also made outlines of their hands. The outlines give us clues about the people. Picture 1 shows the outlines of two hands.

PICTURE 1

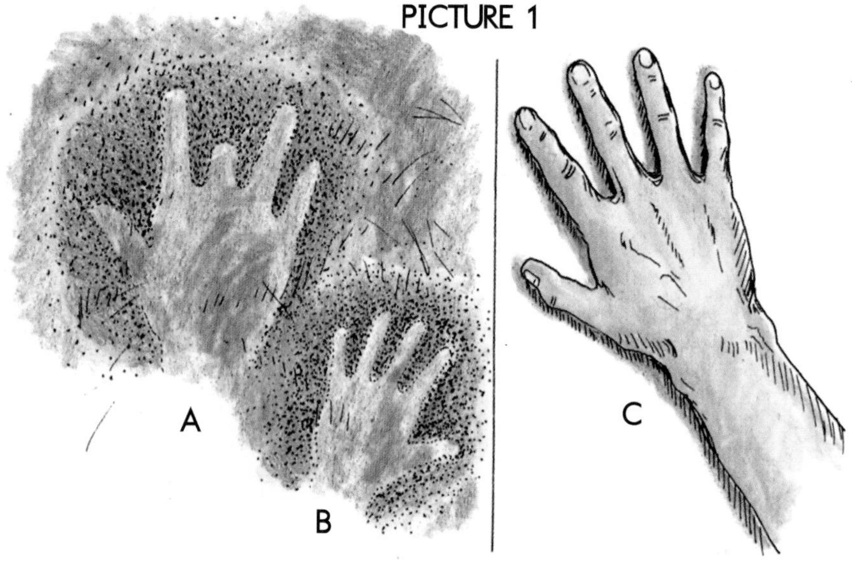

Name two things you can tell about hand A.

Name one thing you can tell about hand B.

Hand A is the hand of a man who lived in the cave 80 thousand years ago.

Hand C is the hand of a full-grown man who is alive now. That man is not bigger than most other men who are alive now. Compare that hand with hand A.

How have adult men changed in 80 thousand years?

The adult men who lived in caves 80 thousand years ago were not as tall as most women who live in the United States today.

Can you figure out how the people who lived in the caves made pictures of their hands?

Here's how the man made the picture of hand A. First he mixed up some paint. To make the paint, he used earth that he mixed with other things. By mixing earth with something like animal fat or blood, he could make red paint, black paint, brown paint, or yellow paint.

After he had mixed paint of the color he wanted, he put his hand against the wall of the cave. Picture 2 shows the man holding his hand against the wall.

Then he filled his mouth with the paint.

Then he put one end of a small bone in his mouth. The bone was hollow. So it worked just like a drinking straw.

PICTURE 2

The man pointed the bone at his hand. Picture 3 shows the man with the bone in his mouth.

PICTURE 3

Then the man blew. A stream of paint came out of the end of the bone. Some paint went on the man's hand. Some went on the wall. The man kept blowing paint until the wall around his hand was covered with paint.

PICTURE 4

Then the man pulled his hand away from the wall. And there was an outline of his hand on the wall.

PICTURE 5

The people who lived in caves used paint to draw things other than hands. They painted pictures of the animals they hunted.

Picture 6 shows two animals they painted—a horse and a cow that you might see today.

PICTURE 6

Picture 7 shows horses and a cow found on the wall of a cave. You can see how small the horses are.

PICTURE 7

Picture 8 shows a cave picture of an animal that looks something like an elephant of today. But no elephant like this one is alive today.

PICTURE 8

We know that animals like the one in picture 8 lived thousands of years ago. We know about these animals because we have found the bones of large animals with very large tusks. People have put the bones together and have shown what the animal must have looked like.

PICTURE 9

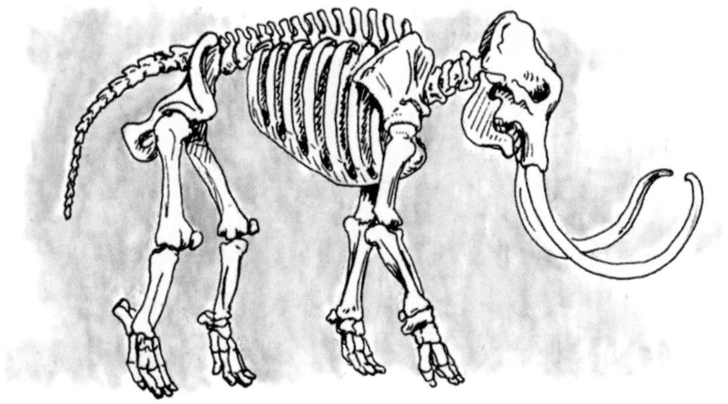

Picture 9 shows the bones.

Picture 10 shows the animal that had those bones. Although we have never seen living elephants like this one, the bones tell us how they looked.

PICTURE 10

The elephant in picture 8 shows how those elephants must have looked.

THE END

C Number your paper from 1 through 23.

Review Items

1. What clues would tell us that people used fire to cook their food?

2. Did the people who first lived in caves cook their food?
3. How do we know?

4. Which letter shows the trunk?
5. Which letter shows the fronds?
6. Which letter shows the coconuts?
7. Which letter shows the roots?

8. All machines make it easier for someone to ___.

9. When did the story of Troy take place?
   - 1 thousand years ago
   - 1 hundred years ago
   - 3 thousand years ago
10. Why didn't the people of Troy have cars?
    - Cars were too much trouble.
    - There were no cars yet.
    - They didn't like cars.
11. The people of Troy got in and out of the city through the great ___.

12. Write the letters of the 4 kinds of weapons that soldiers used when they had battles with Troy.

    a. planes c. rockets e. guns g. spears
    b. swords d. arrows f. bows h. tanks
13. Name **2** kinds of wells.
14. During a storm, which comes first, lightning or thunder?
15. How does fire like to move, up or down?
16. Let's say that Tony sits down. What would you do to imitate Tony?
17. The cave people learned two rules about fire: If you put things in the fire, those things will get ___.
18. The fire makes the cave ___.

19. When we dig into the pile in the picture, what's the first thing we find?
20. What's the next thing we find?
21. What's the next thing we find?
22. What's the next thing we find?
23. What's the last thing we find?

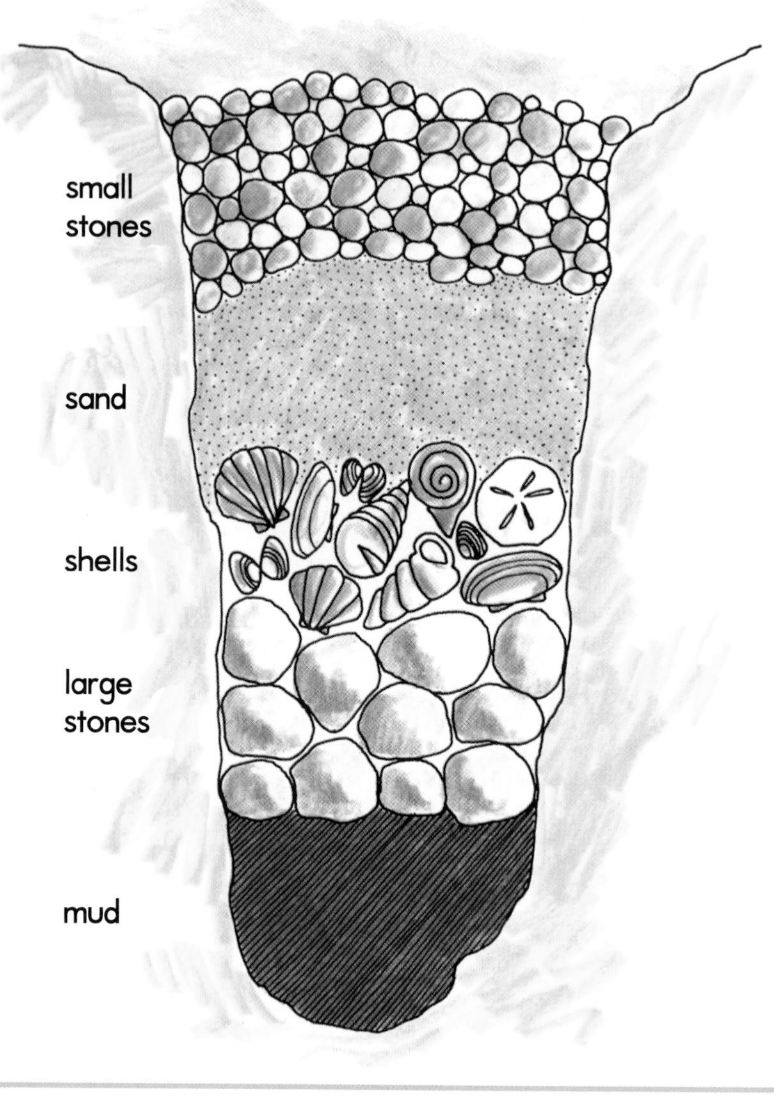

A

1
1. eohippus
2. enough
3. skeleton
4. daydream
5. Mongolian
6. basketball

2
1. hooves
2. third-graders
3. layers
4. muscles
5. cowboys

3
1. quarter
2. pony
3. itself
4. drawn
5. rough

4
1. draft
2. baseball
3. size
4. racehorse
5. sized
6. classroom

B Different Kinds of Horses

Not all dogs look the same. Some are big. Some are small. Some have long hair. Some have short hair.

Not all horses that live today are the same. Some are bigger. Some are smaller. Some have big heavy legs. Some have thin legs. Some horses that are alive today look like the horses that lived 30 thousand years ago.

Some types of horses that are alive today have been around for only two hundred years.

Picture 1 shows some types of horses.

Horse A is a big strong horse called a draft horse. A draft horse cannot run as fast as some horses. But this horse is good at pulling heavy things.

One draft horse may weigh as much as all the children in a third-grade classroom. Think of that. One horse that weighs as much as 30 third-graders.

Horse B is a racehorse. Racehorses are small next to draft horses. But racehorses are fast. In a race, the racehorse runs faster than any other kind of horse. But compare the legs of the racehorse with the legs of the draft horse. Look at their hooves and the bones right above their hooves.

A big racehorse may weigh half as much as a big draft horse. But that racehorse weighs as much as 15 third-grade students. ★ A racehorse is about 2 meters tall at the head.

Horse C is a quarter horse. Compare the quarter horse with the racehorse. Which horse has a longer back? Here's a surprise. The quarter horse weighs as much as the racehorse. If you want to know why, compare the hind legs of each horse. One horse has great, heavy muscles. One horse has long, slim legs.

Quarter horses cannot run a race as fast as racehorses, but here's the rule about quarter horses: **They can stop, start and turn faster than racehorses because they**

are stronger than racehorses. Cowboys ride quarter horses. Quarter horses are good for chasing cows and for riding over rough ground.

PICTURE 1

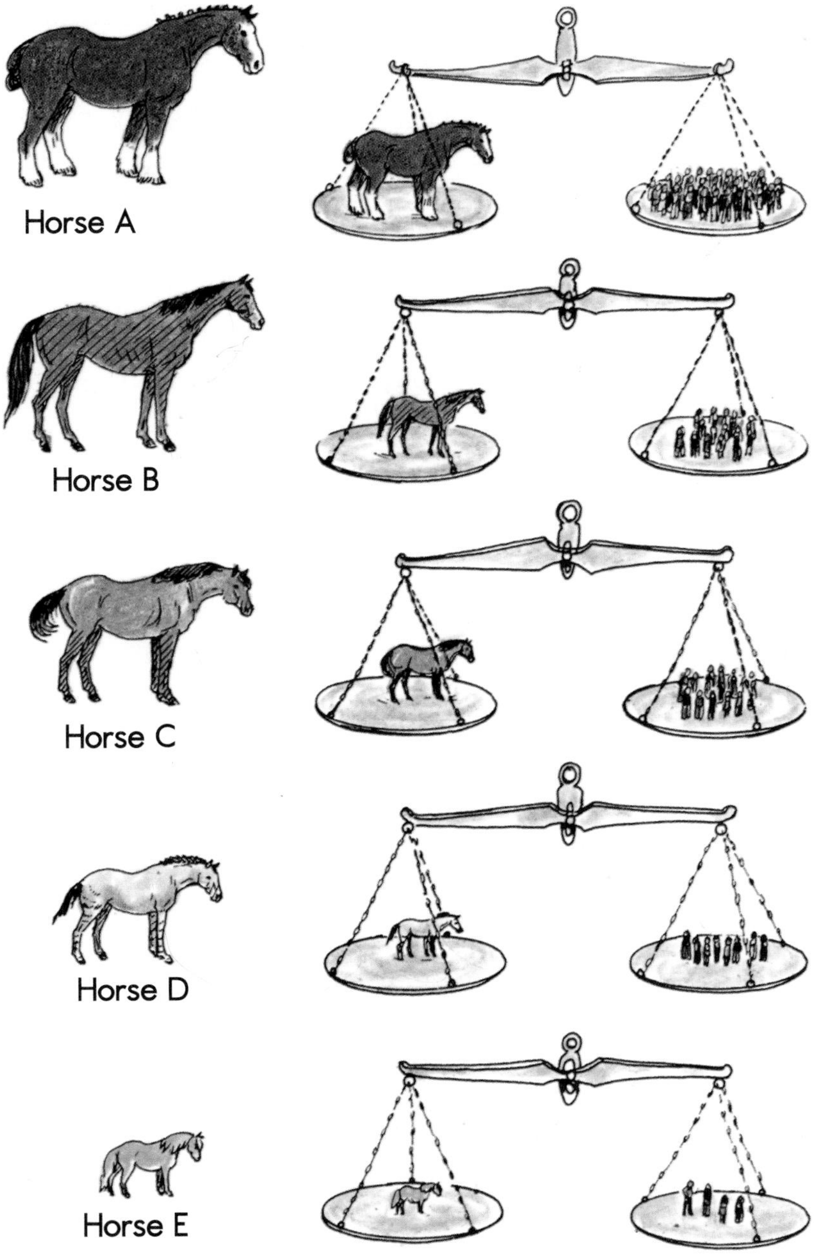

Horse D is a small horse called the Mongolian horse. Not many Mongolian horses are still alive. The Mongolian horse is much smaller than the quarter horse or the racehorse. It weighs about as much as eight third-graders. The Mongolian horse looks like the kind of horses drawn on the walls of caves. The Mongolian horse was the kind of horse that lived 30 thousand years ago.

Horse E is a pony. The pony is full grown, but it gets no bigger than a large dog. It is a little over a meter tall at the shoulders. It weighs about the same as four third-graders.

MORE NEXT TIME

C Number your paper from 1 through 15.

Review Items

1. Which letter shows where New York City is?
2. Which letter shows where San Francisco is?

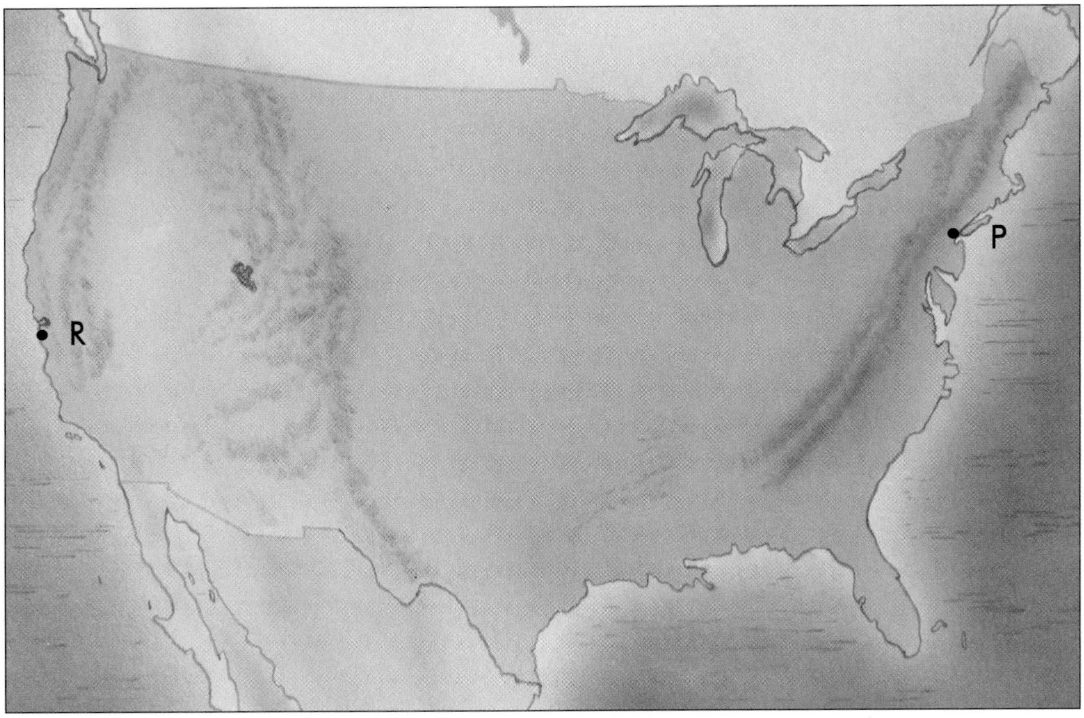

3. Palm trees cannot live in places that get ▭.
4. What are the branches of palm trees called?
5. Name **2** things that grow on different palm trees.

6. Write the letter of each island on the map.
7. **B** is not an island. Tell why.

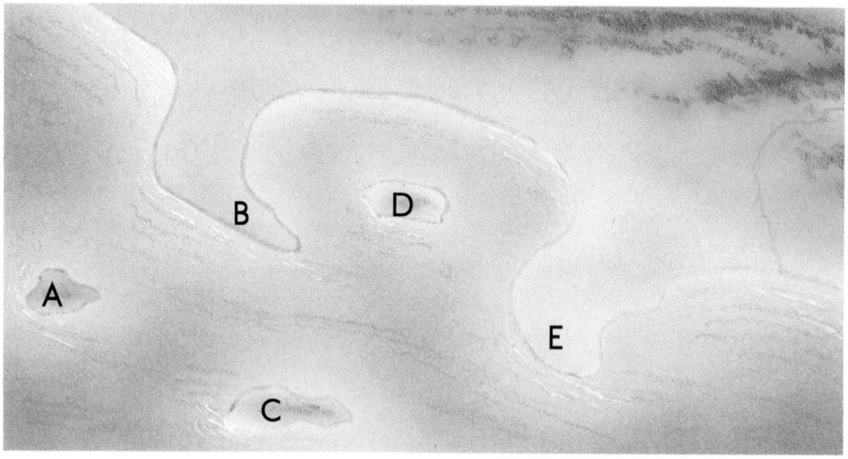

8. Greece went to war with Troy because of a woman named _____.
9. The woman from Greece was important because she was a _____.
10. The woman from Greece went away with a man from _____.
11. Which army was Achilles in during the war between Troy and Greece?
12. How long was Achilles in the war?
13. Who was the greatest soldier of Troy?
14. Who won when Hector and Achilles fought?
15. Achilles rode around the wall of Troy in a _____.

87

A

1	2
1. customer	1. in fact
2. valuable	2. herd
3. thousand	3. layers
4. enough	4. tusks
5. eohippus	5. different
6. skeletons	6. earliest

B

Horses from Millions of Years Ago

The people who lived in caves 30 thousand years ago drew pictures of the things around them. They drew pictures of elephants with huge tusks and pictures of horses. People have found bones of these horses, and the horses were small.

The kinds of horses that lived 30 thousand years ago are different from most of the horses that live today. The horses that lived millions of years ago are different from those that lived 30 thousand years ago. Over the millions of years, horses have changed a lot.

How do we know that horses have changed a lot?

We use the rule about piles. If we look into a pile of rock, we can figure out which things came earlier. We can also figure out which things came later.

Look at picture 1. There is a large cliff. There are rows of stones and rocks and sea shells. Each row is called a layer. The layers are piled up. That means that the layers near the bottom of the pile came earlier than the layers near the top of the pile.

The time line next to the cliff shows how long ago each layer of rock went into the pile. Layer E went into the pile 30 thousand years ago. Layer D went into the pile 1 million years ago.

When did layer C go into the pile?

When did layer B go into the pile?

When did layer A go into the pile?

The person who is looking at the cliff in the picture will see some things that went into the pile 11 million years ago. The person will also see some things that went into the pile more than 38 million years ago.

There are clues in these layers. The clues tell us about the animals that lived when each layer went into the pile. Look at layer C. It has two clues in it. Look at layer E. It has two clues in it.

When we look through layers of rock, we find skeletons of horses. The earliest horse skeletons are found in layer A. The skeleton of that horse is very small. In fact, it's no bigger than a small dog. The skeleton that is found in layer B is about as big as a large dog. The horse in layer C is about as big as a small pony. The horse in layer D is not the same size as the horse in layer C. The horse that is

PICTURE 1

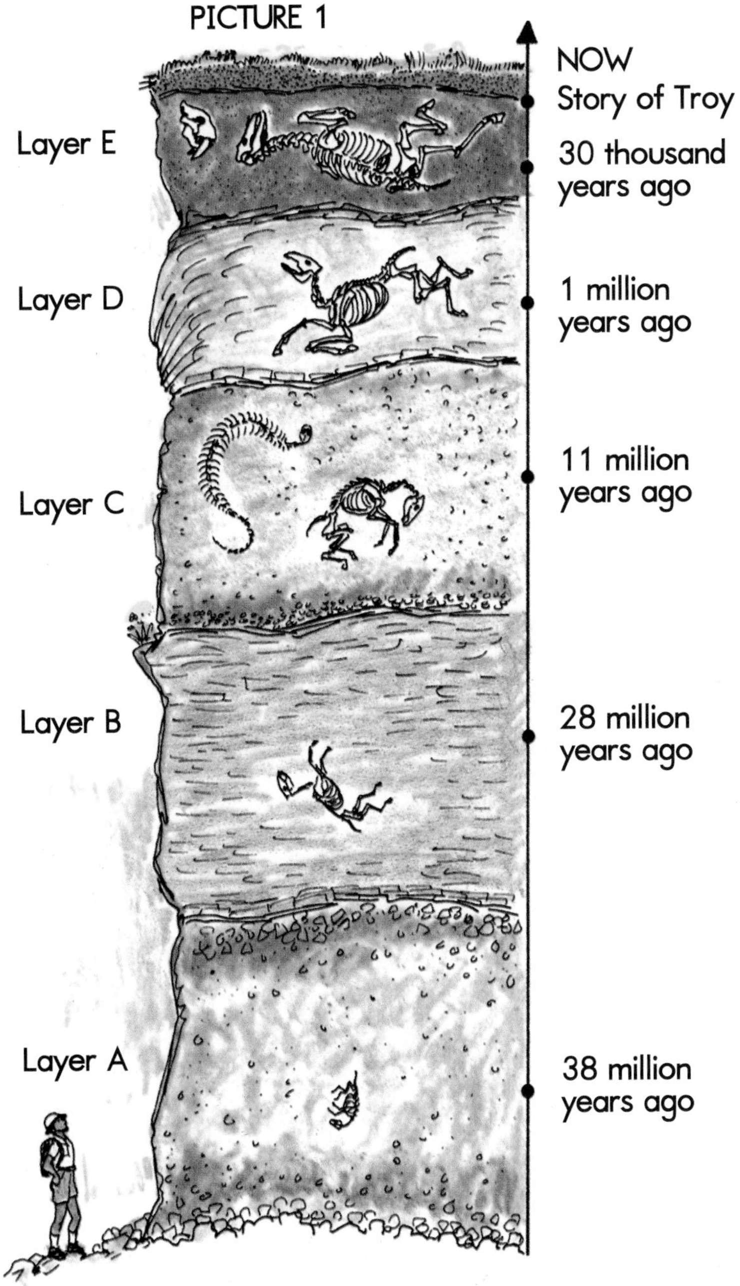

found in layer E is the horse that the cave people hunted. That horse weighed as much as 8 third-graders.

Picture 2 shows the skeletons of horses. The horse from layer A is at the bottom.

Look at the skeleton of the earliest horse. Then look at the skeleton of the horse from layer E. They are different.

PICTURE 2

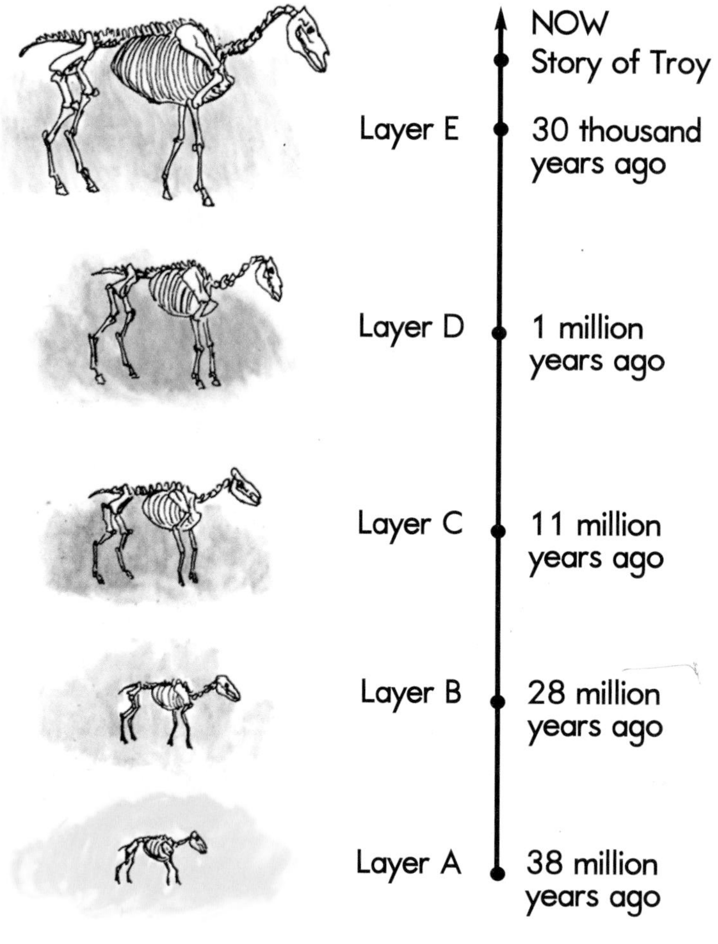

PICTURE 3

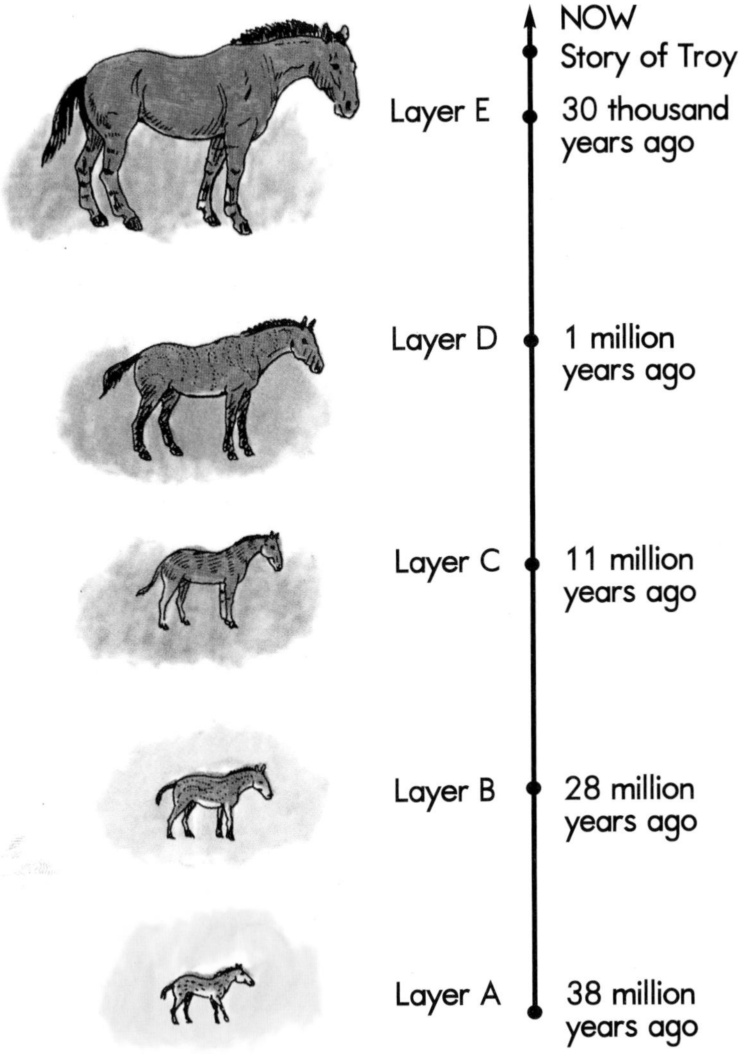

Picture 3 shows what the horses probably looked like. The horse from 38 million years ago didn't look very much like horses of today. The horse from 28 million years ago looked more like the horses of today. The horse from 30 thousand years ago looked just like some horses that live today, but it was different from most of today's horses.

MORE NEXT TIME

C Number your paper from 1 through 20.

Skills Item

1. Compare the way people ate 80 thousand years ago and the way we eat today. The people who lived 80 thousand years ago ____.

Review Items

2. Which letter shows the crude oil?
3. Which letter shows the refinery?
4. Which letter shows the pipeline?

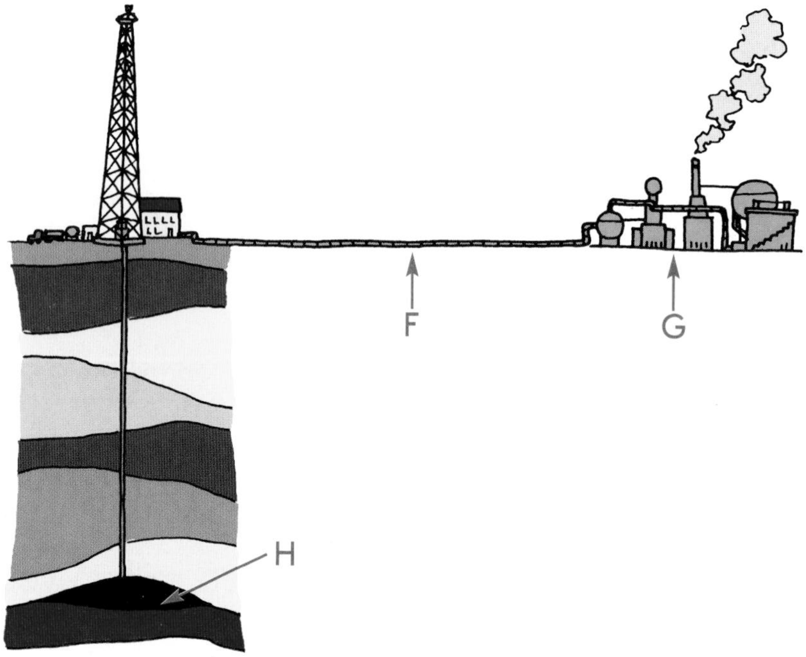

5. Which arrow shows the direction the crude oil is moving at A?
6. Which arrow shows the direction the crude oil is moving at B?

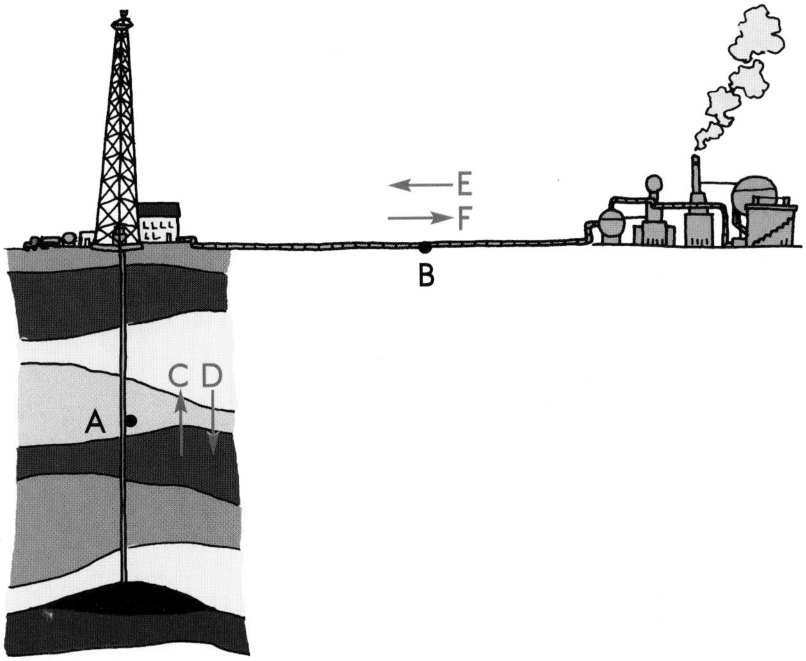

Write each sentence using other words for the word **weakness.**

7. Her **weakness** was her weak knees.
8. His anger was his **weakness.**

9. The arrow that killed Achilles hit him in the ____.
10. That arrow had something on it that killed Achilles. What did it have on it?

11. People who lived 80 thousand years ago did not have many things that we have today. Write the letters of **4** things they did not have.

a. dogs	d. trees	g. telephones
b. bones	e. TV sets	h. books
c. refrigerators	f. food	i. dirt

12. Name 1 clue that tells us that dogs may have lived with people 8 thousand years ago.
13. Name one clue that tells us how people may have hunted large animals like buffalo.
14. Name 2 clues that tell us that people used fire to cook their food.

15. How many third-graders weigh as much as a Mongolian horse?
16. How many third-graders weigh as much as a draft horse?
17. How many third-graders weigh as much as a racehorse?

18. Which horse has a shorter back, a racehorse or a quarter horse?

19. The picture shows the outline of a hand on a cave wall. Which letter shows the part of the wall that was covered with paint?
20. Which letter shows the part of the wall that was not covered with paint?

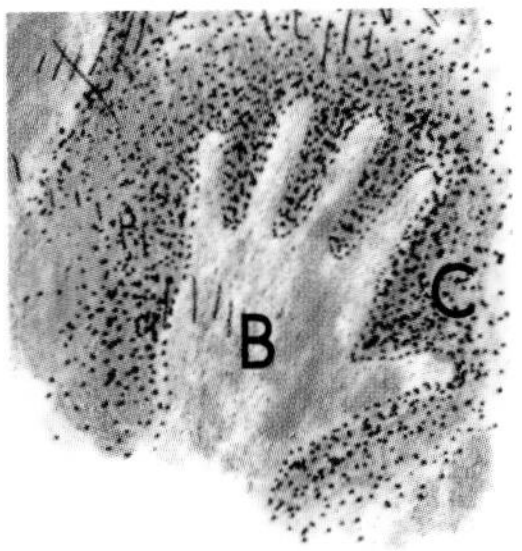

88

A

1
1. Andrew Dexter
2. Sidney Williams
3. magnetic
4. research
5. address

2
1. open field
2. customer
3. eohippus
4. valuable
5. member
6. bubble

3
1. coach
2. lighter
3. hiding
4. family
5. danger

4
1. itself
2. blast
3. worth
4. front
5. herd

B

How Horses Changed

Picture 1 shows horse A. That horse lived 38 million years ago. Horse A is named eohippus. Eohippus is standing next to a horse of today. Next to the picture is a box that shows the front leg bones of eohippus next to the front leg bones of the horse that lives today. Name two ways that the front leg of eohippus is different from the front leg of a horse that lives today.

PICTURE 1

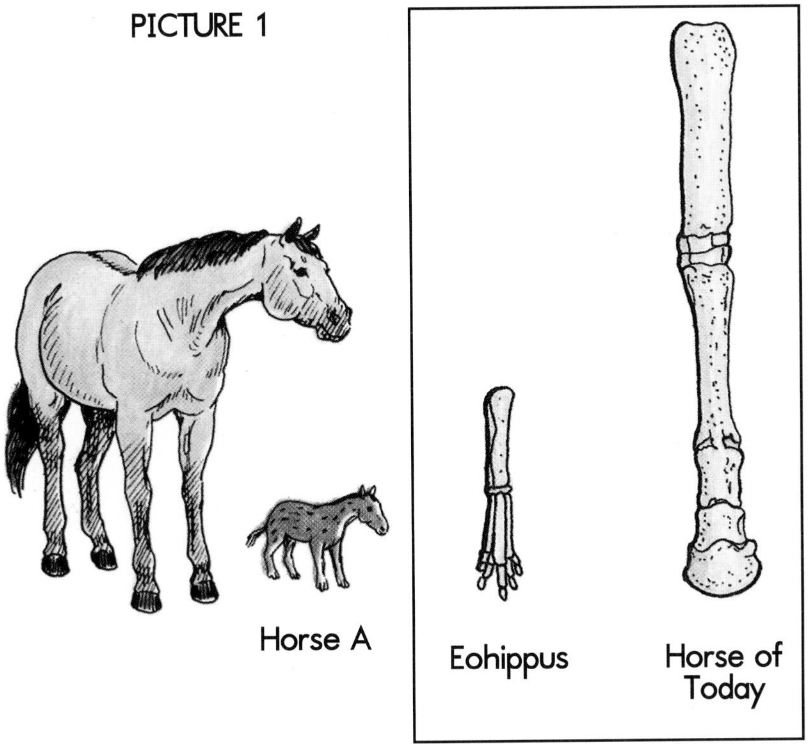

Eohippus did not stand on a hoof. Eohippus stood on toes.

Here are good questions. If eohippus does not look like a horse of today, how do we know that eohippus was a horse? How do we know that eohippus was not a member of the dog family?

We know that eohippus is a member of the horse family because we have found skeletons of other horses that lived long ago. When we put the skeletons in a row

PICTURE 2

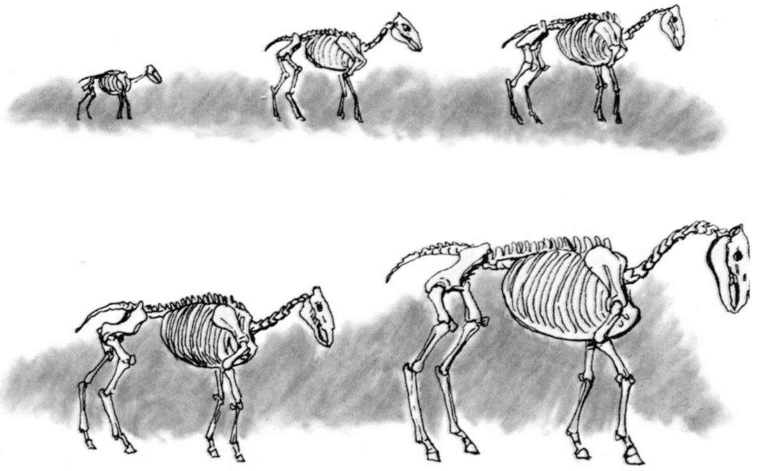

we can see small changes. Picture 2 shows just how horses changed over millions of years. It shows that eohippus did not change into a dog. It changed into the horses of today.

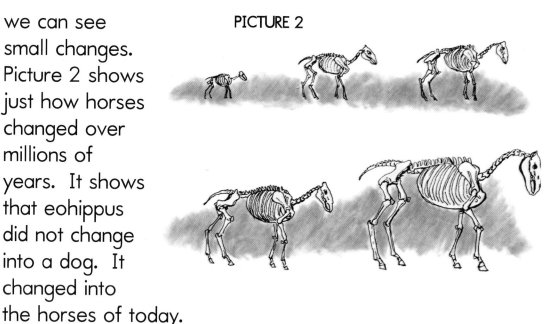

Why did horses change? Here's the rule about the changes in the legs: **The changes in the legs made the horse faster.** Eohippus was a hiding animal. It couldn't run as fast as a large cat like a lion. Eohippus stayed away from large cats. Eohippus ate grass and hid from danger. As millions of years went by, there was more food for animals like horses in the open fields. But an animal in the open had to run faster than eohippus. The horse that came after eohippus could run faster than eohippus. So the horse that came after eohippus could go out into the open more than eohippus did. If a large cat came near, the horse could run away.

Here's the rule about why horses got bigger: **Bigger animals are safer.** Why is a bigger animal safer? Bigger animals are safer because there aren't many animals that hunt bigger animals. An elephant is a very big animal.

Not many animals hunt elephants. A rabbit is a very small animal. Many animals hunt rabbits.

When horses were very small, many animals hunted them. When horses got bigger, not as many animals hunted them. So the bigger horses could go out into the open more than smaller horses. Large cats hunted big horses, but if a large cat came along, the big horse could run away from the cat.

Here's the last rule about horses: **Animals are safer when they run together in a herd.** Wild horses run together in herds.

So horses changed in three ways. They became bigger. They became faster. They ran in herds.

THE END

C Number your paper from 1 through 20.

Story Items

1. Horses changed in 3 ways. **Write the letters** of those 3 ways.
   a. They became slower.
   b. They lived in caves.
   c. They became faster.
   d. They became smaller.
   e. They lived alone.
   f. They became bigger.
   g. They ran in herds.

Review Items

2. When the Greek army dug holes under the wall, what did the people of Troy do?
3. When the Greek army put ladders against the wall of Troy, what did the people of Troy do?
4. Why couldn't the Greek army starve the people of Troy?
5. When the Greek army tried to knock down the gate, what did the people of Troy do?

6. What is the name of the vehicle in the picture?
7. How many wheels does the vehicle have?
8. What is pulling the vehicle?
9. What is soldier R doing?
10. What is soldier S doing?

11. What's a good place to look for clues about people who lived long ago?
12. Some people who lived 80 thousand years ago lived in ___.
13. Did the first people who lived in caves cook their food?
14. Did the people who lived in caves many years later cook their food?

15. When we dig into the pile in the picture, what's the first thing we find?
16. What's the next thing we find?
17. What's the next thing we find?
18. What's the next thing we find?
19. What's the last thing we find?

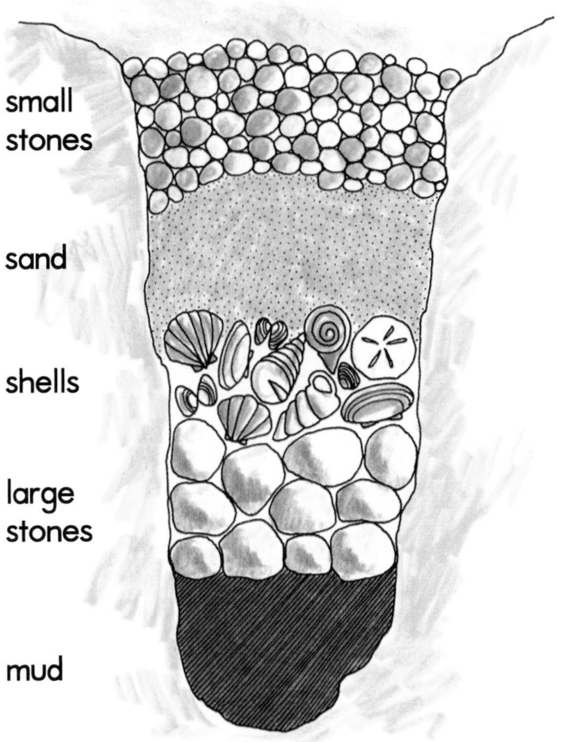

20. The earliest horses on Earth are not alive today. How long ago did the earliest horses live?
    - 38 million years ago
    - 38 thousand years ago
    - 38 years ago

89

A

1
1. uniform
2. package
3. favorite
4. address
5. important
6. magnetic

2
1. Sidney Williams
2. Andrew Dexter
3. strong-looking
4. research
5. enough
6. counter

3
1. go out for a team
2. at bat
3. shove
4. stack
5. shoved
6. phone

4
1. stars
2. coach
3. blasts
4. course
5. bread
6. worth

B

Filling Out a Bank Form

Today's story will tell about banks. People keep money in banks. When you put money in a bank, you must fill out a form.

Bertha wants to keep her money in a bank. Before she can do that, she has to fill out the form that you see on the next page.

Here are some facts about Bertha.

- Her name is Bertha Turner.
- Her phone number is 345-1101.
- She lives at 2233 Forest Street, San Francisco, California.
- She is going to put $500 in the bank.

1. Last Name ____________ 2. First Name ____________
3. Street Address ________________________________
4. City ________________ 5. State ________________
6. Phone number ____________
7. How much money are you putting in the bank? $________

C

Andrew Dexter Has Daydreams

Andrew Dexter worked in a bank. A bank is a place that holds money for people. If you have money and you want to keep it safe, you can take it to a bank. You go inside the bank and walk up to a counter. Behind the counter will be a person called a bank teller. You tell the bank teller that you would like to put your money in the bank. The teller helps you fill out a form. Then the teller takes your money. When you want your money, you can go back to the bank and get it.

Look at the picture. It shows a person leaving a bank. It shows a person standing at the counter giving money to a bank teller. Touch the person giving the money to the teller. Touch the teller.

The teller in the picture is Andrew Dexter. As you can see from the picture, Andrew Dexter was not a very strong-looking man. He was not very big. When you look at him in the picture, you would not believe that he became the strongest man who ever lived. But that is just what happened.

Of course, the picture shows Andrew before he became the strongest man who ever lived. When Andrew was a boy, he was not strong. There were many kids who were stronger than he was.

When Andrew went to high school, he went out for the baseball team. He wasn't good enough to stay on the team. Andrew went out for the football team. He wasn't big enough or fast enough or strong enough for the football team. Andrew went out for the basketball team. He wasn't tall enough or fast enough for that team, either.

So Andrew did two things. He watched, and he did a lot of daydreaming. He watched all the games. He watched football games and baseball games. He watched games on TV and games at the playgrounds. He loved to watch.

But he also dreamed. Everybody has dreams. Andrew had dreams about being a big star at football and baseball and basketball. When he was at work, he would dream. Here is one of his favorite dreams.

Andrew is at a baseball game. Suddenly, the star player gets hurt. The crowd says, "Oh, no! We'll never win without our star player!"

The coach of the team looks around and sees Andrew. "Can you play?" the coach asks.

"Yes," Andrew says.

Andrew walks onto the field. The crowd says, "Who is that guy? He can't take the place of our star." But then Andrew does things that are greater than anything anybody ever saw. He makes catches that the best star in the world can't make.

The crowd cheers. "That guy is great," they yell.

Then Andrew has a turn at bat. BLAM—he blasts the ball completely out of sight.

The crowd goes wild. "We love Andrew," they yell. "We love him. He's the greatest player in the world."

And Andrew becomes a star: a super, super, super star.

Andrew's dreams were just like the dreams that you may have. In Andrew's dreams, people loved him. But Andrew's dreams were just dreams. In real life, not many people loved him. In fact, not many people noticed that he was around.

Get a picture of Andrew. There he was, working in the bank. He did his job, but his mind was often far from the bank. He dreamed about being important. He wanted to be the star. He wanted people to love him.

MORE NEXT TIME

D Number your paper from 1 through 16.

Skill Items

The customer bought a valuable gift.

1. What word tells that something is worth a lot?
2. What word names a person who buys things?

Review Items

3. During a storm, which comes first, lightning or thunder?
4. How does fire like to move, up or down?
5. Let's say that Sally claps her hands. What would you do to imitate Sally?

6. The cave people learned two rules about fire: If you put things in the fire, those things will get ____.
7. The fire makes the cave ____.

8. The people who lived in caves drew pictures on the cave walls. Write the letters of **4** things they made pictures of.

   a. cows　b. horses　c. birds　d. elephants
   e. fish　f. hands　g. bears　h. dogs

9. Cave people painted pictures of horses on cave walls. How are those horses different from horses that live today?

10. Eohippus lived ____ million years ago.
11. The front legs of eohippus were different from the front legs of a horse that lives today. Write the letters of **2** ways that they were different.

    a. They were faster.
    b. They were smaller.
    c. They had smaller hooves.
    d. They didn't have hooves.

12. Over millions of years, horses changed in size. What happened to the size of horses?
13. Bigger animals are safer because ____.
    - not as many animals are smaller
    - not as many animals hunt bigger animals
    - not as many animals run faster

14. Which animal is safer, a horse or a mouse?
15. Why?

16. Horses changed in 3 ways. Write the letters of those 3 ways.
    a. They became slower.
    b. They ran in herds.
    c. They lived alone.
    d. They became bigger.
    e. They lived in caves.
    f. They became faster.
    g. They became smaller.

Number your paper from 1 through 30.

1. Which army was Achilles in during the war between Troy and Greece?
2. How long was Achilles in the war?
3. Who was the greatest soldier of Troy?
4. Who won when Hector and Achilles fought?
5. Achilles rode around the wall of Troy in a ____.
6. What's a good place to look for clues about people who lived long ago?
7. Some people who lived 80 thousand years ago lived in ____.
8. Things closer to the bottom of the pile went into the pile ____.
9. Things closer to the top of the pile went into the pile ____.

10. Which thing went into the pile earlier, thing R or thing X?
11. Which thing went into the pile later, thing R or thing T?

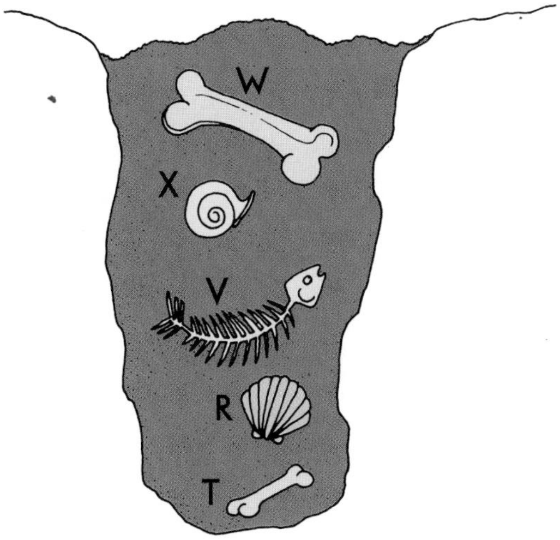

12. When we dig into the pile in the picture, what's the first thing we find?
13. What's the next thing we find?
14. What's the last thing we find?

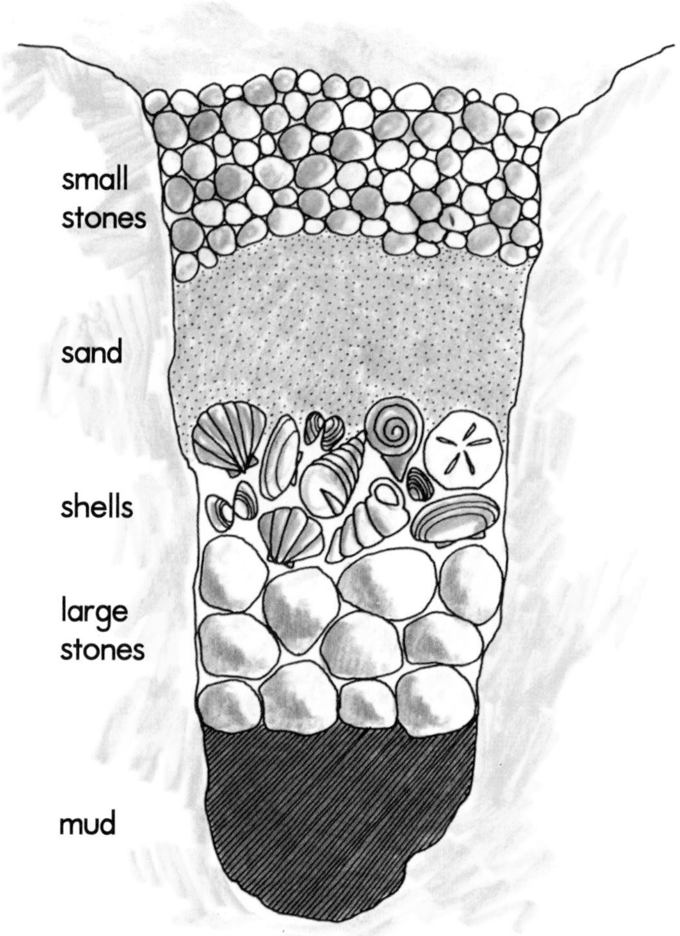

15. During a storm, which comes first, lightning or thunder?
16. How does fire like to move, up or down?
17. The people who lived in caves drew pictures on the cave walls. Write the letters of 4 things they made pictures of.

a. dogs	e. cows
b. bears	f. horses
c. fish	g. elephants
d. hands	h. birds

Write what kind of horse each picture shows.

- racehorse
- quarter horse
- pony
- Mongolian horse
- draft horse

18.

19.

20.

21.

22. How many third-graders weigh as much as a draft horse?
23. How many third-graders weigh as much as a Mongolian horse?
24. How many third-graders weigh as much as a racehorse?
25. Eohippus lived ______ million years ago.

26. Horses changed in 3 ways. Write the letters of those 3 ways.
   a. They lived in caves.
   b. They became bigger.
   c. They ran in herds.
   d. They lived alone.
   e. They became smaller.
   f. They became faster.
   g. They became slower.

Skill Items

For each item, write the underlined word from the sentences in the box.

The <u>adults</u> <u>huddled</u> around the fire. The <u>customer</u> bought a <u>valuable</u> gift.

27. What underlining means **grown-ups?**
28. What underlining tells that something is worth a lot?
29. What underlining tells that the adults crowded together?
30. What underlining names a person who buys things?

END OF TEST 9

A

1	2
1. electricity	1. package
2. examine	2. research
3. electromagnet	3. wrecking
4. interrupt	4. power
	5. oily

3	4
1. magnet	1. boss
2. uniform	2. loaf
3. magnetic	3. tingle
4. shoved	4. reason
5. switch	5. tingled

B Learning About Checks

When you have money in a bank, you can write checks. Here's the rule about a check: **A check tells the bank how much money to pay somebody.**

If you write a check to Luis Gomez for 10 dollars, the check tells the bank to pay Luis Gomez 10 dollars.

If you write a check to Jan Smeed for 5 dollars, the check tells the bank to pay Jan Smeed 5 dollars.

Look at check A. Line 1 shows when the check was made out. When was it made out?

Check A

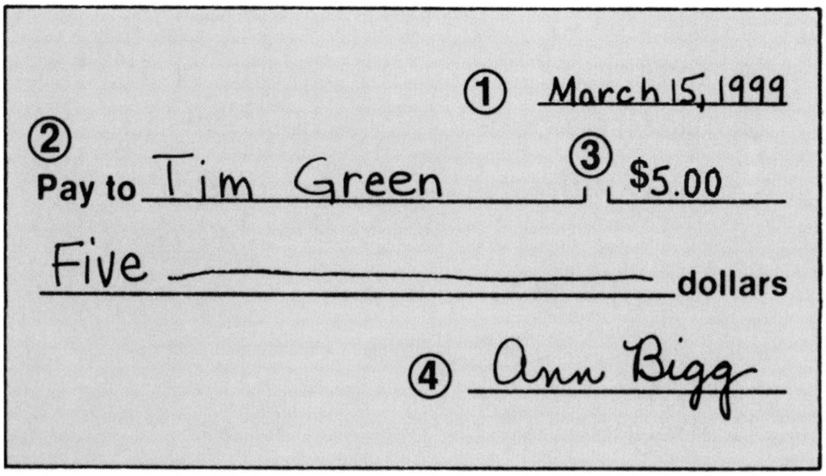

Line 2 tells who the bank should pay. Who is that?

Line 3 tells how much money the bank should pay Tim Green. How much?

Line 4 tells who wrote the check. Who is that?

The bank is holding money for Ann Bigg. So the bank takes five dollars from Ann Bigg's money and pays it to Tim Green.

Look at check B.

Check B

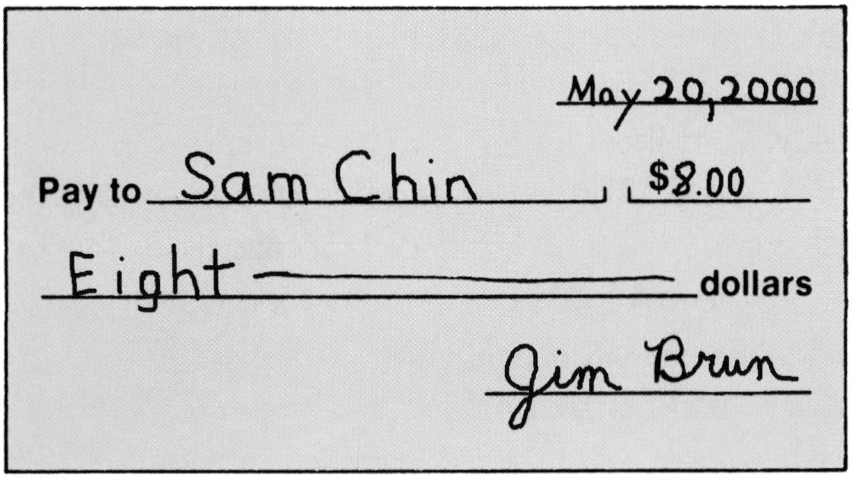

When was the check written?
Who should the bank pay?
How much should the bank pay?
Whose money does the bank use to pay Sam Chin?

C Andrew Visits Magnetic Research Company

"Good morning," Andrew said to a customer.

The customer shoved a stack of checks toward Andrew. Andrew took care of the customer. "Thank you," Andrew said when he had finished. The customer didn't say one word to Andrew. The next customer was in front of Andrew, but Andrew's mind was moving from the bank.

Andrew is in a basketball uniform. The coach is saying to him, "I don't think I should let you play in this game because it's the most important game of the year. But our star player is hurt."

"I'll do a good job," Andrew says to the coach.

Andrew is in the game now. There is almost no time left in the game. The other team is ahead by one basket. The ball comes to Andrew. He's too far from the basket, but he's got to take a chance at making a long shot. Time is running out. Andrew shoots and makes it. The crowd goes wild. "Who is that guy?" the fans ask.

"That's Andrew Dexter," somebody answers.

The other team passes the ball in. The clock is running down. Andrew leaps up and grabs the pass. Only four seconds are left in the game. Time for just one last shot. Andrew . . .

"Andrew, you have a customer." Andrew was suddenly back in the bank. Andrew's boss, Mr. Franks, was standing next to him. "Take care of your customer, Andrew," Mr. Franks said.

"Yes, Mr. Franks," Andrew said and smiled at the customer.

After finishing with the customer, Andrew noticed that the first customer had left a small package on the counter. Andrew picked up the package and brought it to Mr. Franks.

Mr. Franks made a phone call and then told Andrew, "I want you to take this package to Magnetic Research Company." Mr. Franks continued, "Magnetic Research Company is a very good customer of this bank, and this package is very valuable. So take the package over there right away."

"Yes, sir," Andrew said. Andrew took the package, got in his old car, and began driving toward Magnetic Research Company. For a moment, Andrew wondered what was in the package. It wasn't any larger than a loaf of bread. But it was pretty heavy. What could it be?

Andrew has the basketball. The ball almost slips from his hands. The crowd is counting down the seconds that are left in the game. "Four . . . three . . . two . . . " Andrew jumps up and shoots. The ball slowly sails toward the basket. Then it slowly drops—right through the basket.

The sound of the crowd is so loud that the floor shakes. The fans are yelling, screaming, leaping from their seats. People are lifting Andrew onto their shoulders. They are carrying him from . . .

"Watch where you're driving," yelled the woman in the car next to Andrew's car. "Stay in your own lane."

"Sorry," Andrew said softly. He told himself to pay attention to his driving.

MORE NEXT TIME

D **Number your paper from 1 through 21.**

Skill Items

Use the words in the box to write complete sentences.

valuable	dollars	hollow	adults	dozen
noticed	huddled	enough	customer	million

1. The _____ _____ around the fire.
2. The _____ bought a _____ gift.

Review Items

3. Which letter shows where the ground gets warm first?
4. Which letter shows where the ground gets warm last?

5. In which season is the danger of forest fires greatest?

6. Which arrow shows the way the air will leave the jet engines?
7. Which arrow shows the way the jet will move?

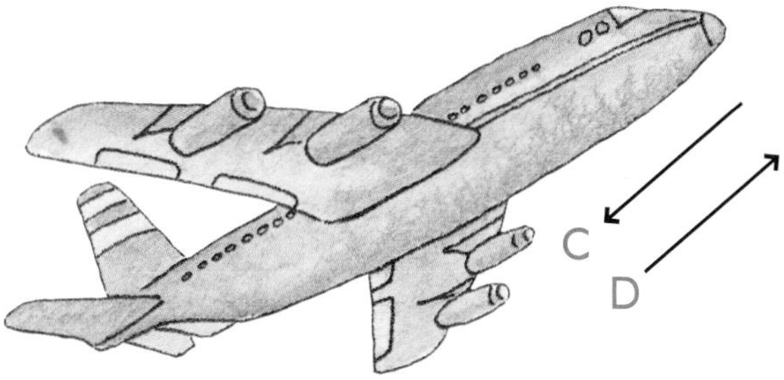

8. You can see drops of water on grass early in the morning. What are those drops called?

9. The picture shows objects caught in a giant whirlpool. The path is shown for object A. Will the path for object B go around **more times** or **fewer times?**
10. Which path will go around the fewest times, the path for A, B, or C?

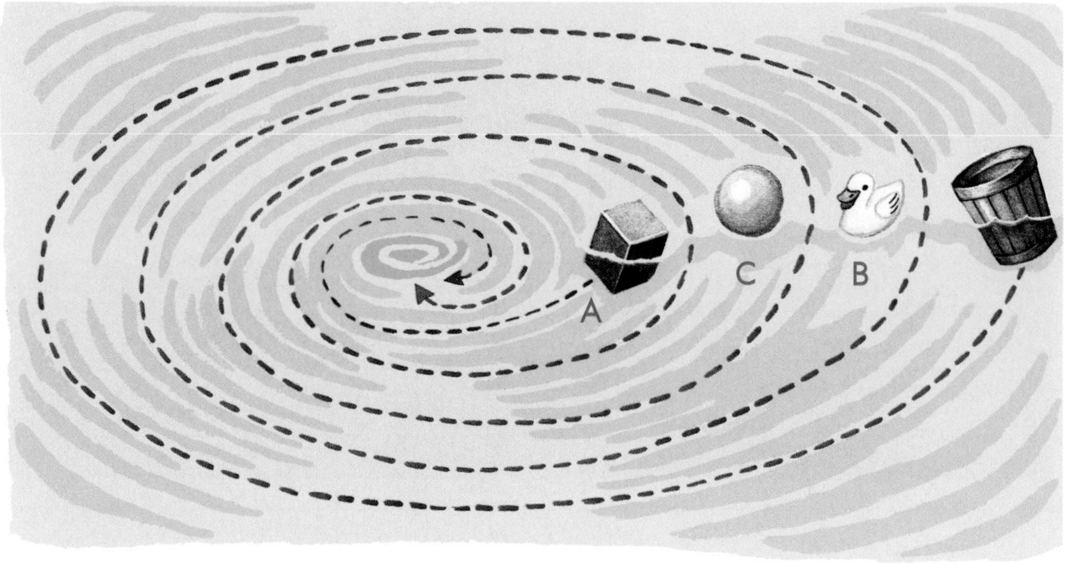

11. Airplanes unload at gates. Ships unload at ____.
12. Airplanes are pulled by little trucks. Ships are pulled by ____.
13. Airplanes land at airports. Ships land at ____.
14. How many ships sailed to Troy?
15. How long did the war between Greece and Troy go on?

16. If the Greek army could get a few men inside the wall of Troy, these men could ____.

17. What kind of place is in the picture?
18. What do we call the person who stands behind the counter and takes people's money?

19. What part of the world is shown on the map?
20. How far is it from **H** to **G?**
21. How far is it from **T** to **S?**

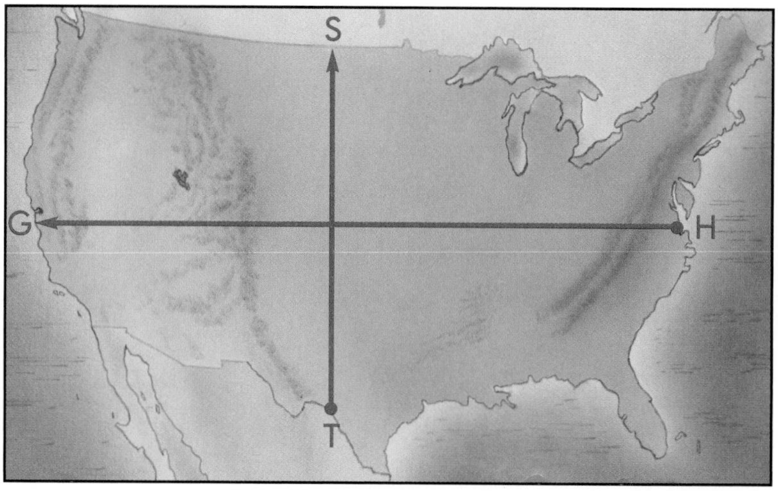

A

1

1. leopard
2. African
3. groceries
4. chimpanzee

2

1. eyebrows
2. stopwatch
3. airline
4. touchdown

3

1. tingled
2. wrecking
3. tingling
4. catcher
5. interrupting

4

1. examine
2. teenagers
3. electricity
4. switch
5. electromagnet

5

1. power
2. scold
3. oily
4. scolded

6

1. knock
2. reason
3. streak
4. yard

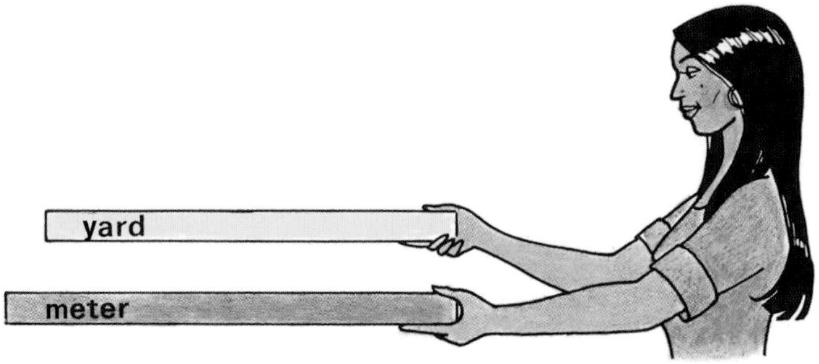

B Andrew Is a Changed Person

Twenty minutes after leaving the bank, Andrew was outside the Magnetic Research Company. He was standing in front of a building that looked something like a school. There were many doors leading into the building. Andrew tried to open two of them, but they were locked. He walked around the building to a large steel door. It was in a part of the building that had no windows. Andrew paused for a moment before trying the door. He could hear a strange buzzing sound inside. He tugged on the door and it opened. He walked inside. And that is when it happened.

You know how magnets work. Some things actually stick to magnets. If you have a strong magnet, you can pick up things like paper clips or nails.

Here's something you may not know about magnets. You can use electricity to turn any steel bar into a magnet. These magnets are called electromagnets. They are used in automobile wrecking yards. Look at the picture. It shows a large electromagnet picking up a car. If the person who is running the magnet wants to drop the car, the person just turns off the switch for the electricity. The electricity stops running through the electromagnet. And the electromagnet loses its power.

Why are we talking about magnets in the middle of the story about Andrew? We're talking about electromagnets because Andrew walked right into a room that was filled with electricity. Nobody knows exactly what happened or how it happened. We know that Andrew was holding the package. We also know what was in the package. It was a new motor that could pick up very small amounts of electricity from the air. These small amounts of electricity would run the motor.

The Magnetic Research Company had planned to make car motors like the one in the package. These car motors wouldn't use gasoline. They would run on the electricity that is  in the air. The motor that was in the package was very small. It was a model of the bigger motors. But the model worked. It ran by picking up very small amounts of electricity from the air.

There were very large amounts of electricity in the room where Andrew was standing. When Andrew walked into the room, the motor began to work so fast that it actually melted. It burned Andrew's hands. But it did more than that. It put millions of pounds of power into Andrew's body. Of course he didn't know it. In fact, he didn't know exactly what happened. He had opened the steel door and walked into a large dark room. A loud, strange noise made him feel very dizzy. The noise got louder and louder. He could hear somebody's voice saying, "You can't come in here. We're . . . " Then he noticed that his hands felt like they were on fire. He tried to drop the package, but he couldn't. It was stuck to his hands.

Suddenly, the noise stopped. Lights came on. Three men and a woman were in front of Andrew. The woman was saying to one of the men, "Wasn't that door locked? I told Jimmy that we were going to run a test."

One man was saying to Andrew, "Are you all right? You don't look well."

Andrew didn't feel well. His hands hurt, but he couldn't let go of the package. One of the men said, "Let me take that." He grabbed the package and jumped back. "Wow," he said. "Did I ever get a shock."

The man touched the package again. This time he didn't get a shock. He pulled Andrew's fingers from the package. Then he opened the package. "Oh no," he said. "Look at it. It's completely wrecked."

The woman shook her head. "Two years. It took us two years to make that machine. And look at it now."

Before Andrew left the building, a doctor examined him. The doctor put some oily stuff on Andrew's hands. He asked, "How do you feel?"

Andrew said, "I'm all right," but he felt very strange. His hands and arms tingled. His legs tingled. Even his eyes had a kind of tingling feeling. "I'm all right," he repeated.

But Andrew was not the same person that he had been. Andrew started to find out just how different he was when he left the Magnetic Research Company. His car door was stuck. So he gave it a tug. He pulled the door completely off the car.

MORE NEXT TIME

C Number your paper from 1 through 11.

1. Write the letters of the 5 names that tell about length.

a. minute	d. centimeter	g. mile	j. inch
b. hour	e. second	h. meter	k. week
c. day	f. yard	i. year	

Review Items

2. Which liquid does the **A** show?
3. Which liquid does the **B** show?
4. Which liquid does the **C** show?

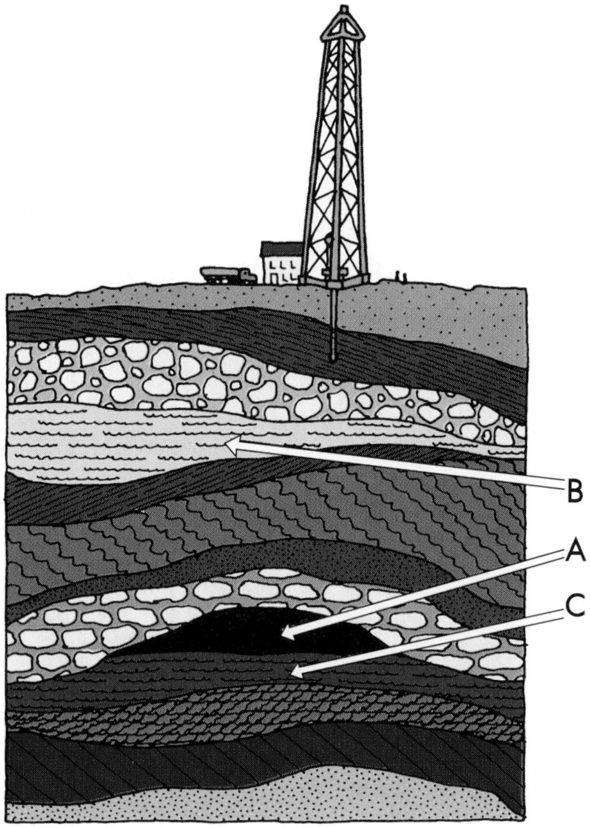

5. What do all living things need?
6. What do all living things make?
7. Do all living things grow?
8. Gasoline comes from a liquid called ▒▒▒.

9. What place does the **A** show?
10. What place does the **B** show?
11. What place does the **C** show?

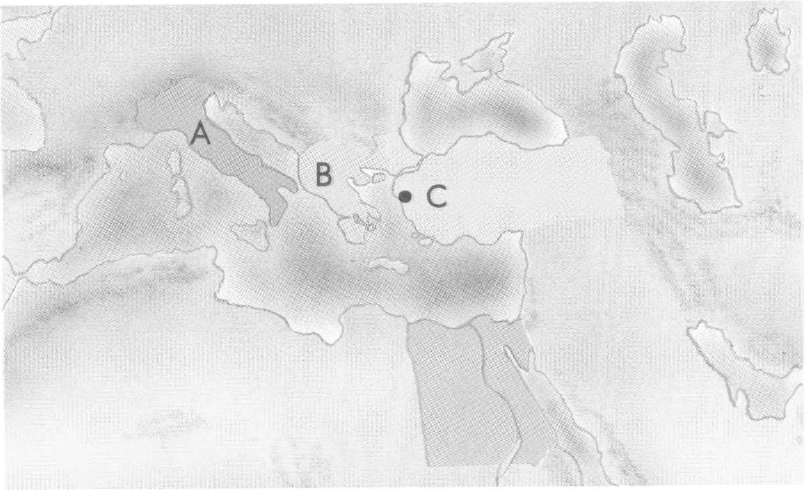

93

A

1

1. deaf
2. Titans
3. league
4. pardon
5. whistle
6. professional

2

1. fired
2. easily
3. groceries
4. scolded
5. teenagers
6. catcher

3

1. stopwatch
2. touchdown
3. hang-time
4. airline
5. full-grown

4

1. Denny Brock
2. home run
3. first base
4. chimpanzee
5. eyebrows
6. leopard

5

1. tackle
2. worth
3. sorry
4. trunk
5. streak

B The Strength of Animals

The story that you will read today tells about the strength of humans. Humans are very weak when we compare humans with some other animals. Picture 1 shows a leopard. The leopard may weigh only 100 pounds. Yet a leopard can carry an animal that weighs 150 pounds while the leopard climbs a tree.

A lion is much stronger than a leopard. People have seen this: A large lion carries an animal that weighs about

200 pounds. The lion then jumps a fence that is over 2 yards high. Picture 2 shows a large lion.

PICTURE 2

Chimpanzees are very strong. If a strong man pulls down on a rope as hard as he can pull, he may pull with a force of over 200 pounds. A chimpanzee can pull with a force of over 500 pounds. And a chimpanzee weighs only about 100 pounds. Picture 3 shows a chimpanzee.

PICTURE 3

The strongest land animal is the elephant, and the strongest elephant is the African elephant. An African elephant can pick up a horse as easily as you would pick up a baby. It can lift logs that 30 men could not lift. It can tear trees out of the ground. It can knock down buildings or tip over a large truck. Look at what the elephant in picture 4 is doing.

PICTURE 4

C Andrew Gets Fired

Andrew felt silly driving back to the bank in a car that had no door. The door was in the trunk of the car. People looked at Andrew and smiled. "What a nut," he heard one driver say. But Andrew still felt strange, and he still didn't know that he was just about as strong as a full-grown African elephant.

When Andrew walked inside the bank, Mr. Franks walked up to him. Andrew could tell that Mr. Franks was not happy. When Mr. Franks was mad at somebody, he would make his eyebrows come together and he would stare at the person. That's just what he was doing now.

"Andrew," he said. "I would like to talk with you. Follow me." So Andrew followed. Mr. Franks led the way to a small room in the back of the bank. Mr. Franks told Andrew, "You don't think about what you are doing. Why didn't you ring the bell by the front door at Magnetic Research Company instead of going in the side door?"

"Well, I didn't see a bell," Andrew said.

"That's your problem. You don't see. You don't think. Your mind is always a million miles away. The people at Magnetic Research Company are very, very unhappy. And so am I." Mr. Franks scolded Andrew for a few more minutes. Then he told Andrew, "I'm very sorry, but you can't work here anymore. You're fired."

Andrew didn't feel bad when he heard this announcement. He still felt a little strange. "All right," he said, and went back to his teller window to get his coat.

Then he went out for a walk. He walked to a playground. A bunch of teenagers were playing baseball. When Andrew was just outside the fence, one of the boys hit a home run. The ball sailed over the fence. It was just about three meters over Andrew's head. But for some strange reason, Andrew jumped up to catch the ball. Nobody had ever seen a person jump three yards high because nobody had ever jumped three yards high before Andrew did it. He jumped up, and up, and up. He reached out and . . . he caught it.

The boys stopped playing. The boy who had hit the ball was not running toward first base. He was standing and staring at Andrew. His eyes were very big. The other boys who had been watching the ball were now watching Andrew. Their eyes were very big.

Andrew smiled. He jumped again and threw the ball to the catcher. The ball went through the air like a streak. The ball moved over 100 miles per hour. When the ball hit the catcher's mitt, it made a sound—WHAP—that you could hear nearly a mile away. The catcher fell over backwards. The catcher shook his mitt from his hand and ran around shaking his hands and blowing on them.

MORE NEXT TIME

D Number your paper from 1 through 18.

Skill Items

They had reasons for interrupting her talk.

1. What word tells about why they interrupted her talk?
2. What word tells that they didn't let her finish talking?

Review Items

3. Name 2 things that a strong magnet can pick up.
4. Electricity can turn any steel bar into a magnet. What are these magnets called?
5. Name a place where these magnets are used.

6. A forest fire may burn for ____.
   - hours
   - weeks
   - minutes
7. A forest fire kills both ____ and ____.
   - plants
   - whales
   - fish
   - animals
8. About how many years could it take for the forest to grow back?
   - 20 years
   - 200 years
   - 100 years

Each statement tells about how far something goes or how fast something goes. Write **how far** or **how fast** for each item.

9. He ran 5 miles.
10. He ran 5 miles per hour.
11. The plane was 500 miles from New York City.
12. The plane was flying 500 miles per hour.

13. Write the letter of the tree that has deeper roots.
14. Write the letter of the tree that begins to grow first every year.

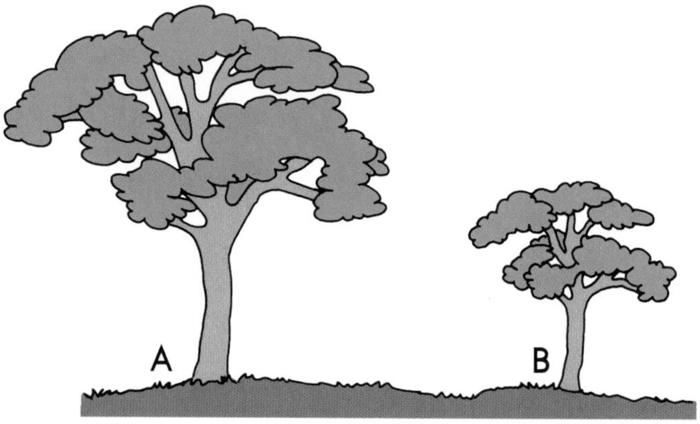

15. When was the check below written?
16. Who should the bank pay?
17. How much should the bank pay?
18. Whose money should the bank use to pay Kim Johns?

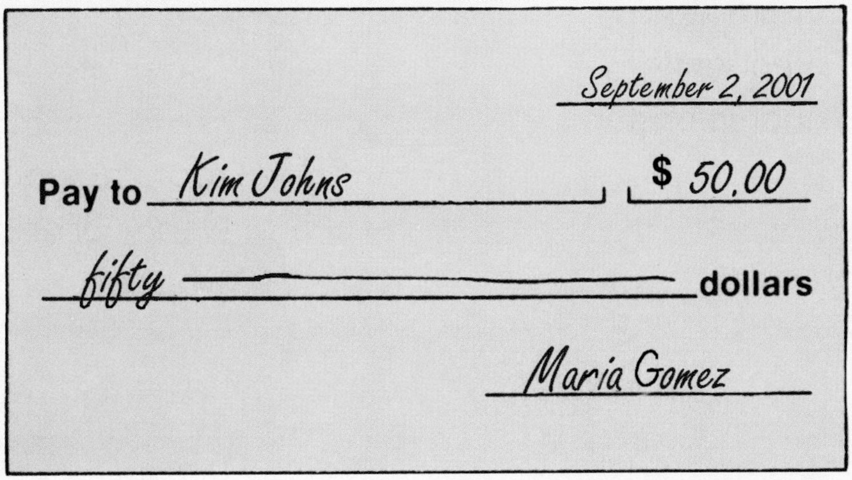

94

A

1
1. interrupt
2. Charlie
3. champion
4. frequently
5. championship

2
1. show up
2. professional football league
3. Denny Brock
4. whistles
5. tackles
6. pardon

3
1. blame
2. argued
3. deaf
4. blamed
5. Titans
6. worth

B Learning About Football

You're going to read about a football team. So you have to know some things about football games.

Picture 1 shows the things the player wears. These things are part of the football uniform.

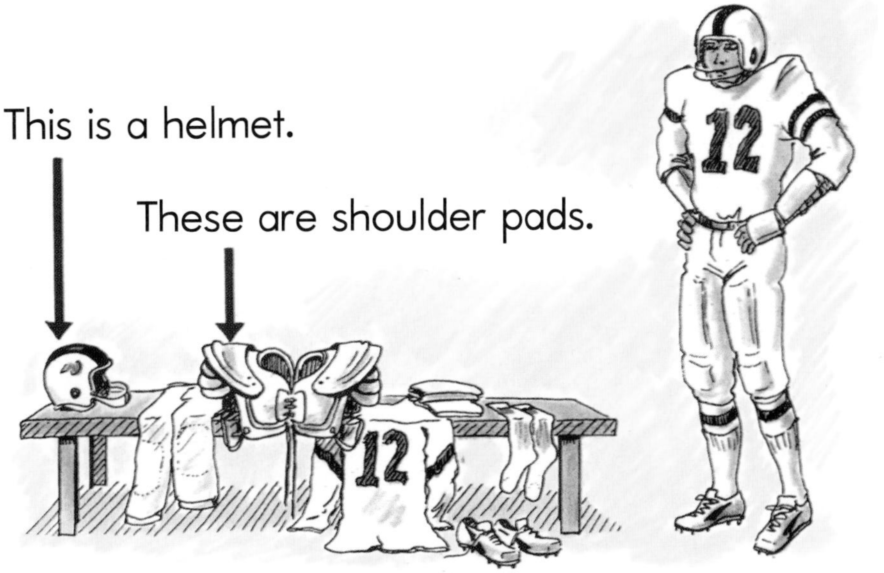
This is a helmet.
These are shoulder pads.
12
12

PICTURE 1

Here are facts about the game of football:

- Football is played with 11 players on a team.
- Two teams play.
- The field is 100 yards long.
- The team that has the ball tries to move the ball to the goal line at the other end of the field.
- If the team gets all the way to the other end of the field, the team scores a **touchdown.** That is worth 6 points.
- To move down the field, the team runs with the ball or passes the ball.
- The other team tries to stop the team that has the ball. This team tries to tackle players who have the ball and tries to catch any passes.

- Each team has kickers. The kicker can kick the ball to score points. The kicker also kicks the ball if a team has to turn the ball over to the other team.
- Picture 2 shows the red team running with the ball. The blue team is trying to tackle the player with the ball.

PICTURE 2

C Andrew Meets Denny Brock

Andrew was standing outside the playground fence. He was smiling. The boys walked over to the fence. They were smiling. “Hey, man,” one of them said. “What’s your name?”

Andrew told them.

Another boy asked, "Are you a baseball star?"

"No," Andrew said. He was going to say, "I work in the bank," but then he remembered that he had been fired. "No," he repeated. "I'm looking for a job."

"Wow," one boy said. "You should get a job playing baseball. I have never seen anybody throw or catch the way you do."

Andrew talked to the boys for a few minutes. Then he said goodbye and walked away from the playground. His mind was still dizzy. What had happened? He had just done two things that are impossible. Yet he did them. He—Andrew Dexter—had just caught a ball that nobody could catch, and he had just thrown it the way nobody could throw it. Wow, it really happened. It really, really happened.

• • •

Denny Brock was mad. Denny Brock was almost always mad. He was the coach of the worst team in the Professional Football League, the Titans. Last year, his team had won one game. The year before that, his team had not won a single game. Denny's players were unhappy. The players blamed each other. They blamed the coaches. They blamed the rain or the snow or anything else they could blame. The people who owned the team were as unhappy as the players. At least once a week they would remind Denny, "We pay a lot of money for good football players. We should have a good team.

But we don't. And if the team doesn't get any better, we'll have to fire you."

The players and the owners were not the only people who were unhappy. The fans were unhappy, too. When most teams in the Professional Football League play, more than 50 thousand fans come to the ball park and watch the game. When the Titans played, less than 15 thousand people showed up. The team didn't have many fans, so the team didn't make much money, so the players didn't get paid as much as they wanted, so the players were unhappy, so they didn't play well, so the owners were unhappy.

If you understand the kind of problems that Denny had every day, you can see why he was mad most of the time. You can also see why he wasn't very happy when Andrew came to the ball park of the Titans and tried to talk to Denny. The team was on the field trying to practice some running plays. The coaches were doing as much running as the players. The coaches were blowing whistles and trying to tell the players how to run the play the right way. Denny was standing on the sidelines, with his arms folded. Every now and then, Denny would yell, "No, you clowns. Use your head and think about what you're doing." Then Denny would mumble something like, "I think they're daydreaming half the time."

"Pardon me," Andrew said. "I would like to try out for your team."

Andrew was standing behind Denny.

Andrew had told a guard at the gate that he had a meeting with Denny. That wasn't true, but it was the only way that Andrew could think of to meet Denny.

Denny turned around and gave Andrew a mean look. "Who let you in here?" he demanded.

"I told a guard that I had a meeting with you so . . ."

Denny yelled, "That guard should know better than that. Now get out of here. We're having a practice."

"I can help your team," Andrew said. "I'm very good at . . . "

"Are you deaf?" Denny yelled. "I said get out of here."

"But I can help your . . . "

"Listen, buddy, get out of here or I'll have you thrown out."

MORE NEXT TIME

D **Number your paper from 1 through 19.**

Skill Items

Use the words in the box to write complete sentences.

interrupting	power	tingling	company
customer	magnetic	valuable	reasons

1. The _____ bought a _____ gift.
2. They had _____ for _____ her talk.

Review Items

3. When do trees begin to grow?
   - in the winter
   - in the spring
4. Trees begin to grow when their roots get _____.

5. Write the letter of the tree that has deeper roots.
6. Write the letter of the tree that begins to grow first every year.

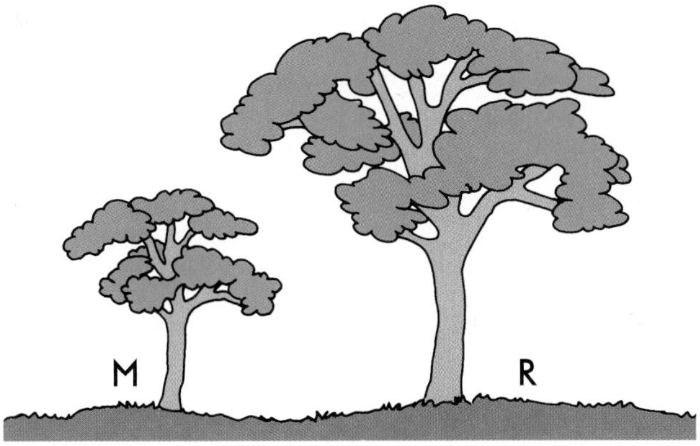

7. A forest fire may burn for ____.
   - hours
   - minutes
   - weeks
8. A forest fire kills both ____ and ____.
   - whales
   - plants
   - fish
   - animals
9. About how many years could it take for the forest to grow back?
   - 20 years
   - 100 years
   - 200 years

10. The names in one box tell about time. Write the letter of that box.
11. The names in one box tell about length. Write the letter of that box.

A	yard	centimeter	inch	meter	mile	
B	week	year	second	month	minute	hour

12. Does a housefly weigh **more than a gram** or **less than a gram?**
13. Does a long pencil weigh **more than a gram** or **less than a gram?**
14. If you get smaller, your voice gets ______.
15. Jean got smaller. So what do you know about Jean's voice?

Use these answers:

- 100 pounds
- 150 pounds
- 500 pounds

16. About how much does a chimpanzee weigh?
17. About how much force can a chimpanzee pull with?
18. About how much does a leopard weigh?
19. About how much weight can a leopard carry?

A

1

1. treat
2. sweat
3. uneasy
4. breath
5. treating

2

1. pretended
2. becoming
3. laughter
4. interrupted

3

1. frequently
2. hang-time
3. champion
4. coaches
5. Charlie

4

1. slight
2. muscle
3. believe
4. couple
5. argued

B

Seconds

The story that you will read today tells about seconds. A second is a unit of time. It is not a very long unit of time. If you count slowly, one . . . two . . . three . . . four . . . , you're counting seconds.

Find a clock or a watch with a second hand. Count the seconds. Remember to count each time the second hand crosses a dot.

A stopwatch is used to measure seconds. A stopwatch starts with the second hand pointing straight up. Each time one second passes, the second hand moves one dot this way: 

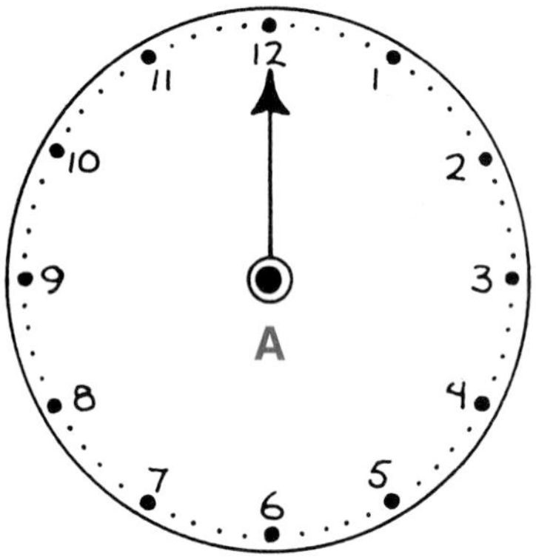

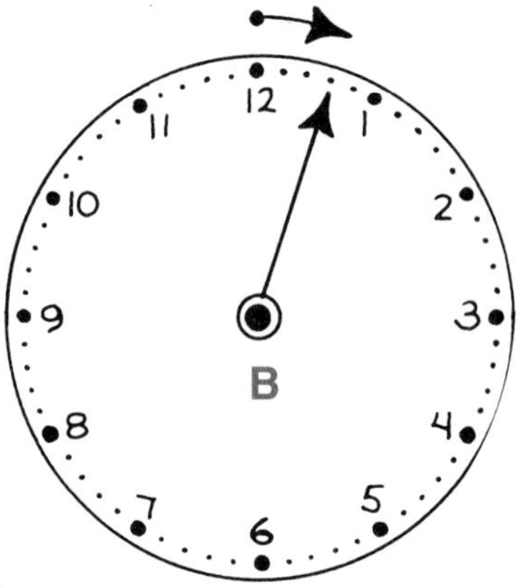

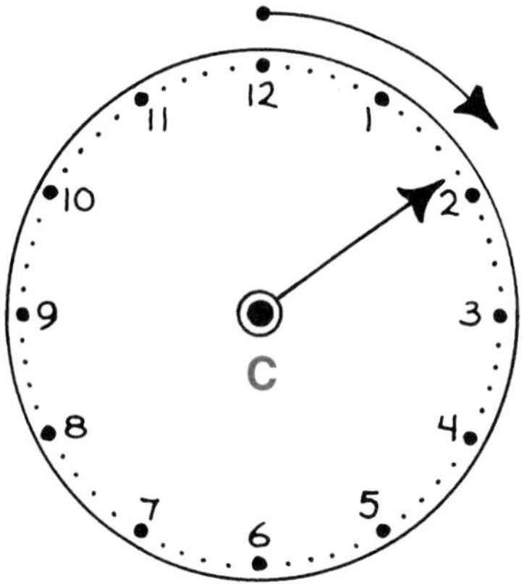

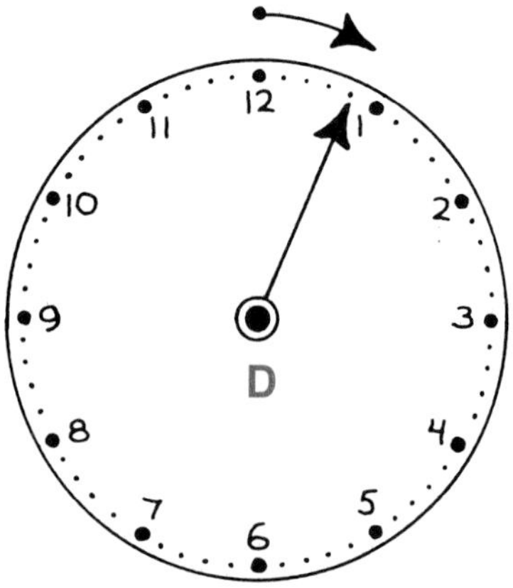

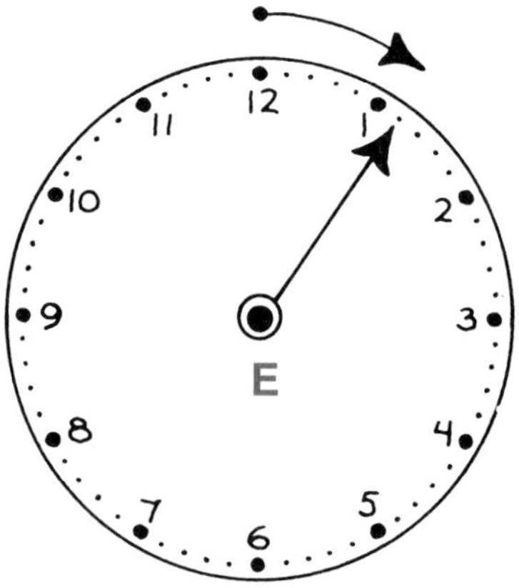

Touch stopwatch A. Stopwatch A shows that no seconds have passed.

Which stopwatch shows that 3 seconds have passed?
Which stopwatch shows that 4 seconds have passed?
Which stopwatch shows that 6 seconds have passed?
Which stopwatch shows that 9 seconds have passed?

C

The Titans Make Fun of Andrew

Andrew was trying to get a job with the Titans. Denny Brock wouldn't listen to Andrew. Just then, one of the coaches who worked for Denny ran up. "Denny," he said. He was out of breath. "You're not going to believe this, but Charlie just pulled a leg muscle. It looks bad, and I don't think he'll be able to kick the ball for a couple of weeks. The doc is looking at him now and maybe he'll be all right, but . . . "

"The only good player we have on this team," Denny shouted. "And he pulls his leg muscle. I don't believe this. I just don't believe it."

Denny kicked a helmet that was on the field next to him. He hurt his toe and hopped around.

"I can kick," Andrew said. "I think I can kick as far as anybody."

Denny was still hopping. "You can kick as far as anybody. Did you hear that, Joe?" Denny pretended to laugh. "This guy walks in off the street and tells us he can kick as far as anybody. All right, smart guy. What's the hang-time on your best kick?"

"I really . . . I don't know."

Denny said, "Here he is, Joe. A guy who can kick as well as anybody, but he doesn't know what his hang-time is. I'm not even sure he knows what hang-time means. Do you, buddy? What is hang-time?"

"Well, the hang-time . . . " Andrew knew what hang-time was. He'd watched a lot of games. But Denny was making him uneasy. "The hang-time . . . "

Denny interrupted. "It's how long the ball stays in the air. That's what hang-time is. Now get out of here."

Andrew was becoming angry. "I can kick the ball as well as anybody," he said loudly. "I can do it," Andrew yelled. He ran onto the playing field and picked up a football. One of the players called to Denny, "You want me to throw him out?"

"No, don't throw him out until he shows us how well he can kick," Denny shouted. "He tells us he can kick the ball as well as anybody. Of course, he doesn't know what his best hang-time is. And of course nobody knows who this guy is. But he just happens to be as good as any kicker in professional football."

The players started to laugh. Some of them took off their helmets and wiped the sweat from their faces. Soon, all the players and the coaches were watching Andrew. He was standing in the middle of the field holding a football and feeling very silly. "Where do you want me to kick it?" Andrew asked.

The players and the coaches laughed. "Up," Denny shouted, and pointed up. "I want to see a four-second hang-time." Everybody was laughing.

A couple of players pointed up. "That's it, man," one player yelled. "Just put that ball up there long enough for us to run down the field and catch it."

The laughter continued and Andrew tried not to listen to it. It bothered him, though. "Think about what you're doing," he told himself. He held the ball in front of him.

He heard a couple of the players yelling, "Look at that. He's holding the ball all wrong." They laughed louder.

MORE NEXT TIME

D Number your paper from 1 through 18.

Review Items

Some of the lines in the box are one inch long and some are one centimeter long.

1. Write the letter of every line that is one centimeter long.
2. Write the letter of every line that is one inch long.

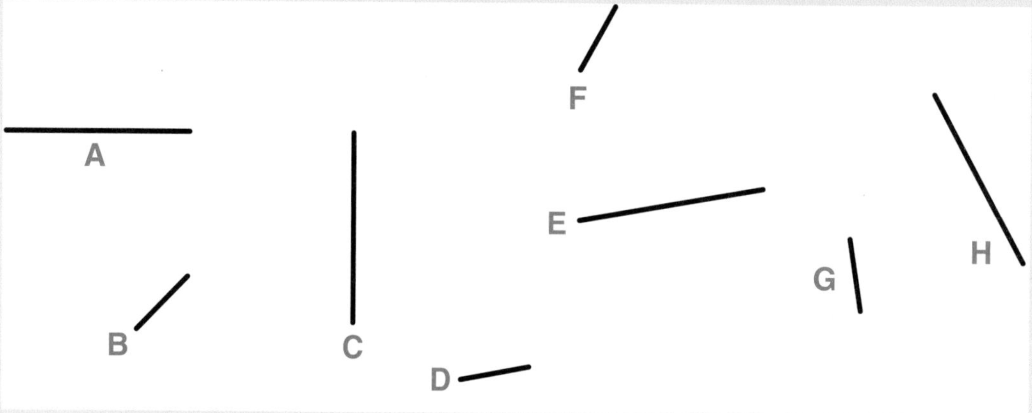

3. When we weigh very small things, the unit we use is ____.
4. If you get smaller, your voice gets ____.
5. Lynn got smaller. So what do you know about Lynn's voice?

Each statement tells about how far something goes or how fast something goes. Write **how far** or **how fast** for each item.

6. Jean walked 4 miles per hour.
7. Jean walked 4 miles.
8. The train was going 100 miles per hour.
9. The train was 100 miles from Denver.

Here's how fast different things can go:

- 20 miles per hour
- 35 miles per hour
- 200 miles per hour
- 500 miles per hour

10. Which speed tells how fast a jet can fly?
11. Which speed tells how fast a fast man can run?
12. Which speed tells how fast a fast dog can run?

13. How long is a football field?
14. Write 2 ways that a football team can move the ball down the field.
    - roll
    - slide
    - pass
    - run
15. How many parts does the body of an insect have?
16. How many legs does an insect have?
17. How many legs does a spider have?
18. How many parts does a spider's body have?

96

A

1

1. sideline
2. mention
3. offer
4. upright

2

1. stands
2. treating
3. argued
4. frequently

3

1. time
2. chirp
3. earn
4. chirping
5. paid
6. slight

B

Andrew Kicks

Everybody was laughing at Andrew, but he tried not to think about it. He thought about kicking the ball. Andrew dropped the ball and kicked it as hard as he could with his right foot. CRACK. The sound of his foot hitting the ball was so loud it sounded like a gunshot. "Crack, Crack, Crack," it echoed around the stands. The ball went almost straight up. It moved so fast that some of the players didn't even see it leave Andrew's foot. Within a second, it was a small speck, hundreds of yards overhead. If you looked very hard, you could see the ball. "Rack, rack," the sound was still echoing around the stands.

Then there was silence. You could hear a slight breeze and the flapping of the flag at the far end of the playing field. There was the sound of a bird chirping in the stands. In the distance was the sound of a bus and a few car horns. But there was not one sound from Denny, not one sound from the football players or from the other coaches. Not a word. They stood there staring straight up into the sky. And they stood there and they stood there and they watched and they waited. Finally, the ball seemed to get bigger and bigger. Now you could see that it was coming down very fast. It didn't land in the field. It landed in one of the stands. BLAM. Then the ball bounced up ten yards. Again it came down and bounced and finally rolled to a stop.

The first person to talk was one of the players. "I don't believe this," he yelled. "This is amazing." Then other players began to yell. "Do it again," one yelled. "Yeah, man, once more."

The coach standing next to Denny held out a stopwatch. The coach explained to Denny, "I timed his hang-time. You probably saw that it was more than four seconds."

Denny looked at the stopwatch. His eyes became very large. Yes, Andrew's hang-time was more than four seconds. It was more than five seconds and more than six seconds. The picture shows what his hang-time was.

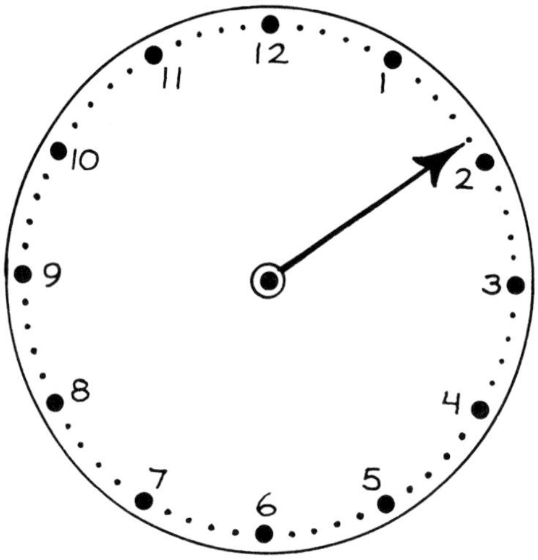

The players were crowding around Andrew now. "What's your secret?" one asked. "Is it the funny way you hold the ball before you kick?"

"Get out of the way," another player said. "I want to see him do it again." The player handed Andrew a ball. "Do it again, man," the player said.

So Andrew did. It was a better kick than the first one. The noise of his foot hitting the ball was so loud that a couple of players put their hands over their ears. The ball went up, up, almost out of sight. Then down, down it came, this time landing about 30 yards away, right in the middle of the field. All the players looked at the coaches' stopwatches to see what the hang-time was.

"Come on," one of the players said. "This isn't happening. Nobody can kick a ball with a hang-time of 11 seconds." That player was almost right. There was only one person who could kick a ball with a hang-time of 11 seconds.

"Okay, you guys," Denny shouted to his football players. "Get back to your practice." Denny blew three short blasts on his whistle. "Now," he shouted.

Slowly, the players put on their helmets and trotted away from Andrew. Before leaving, some of them slapped him on the back. "Good kicking, man," they said.

"Thanks," Andrew replied. He felt very strange. The other players were treating him like a star.

"Let's talk," Denny said, putting his arm around Andrew's shoulder. "Let's go have a soft drink and do a little talking." Denny's voice was not mean. It was very friendly. He was being nice to Andrew because he wanted Andrew to play for the Titans.

MORE NEXT TIME

C Number your paper from 1 through 21.

Review Items

1. Which is longer, a yard or a meter?
2. Which is longer, a centimeter or a meter?
3. How many centimeters long is a meter?

4. How fast is truck **A** going?
5. How fast is truck **B** going?
6. Which truck is going faster?

A 50 B 35

Write what kind of horse each picture shows.

- racehorse
- quarter horse
- pony
- Mongolian horse
- draft horse

7.

8.

9.

10. A second is a unit of ▬▬.
    - length
    - weight
    - time
    - distance

11. What is the name of the vehicle in the picture?
12. How many wheels does the vehicle have?
13. What is pulling the vehicle?
14. What is soldier P doing?
15. What is soldier J doing?

16. Which stopwatch shows that 3 seconds have passed?
17. Which stopwatch shows that 9 seconds have passed?
18. Which stopwatch shows that 5 seconds have passed?

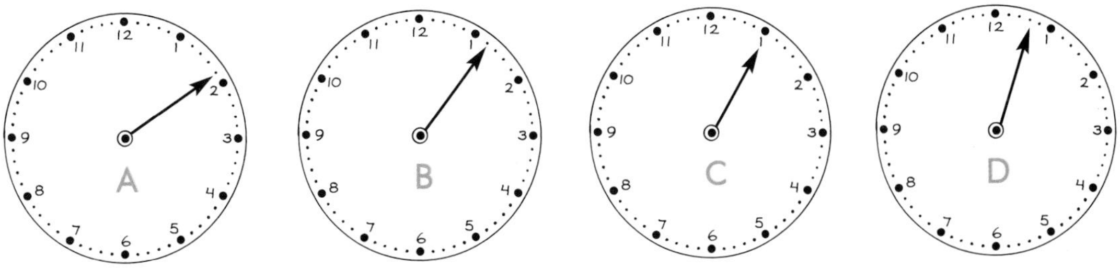

19. Write the letter of the sun you see at noon.
20. Write the letter of the sun you see at sunset.
21. Write the letter of the sun you see early in the morning.

A

1
1. often
2. allow
3. referee
4. bury
5. earn
6. paid

2
1. championship
2. sideline
3. upright
4. Wildcats

3
1. roar
2. scratch
3. scratched
4. argues
5. mistakes

4
1. kid around
2. fumble
3. mention
4. fumbled
5. offer

B

Professional Football Players

Some football players play football for fun. But the best players play professional football. For these players, playing football is their job. These players make money playing football. The work is very hard because only the best players play professional football. So if you are a professional football player, you play against the best players there are. These players tackle very hard and run very fast.

Professional football players earn a lot of money. A player who is very good at running with the ball may earn over 3 million dollars a year. Most players do not earn that much. Some players make only 250 thousand dollars a year. But 250 thousand dollars a year is a lot of money. It is more money than a teacher earns. It is more money than a flight attendant earns. It is more money than a bank teller earns. Some doctors earn more than 250 thousand dollars a year, and so do the people who are in charge of big companies like Reef Oil Refinery.

The football players that are worth the most money are the players the football fans like. If fans go to a game just so they can see one player, that player is worth a lot of money.

C Denny Gives Andrew a Job

The two men walked over to a bench on the sideline. "Joe," Denny yelled in a mean voice. "Have one of the boys bring us some soft drinks."

Denny mentioned how nice the weather had been. Then Denny said, "Okay, I don't know how you do that kicking, but we want you. You have to remember that kicking out there in an empty field is a lot different from kicking in a game when four monsters are coming after you like trucks. I mean, we'll have to work with you and teach you a lot. But we want you to play for the Titans."

"Okay," Andrew said, and smiled.

Denny didn't jump up and down with joy. He thought that Andrew was trying to play a joke on him. Players don't just say, "Okay, I'll be on your team." Here's what almost every player says: "How much do I get paid?"

Then Denny offers a small amount of money and the player argues for more money. And they argue and argue.

Denny had been ready to argue with Andrew. Denny knew that fans would come from all over to see somebody kick the ball hundreds of meters into the air. Even if the Titans lost, people would pay money just to see Andrew kick the ball. Here's what Denny was thinking: If the team had Andrew, at least 10 thousand more fans would come to each game. So the team would make at least 250 thousand dollars each game if Andrew played. The team could probably make another million dollars by letting the games go on TV. So Andrew was worth more than a million dollars for each game that he played. Denny was ready to pay Andrew a lot of money—a lot of money. But when Denny had asked Andrew to play for the Titans, Andrew didn't argue about the money. Denny didn't know what to say.

Denny looked at Andrew. Then he said, "Well—I don't even know your name." Andrew told him, and the men shook hands. Then Denny continued, "Well, how much money do you think you should get?"

Andrew scratched his cheek and made a face. "I think I should make at least as much as I made at my last job."

"Tell me how much and I'll tell you if we can do it."

"Two thousand dollars a month," Andrew said.

First Denny smiled, and then shook his head. Then he smiled again. Then he made a face. Then he said, "Come on, now. I don't know if you're kidding around with me or what you're doing. No player of mine is going to work for only 2 thousand dollars a month. I'll pay you 20 thousand dollars a month. That's 240 thousand dollars a year."

Andrew had seen a lot of money when he worked in the bank. He had counted piles of money worth more than 20 thousand dollars, but he never thought that he would earn 20 thousand dollars a month. "That's great," Andrew said, smiling. "That's really great."

The men shook hands again. Denny was very happy because he didn't pay Andrew very much. Andrew was very happy because he was going to make more money than he ever thought he'd make.

MORE NEXT TIME

D Number your paper from 1 through 19.

Skill Items

He frequently argued about the championship.

1. What word names a contest between the two best teams?
2. What word means **often?**
3. What word tells what he did that showed he didn't agree?

Review Items

4. Things closer to the top of the pile went into the pile ____.
5. Things closer to the bottom of the pile went into the pile ____.
6. The people who lived in caves drew pictures on the cave walls. Write the letters of 4 things they made pictures of.

   a. cows   b. horses   c. elephants   d. birds
   e. fish   f. hands   g. dogs   h. bears

7. If the hang-time for a kick is 7 seconds, how long does the ball stay in the air?

8. Write the letter of the shortest hang-time.
9. Write the letter of the longest hang-time.

   a. 9 seconds   b. 4 seconds
   c. 6 seconds   d. 3 seconds

10. The temperature inside your body is about ____ degrees when you are healthy.
11. Most fevers don't go over ____ degrees.

12. How many years ago did layer A go into the pile?

13. How many years ago did layer B go into the pile?

14. How many years ago did layer C go into the pile?

15. How many years ago did layer D go into the pile?

16. How many years ago did layer E go into the pile?

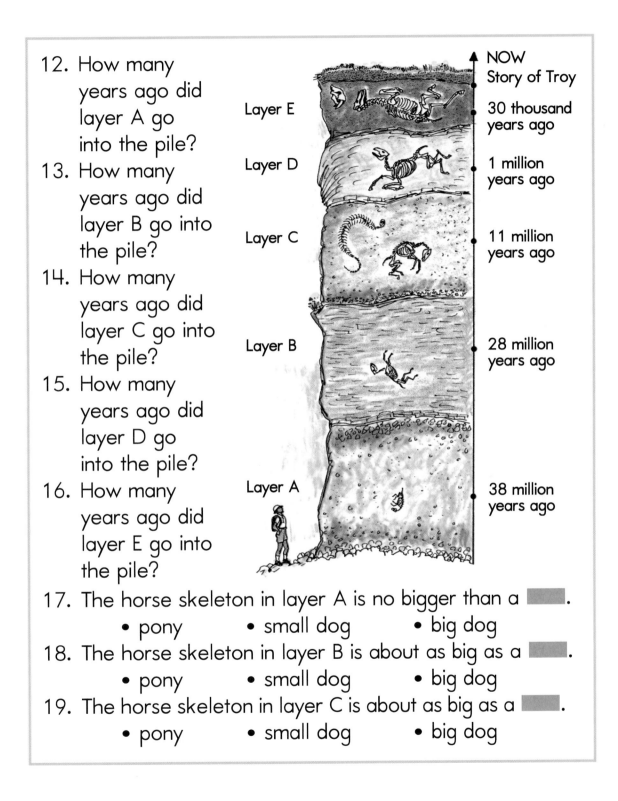

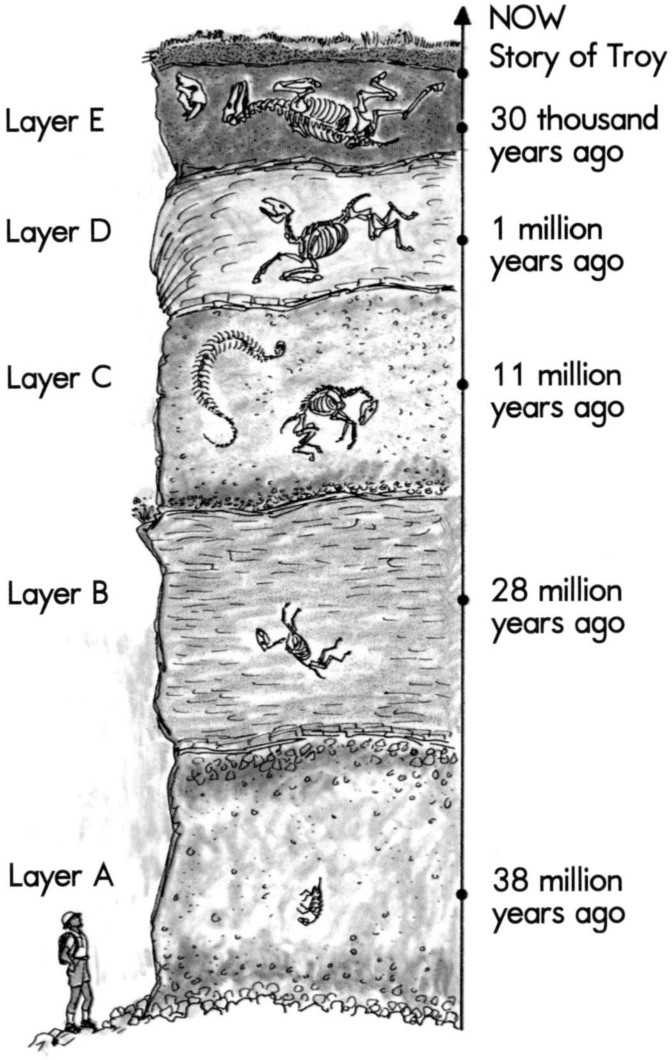

17. The horse skeleton in layer A is no bigger than a ___.
   • pony • small dog • big dog

18. The horse skeleton in layer B is about as big as a ___.
   • pony • small dog • big dog

19. The horse skeleton in layer C is about as big as a ___.
   • pony • small dog • big dog

98

A

1
1. ruin
2. elbow
3. often
4. buried

2
1. newspapers
2. whenever
3. loudspeaker
4. Wildcats

3
1. mistakes
2. fumbled
3. ruining
4. simply
5. roars

4
1. referee
2. secret
3. reply
4. talents
5. famous

5
1. field goal
2. holler
3. impression
4. reporters
5. allow

B

Andrew Plays in His First Game

Before Andrew's first game, many announcements appeared in the newspapers. These announcements told about the Titans' secret new player. The announcements gave the impression that the Titans had a player who could turn the Titans into a winning team. Through these announcements, the Titans hoped to bring more people to the game. Here's what one announcement said:

> "Coach Denny Brock did not respond when he was asked what his new star player could do. He simply smiled and said, 'Andrew Dexter has some talents that nobody has seen on a football field before.'"

Before Andrew's first game, he was already famous. He talked to reporters from TV stations and from newspapers. But he didn't tell them what he could do for the team. Whenever a reporter asked about what he would do in this game, he would reply, "All I can tell you is this: I can do my part of the game better than anybody else in the world."

• • •

For the first time in four years, the stands were filled with people. Most of the fans were talking about Andrew Dexter. You could hear them talking near the hot dog stand.

"He doesn't look like much," one fan would say.

"Yes," another would say, "this had better not be a trick to get us out here."

But the fans did come to see Andrew. Over fifty thousand fans crowded into the stands. None of the fans really thought that the Titans would win this game, because the Titans were playing the best team in the league—the

Wildcats. The sun was bright, and a slight breeze was blowing. The air was just cold enough so you could see your breath. Most of the fans wore heavy shoes and mittens.

Now came the time when all players start to feel a little uneasy. Just before the game, they know that they will go out on the field. Everybody will be watching them. Will they do well? Will they make mistakes? These questions run through the players' minds. Sometimes the players have daydreams of being a star who wins the game. But there are very few stars on a team. Most of the players must do their job so the stars can look like stars.

The name of each player was announced over the loudspeaker. Each player ran onto the playing field, and the crowd whooped and hollered. They whooped very loudly for Andrew. Now the players on the field were ready. They felt like they couldn't catch their breath. They felt a little exhausted although they hadn't started to play yet.

The teams lined up. The Titans were ready to kick to the Wildcats. Andrew was more frightened than the other players. He had never played in front of a huge crowd. One of the other Titans held the ball. Andrew ran up and kicked it. BOOOOM.

The crowd roared as the ball went up, up, up, up.
Everybody in the stands was standing, looking straight up

into the blue sky at a tiny speck. The ball came down, down, down. But it wasn't caught by a member of the other team. The ball stayed in the air so long that the Titans ran all the way down the field before it came down. And the ball was caught by a Titan. The Titans had the ball only ten yards from the goal line.

As Andrew left the field, the people in the stands were yelling and cheering. The players from the Wildcats were arguing that the Titans should not be allowed to have the ball. The Wildcats insisted that the kick was unfair. But the referee didn't take the ball from the Titans. So the Titans ran three plays and scored a touchdown.

The Titans kicked off again. BOOOOM. This time, the ball floated all the way past the end of the field, and the Wildcats had the ball. The Wildcats moved down the field, passing the ball and running the ball. Then, on one play, a runner fumbled the ball and a player from the Titans fell on it. The Titans had the ball.

The Titans ran two plays and lost over fifteen yards. They ran another play and lost another four yards. The crowd started to boo the Titans. The team was now eighty yards from a touchdown. Andrew came onto the field. The announcer said, "It looks as if the Titans are going to try to kick a field goal—an eighty-yard field goal." The people in the stands didn't laugh, because they had seen how high Andrew could kick the ball.

MORE NEXT TIME

C Number your paper from 1 through 19.

Skill Items

Use the words in the box to write complete sentences.

uniform	interesting	frequently	scolded	interrupting
arranged	reasons	championship	mistake	argued

1. They had ____ for ____ her talk.
2. He ____ ____ about the ____.

Review Items

3. During a storm, which comes first, lightning or thunder?
4. How does fire like to move, up or down?
5. Cave people painted pictures of horses on cave walls. How are those horses different from horses that live today?
6. Which horse has a longer back, a racehorse or a quarter horse?
7. Eohippus lived ____ million years ago.
8. The front legs of eohippus were different from the front legs of a horse that lives today. Write the letters of 2 ways that they were different.
   a. They didn't have hooves.
   b. They had smaller hooves.
   c. They were smaller.
   d. They were faster.

9. Which animal is safer, a bear or a rabbit?
10. Why?

11. How fast is car **A** going?
12. How fast is car **B** going?
13. Which car is going faster?

A	B
15	50

14. The arrow that killed Achilles hit him in the ____.
15. That arrow had something on it that killed Achilles. What did it have on it?

16. Which thing went into the pile earlier, thing **R** or thing **T?**
17. Which thing went into the pile earlier, thing **Y** or thing **J?**
18. Which thing went into the pile later, thing **R** or thing **X?**
19. Which thing went into the pile later, thing **J** or thing **T?**

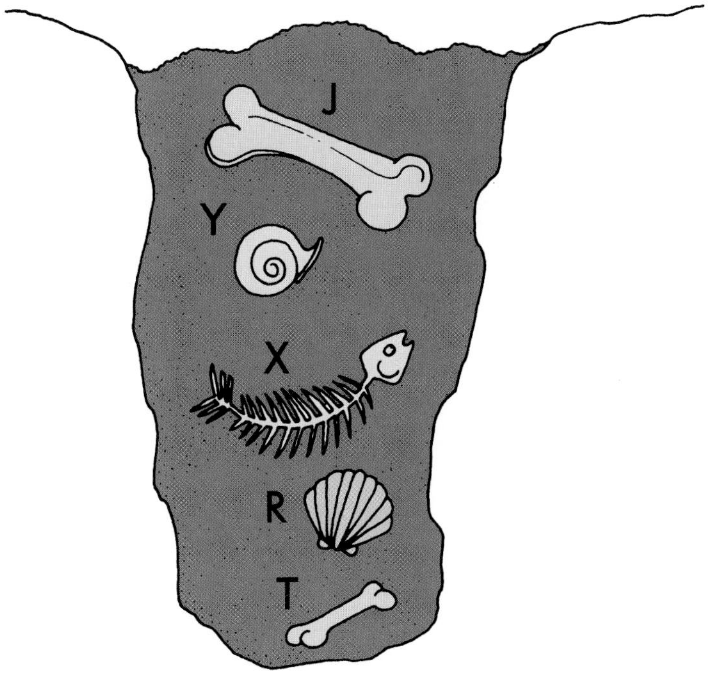

99

A

1	2
1. whooped	1. laughed
2. plowed	2. crowded
3. slapped	3. echoed
4. waited	4. bounced
5. pushed	5. approached

3	4
1. Handy Andy	1. charge
2. elbow	2. awful
3. ruin	3. ruining
4. ka-splat	4. bury
5. cracked	5. buried
	6. kicked

B Andrew Meets Smiling Sam

The Titans had the ball eighty yards away from a score. Andrew was going to try an eighty-yard field goal. No fan had ever seen a field goal that long. They had seen fifty-yard field goals when the wind was blowing in the same direction as the kick. But the wind was blowing against the kick today.

The fans were quiet. The players on the Wildcats were jumping around, yelling things at the Titans. "Come on, you bums," they yelled. "What's that tiny foot going to try to do? You'll never make it, jelly face."

The ball came back. A Titan held it in place and Andrew kicked it. The crowd whooped. The ball sailed 180 yards and went completely out of the ball park. But it did not pass between the upright poles. So it was not a field goal.

Some of the Titan players patted Andrew on the back. "Good try," they said, and Andrew felt a little better. The biggest player on the team, Mean George, said, "You'll get it next time. Just stay cool."

The Wildcats scored a touchdown and the game was tied—7 to 7. Then the Wildcats scored another touchdown. The score was now 14 to 7. And the Wildcats were just running over the Titans. Two Titans were hurt and had to leave the game. The player that was hurting them was Smiling Sam. He was one of the biggest Wildcats. Three of his front teeth were missing, and he smiled. It wasn't a friendly smile, though. It was a very mean smile. "Going to get you guys," Smiling Sam would say to the Titans. Then he would fly into one of them with his helmet down and his legs pushing his huge body as fast as it could go.

Andrew was standing on the sidelines watching Smiling Sam. "He's playing dirty," Andrew said to one of the coaches. "He just hit one of our guys with his elbow."

"Yeah," the coach said. "He's a mean one."

"Well, we should make him stop doing that."

"How could we stop him?" the coach asked. "We would need a truck to stop that animal."

"I'll tell him to stop," Andrew said.

"Hey, Andrew," the coach said. "We need you in one piece. Just stay away from the guy."

The Titans had the ball. The Wildcats pushed them back on three running plays. It was time for Andrew to go out and kick the ball. He trotted out on the field. Then Andrew ran up to Smiling Sam. He looked up at him and said, "Listen, you stop playing dirty. Football is a good game, but you're ruining it. So cut it out."

Smiling Sam gave Andrew a big smile, a very big one. Then, while he was still smiling, he said, "I'm going to get you, you little creep."

"Don't try it," Andrew said. "I'll knock you out of the game."

The Wildcats laughed. Some Wildcats slapped Smiling Sam on the back, and Smiling Sam didn't take his eyes off Andrew. The teams lined up for the kick. The ball came to Andrew. But Andrew didn't try to kick it. He just put it under one arm and waited. Smiling Sam plowed through the Titans and charged at Andrew as hard as he could. Andrew could hear him yelling, "I got you now."

Just as Smiling Sam was ready to bury his helmet in Andrew's chest, Andrew put his head down and charged. KA-SPLAT. A terrible sound, almost like a clap of thunder, echoed through the stands as the players hit head-on. Smiling Sam flew backwards into two of his own players. He knocked them about five yards back. He was knocked out. His helmet was cracked. And two of his teeth were loose.

Andrew ran forward. Two more Wildcats tried to tackle him. They bounced off. He ran down the field. The fans were cheering and yelling and stamping as he approached the goal line. A touchdown. The score was tied.

Titan players crowded around Andrew. "Wow," one of them said. "You're the greatest."

"Yeah," another one said. "I didn't know you could run with the ball."

Andrew ran with the ball three more times during that game and he made three more touchdowns. The Titans won the game, 35 to 21.

MORE NEXT TIME

C **Number your paper from 1 through 14.**

Review Items

1. People who lived 80 thousand years ago did not have many things that we have today. Write the letters of 6 things they did not have.

   a. dogs
   b. computers
   c. food
   d. stoves
   e. bones
   f. TV sets
   g. rocks
   h. cars
   i. refrigerators
   j. dirt
   k. trees
   l. telephones

2. Name 2 things that a strong magnet can pick up.
3. Electricity can turn any steel bar into a magnet. What are these magnets called?
4. Name a place where these magnets are used.

5. When was the check below written?
6. Who should the bank pay?
7. How much should the bank pay?
8. Whose money should the bank use to pay Ann Rogers?

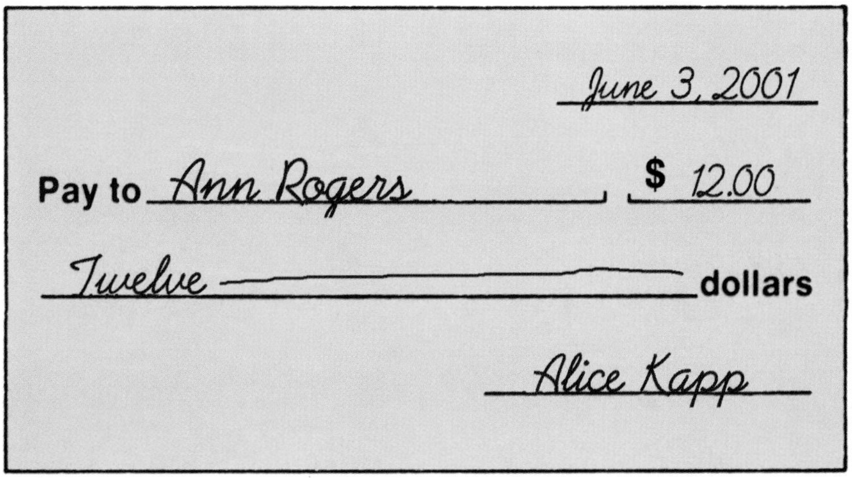

Use these answers:

100 pounds 150 pounds 500 pounds

9. About how much does a leopard weigh?
10. About how much weight can a leopard carry?
11. About how much does a chimpanzee weigh?
12. About how much force can a chimpanzee pull with?

13. How long is a football field?
14. Write 2 ways that a football team can move the ball down the field.
    - run
    - pass
    - slide
    - roll

100 TEST 10

Number your paper from 1 through 27.

1. When was the check below written?
2. Who should the bank pay?
3. How much should the bank pay?
4. Whose money should the bank use to pay Sally Daniels?

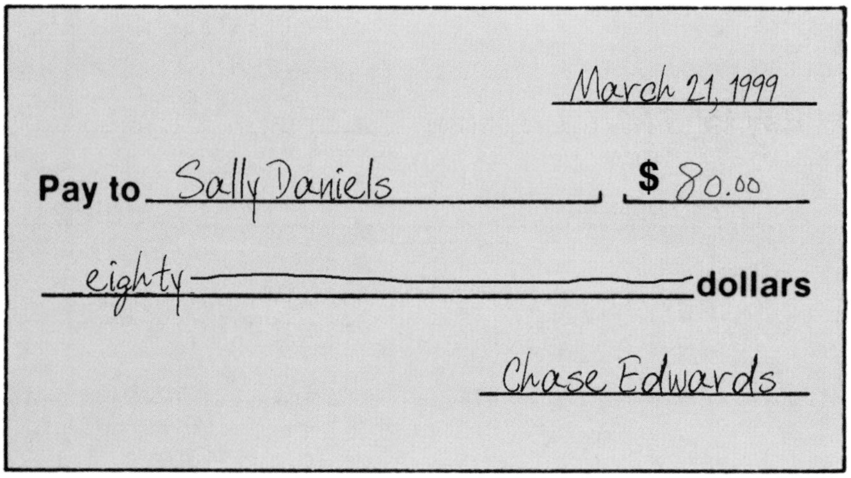
March 21, 1999

Pay to Sally Daniels $ 80.00

eighty dollars

Chase Edwards

5. Name 2 things that a strong magnet can pick up.
6. Electricity can turn any steel bar into a magnet. What are these magnets called?
7. Name a place where these magnets are used.

Use these answers:

500 pounds **150 pounds** **100 pounds**

8. About how much weight can a leopard carry?
9. About how much does a leopard weigh?
10. About how much force can a chimpanzee pull with?
11. About how much does a chimpanzee weigh?

Write the name of each part of a football player's uniform.

- shoulders
- shoulder pads
- knee pads
- helmet
- hat

12. 

13. 

14. How long is a football field?
15. Write 2 ways that a football team can move the ball down the field.
    - run
    - pass
    - slide
    - roll
16. A second is a unit of ___.
    - distance
    - time
    - length
    - weight

17. Which stopwatch shows that 8 seconds have passed?
18. Which stopwatch shows that 4 seconds have passed?
19. Which stopwatch shows that 6 seconds have passed?

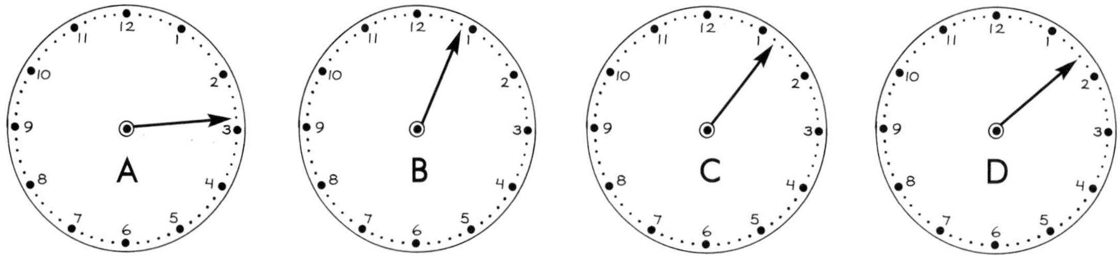

20. If the hang-time for a kick is 4 seconds, how long does the ball stay in the air?

21. Write the letter of the longest hang-time.
22. Write the letter of the shortest hang-time.

a. 3 seconds b. 8 seconds c. 5 seconds d. 6 seconds

Skill Items

They had reasons for interrupting her talk.
He frequently argued about the championship.

23. What underlining means **often?**
24. What underlining tells that they didn't let her finish talking?
25. What underlining names a contest between the two best teams?
26. What underlining tells about why they interrupted her talk?
27. What underlining tells what he did that showed he didn't agree?

END OF TEST 10

Fact Game Answer Key

Lesson 60

2. A, B, E
3. a. X
   b. Y
4. a. X
   b. Y
5. a. J
   b. M
6. A–Italy
   B–Japan
7. C–Turkey
   D–China
8. a. W
   b. Z
9. a. M
   b. J
10. a. Q
    b. P
11. Texas, Alaska, New York City
12. A–roots
    B–trunk
    C–coconuts
    D–fronds

Lesson 70

2. a. 1 thousand
   b. 10 years
   c. Greece
3. a. A wooden horse
   b. Men (or soldiers)
   c. Idea: Opened the gate
4. a. tugboats
   b. docks
   c. harbors
5. a. 98
   b. 101
6. a. 1903
   b. 1776
   c. 3 thousand years ago
7. a. Check with your teacher.
   b. Check with your teacher.
   c. Check with your teacher.
8. a. Check with your teacher.
   b. Check with your teacher.
9. A–Italy
   B–Troy
   C–Greece
10. a. L
    b. N
    c. J
11. a. Helen
    b. queen
    c. Troy
12. Turkey

Lesson 80

2. A–Greece
   B–Troy
3. a. 10 years
   b. A horse
   c. Greece
4. crude oil
5. A–refinery
   B–pipeline
   C–crude oil
6. a. R
   b. T
7. A–fresh water
   B–crude oil
   C–salt water
8. His love of candy was his Achilles heel.
9. oil, water
10. a. J
    b. K
    c. P
11. a. 1776
    b. 3 thousand years ago
12. a. Check with your teacher.
    b. Check with your teacher.

Lesson 90

2. a. Greek
   b. 10 years
   c. Achilles
3. a. Hector
   b. chariot
4. a. garbage (or caves)
   b. 38 million years ago
5. A–pony
   B–Mongolian horse
   C–quarter horse
6. a. later
   b. earlier
7. a. W
   b. H
8. a. X
   b. H
9. a. F
   b. H
   c. W

10. a. 30
    b. 15
    c. 8
11. a. caves
    b. up
12. lightning

Lesson 100

2. a. electromagnet
   b. Idea: wrecking yard
3. a. 1 hundred yards
   b. run, pass (or kick)
4. time
5. a. 100 pounds
   b. 150 pounds
6. a. 100 pounds
   b. 500 pounds
7. A–2 seconds
   B–7 seconds
8. a. May 20, 1998
   b. Ted Rose
9. a. 15 dollars
   b. Rod Mack's
10. a. 2 seconds
    b. 6 seconds
11. A–shoulder pads
    B–helmet
12. 6 seconds

VOCABULARY SENTENCES

LESSONS 1–50

1. You measure your weight in pounds.
2. They waded into the stream to remove tadpoles.
3. The fly boasted about escaping from the spider.
4. The workers propped up the cage with steel bars.
5. Hunters were stationed at opposite ends of the field.
6. He motioned to the flight attendant ahead of him.
7. The traffic was moving forty miles per hour.
8. He is supposed to make a decision in a couple of days.
9. Several paths continued for a great distance.
10. Boiling water will thaw ice in a few moments.
11. They were eager to hear the announcement.
12. The lifeboat disappeared in the whirlpool.

VOCABULARY SENTENCES

LESSONS 51–100

13. The smoke swirled in enormous billows.
14. The occasional foul smell was normal.
15. They constructed an enormous machine.
16. She survived until she was rescued.
17. The soldiers protected their equipment.
18. Lawyers with talent normally succeed.
19. A dozen typists approached the stairs.
20. The job required a consultant.
21. The adults huddled around the fire.
22. The customer bought a valuable gift.
23. They had reasons for interrupting her talk.
24. He frequently argued about the championship.

POEM

The bow is the front and the stern
is the back.

The floors are decks that don't
have a crack.

The walls are bulkheads with
doors that are tight.

They're made to keep water from
spreading, all right.